P9-APQ-155

Decision Against War

Contemporary American History Series
William E. Leuchtenburg, General Editor

DECISION AGAINST WAR

Eisenhower and
Dien Bien Phu, 1954

Melanie Billings-Yun

Columbia University Press
New York   1988

Columbia University Press
New York   Guildford, Surrey
Copyright © 1988 Columbia University Press
All rights reserved
Printed in the United States of America

Library of Congress Cataloging-in-Publication Data
Billings-Yun, Melanie.
    Decision against war: Eisenhower and Dien Bien Phu, 1954 / Melanie
Billings-Yun.
        p.   cm. — (Contemporary American history series)
    Bibliography: p.
    Includes index.
    ISBN 0-231-06622-8
    1. Indochinese War, 1946–54—United States.   2. Diên Biên Phù,
Vietnam, Battle of, 1954.   3. United States—Foreign
relations—1953–1961.   4. Eisenhower, Dwight D. (Dwight David),
1890–1969. I. Title. II. Series.
DS553.1.B54 1988
959.704'1—dc19

Book design by Ken Venezio

To Joe

Contemporary American History Series
William E. Leuchtenburg, General Editor

Contemporary American History Series

Contents

Preface

In the spring of 1954, barely into his second year in the Oval Office, Dwight D. Eisenhower confronted one of the most fateful decisions of his presidency: whether or not to commit United States military forces to the war raging in Vietnam, in what was then the French colony of Indochina. Communist Vietminh forces had a stranglehold on US-backed French troops in the northern outpost at Dien Bien Phu. The government of France made it clear that this was the battle that would decide the war. If Dien Bien Phu were to fall, President Joseph Laniel warned Washington, France would have no choice but to come to terms with the communists, no matter how egregious those terms might be. Previously content to let the United States merely finance the colonial war (indeed, adamant that the Americans intrude no further), Paris now demanded more active intervention. Laniel appealed to Eisenhower to order a bombing mission over Dien Bien Phu.

Eisenhower had to decide a far weightier question than whether to launch a few limited airstrikes. To order them would be to commit America's armies and their prestige to the whole seven-year-old French-Indochina War. The true question before him was whether he wanted to send his nation back to war in another far-off Asian country—this time to win—just eight months after extricating it from the grueling and unpopular Korean stalemate. Or did he want to brand his youthful administration with the stigma of having lost Vietnam to communism, after winning the presidency and his party's control of Congress on the platform of "No More Chinas"? In short, he faced a precursor of the Vietnam dilemma that would tyrannize each successive president over the next two decades.

What makes this story worth reexamining is that the Indochina intervention decision did *not* subjugate Eisenhower. So little did it encumber his presidency that few people even recall that he decided against going to war in Vietnam. In part that is because it was a negative action. A decision not to intervene in a distant foreign conflict has a far less perceptible (if no less real) impact on the life of a nation than does a call to arms. Still, Ike's immediate predecessor, Harry Truman, suffered heavily for a similar "nonaction" in China in 1949, as well as for his decision not to push for total victory over North Korea.

How Eisenhower escaped indictment for standing by at Dien Bien Phu while yet another Asian territory fell to communism is as complex as history itself. One of the key factors, however, is that the president went to great lengths to conceal his role in keeping US forces out of the French-Indochina War. He dissembled before the public, Congress, America's closest allies, and even his own advisers. And, until the recent opening of the Eisenhower archives of those years, he hid his machinations from the historical record.

To uncover the truth of Eisenhower's decision against war is the aim of this book. In so doing, it explores why and how a president would engage in such subterfuge against his own administration. The case of Eisenhower and Dien Bien Phu highlights the maneuverability a "hidden-hand president" can exploit to his political advantage—if he is willing to pay the price.

Acknowledgments

In preparing this book I received invaluable aid from a number of people. Professor Ernest May first introduced me to Dien Bien Phu, later advised me on turning my work into a Ph.D. dissertation, and, as I was rewriting the manuscript in Hong Kong, generously mailed me the latest documents. It is the simple truth to say that without his help this book would not have been possible. The same is true of my friend and colleague, Dr. Carl Brauer, whose faith in me and my work outstripped my own and spurred me on. Professor Richard Immerman helped me with his provocative criticism as much as with his generous aid and advice. Professor William Leuchtenberg provided much-needed editorial criticism. I also owe thanks to Professor Richard Neustadt for his moral support and gentle pressure to complete this work.

For their assistance in providing me with research materials and information I would like to thank the staff of the Dwight D. Eisenhower Library—John Wickman, James Leyerzapf, Herbert Pankratz, and especially Mack Teasley—whose exceptional knowledge, helpfulness, and professionalism made my job significantly easier; Nancy Bressler of the Seeley G. Mudd Manuscript Library at Princeton; Philip Cronenwett of the Baker Library at Dartmouth; and the staffs of the Richard B. Russell Memorial Library at the University of Georgia,

Acknowledgments

the library of the Army War College, the U.S. Navy History Division, and the National Archives. Sherman Adams, James C. Hagerty, and Livingston Merchant kindly allowed me to read their private papers. The Henry L. and Louis H. Kohn Family Fund and its trustees merit a very special thankyou for financing my research travels.

I would like to record my personal debt to my friend and typist, Ruth Martin, and to Sally Makacynas, my friendly link to the resources of the western world. Finally, to Joe I offer my loving thanks for his patience and unflagging support.

Decision Against War

I

Setting the Stage

When Eisenhower assumed the presidency in 1953, he inherited a policy of steadily escalating support for the French war with the Vietminh. The three Associated States of Indochina—Vietnam, Laos, and Cambodia—ranked second only to Korea in US military aid priority. American dollars covered more than 40 percent of France's war costs, well over half a billion dollars by fiscal year 1953. The commitment to France was limited to money and matériel. However, it rested upon an unequivocal strategic interest in the Indochina region, most boldly set out in a June 1952 National Security Council memorandum, NSC 124/2.

Developing what would later be dubbed the "domino principle," President Truman's security advisers had warned that the turn to communism of any single country in Southeast Asia would seriously threaten the survival of the entire free world. Though NSC 124/2 stopped short of advocating direct United States military involvement in wars in the area, unless China first intervened, it stressed the high priority of supporting the French effort:

The loss of any of the countries of Southeast Asia to Commnunust control . . . would probably lead to relatively swift submission to or an alignment with communism by the remaining countries of this group. Furthermore, an alignment with communism of the rest of Southeast Asia and India, and in the longer term, of the Middle East (with the probable exception of at least Pakistan and Turkey) would in all probability progressively follow. Such widespread alignment would endanger the stability and security of Europe.

Communist control of all of Southeast Asia would render the United States position in the Pacific offshore island chain precarious and would seriously jeopardize fundamental United States security interests in the Far East. . . .

The loss of Southeast Asia, especially of Malaya and Indonesia, could result in such economic and political pressure on Japan as to make it extremely difficult to prevent Japan's eventual accommodation to communism.[1]

That the Truman administration took this threat very seriously was emphasized to President-elect Eisenhower in a November 1952 briefing given him by outgoing Secretary of State Dean Acheson. Acheson listed the French-Indochina War as one of the greatest international concerns facing America. "It is urgent," he said, for the Eisenhower administration to decide how far it would be willing to go to help the French. If events took a turn for the worse, "the new administration must be prepared to act."[2]

The French-Indochina War was entering its seventh year when Acheson spoke those words. It had begun as part of the great post-World War II struggle between the drives of national independence and colonial reconquest. In March 1945 Japanese occupiers ousted France from its century-old command of Indochina. Five months later Japan in turn lost its bid for dominance in Asia, and French forces headed back. However, times had irretrievably changed. The Indochinese had seen the once-indomitable white colonizer driven out by an Asian army. Morever, they had gotten an addictive taste of independence in the few weeks that elapsed between the Japanese defeat and the reappearance of the French.

In that month of freedom, Vietnam, the largest and traditionally most independent territory in French Indochina, declared its independence under the leadership of the *Vietnam Doc-Lap Dong Minh Hoi* (Revolutionary League for the Independence of Vietnam), known as the Vietminh. Led by the charismatic Ho Chi Minh, the Soviet-trained founder of the Indochinese Communist Party, the Vietminh had emerged as the predominant nationalist party of Vietnam by 1945. It also boasted the most powerful indigenous army: some 5,000 troops hardened in four years of guerrilla warfare with the Japanese. It was from this strong military and political base that Ho entered the northern Vietnamese capital of Hanoi, demanded the abdication of the Japanese puppet ruler, Emperor Bao Dai, and on September 2 proclaimed the independent Democratic Republic of Vietnam (DRV).

France had no intention of submitting to this *coup de main*. It had suffered enough blows to its prestige since 1940. Three weeks after Ho's proclamation, French forces, aided by British troops in the area, overthrew the DRV government in Saigon and began to push up from the south to restore French authority. For a time the two sides attempted to negotiate a settlement, but there was no basis for compromise. After a year of ineffectual dialogue, tempers snapped. On November 20, 1946, a bloody anticolonial riot broke out in the French-held port of Haiphong. Watching from the harbor, the crew of a French gunboat panicked. It opened fire into a crowd massing on the dock and killed some 6,000 Vietnamese civilians. One month later, on December 19, Vietminh forces replied with a major retaliatory strike directed at both French military garrisons and civilians. The French-Indochina War had begun.

The American government initially adopted a "hands off" policy. Despite its communist affiliation, the Vietminh had won the respect of many Asia-watchers for its anti-Japanese resistance campaign during World War II. Those who had come in contact with the Vietminh's leaders described them as dedicated nationalists representing a broad spectrum of the Vietnamese people. More critically, the Truman administration insisted on maintaining at least a public adherence to the Atlantic Charter and the cause of national self-determination. For several years the government refused France's request to provide military transport or direct financial aid for the war. On the other hand, Truman put no real pressure on France to come to terms with the Vietminh. Washington was far more concerned with strengthening the French government and aligning it securely with the United States than with solving a distant colonial problem. Even before World War II ended in Asia, Roosevelt's administration had agreed unofficially to accept, though not to aid, the reimposition of French sovereignty over Indochina. The conventional wisdom was that the US had little to gain—except enemies—by getting involved.

As the years passed and France failed to bring the war to a successful conclusion, Washington's attitude toward the Indochina War

3

gradually changed. The conflict came to be seen as one more front in the Cold War that was spreading like a glacier across the world. In July 1948, while the Western powers began talks on creating NATO, the State Department charged that Ho Chi Minh was chained to Moscow (though the accusers admitted they could not come up with any hard evidence proving the link).[3] One year later the NSC concluded that "Southeast Asia is the target of a coordinated offensive directed by the Kremlin. . . . If Southest Asia is also swept by communism we shall have suffered a major political rout the repercussions of which will be felt throughout the world."[4] Still, American policymakers held back from giving aid to the French earmarked for the Indochina War. France's nakedly imperialist aims raised Washington's scruples until the winter of 1949–50, when events in China convinced the government that it must adopt a new morality.

On October 1, 1949, Chinese Communist Party Chairman Mao Zedong announced victory over the Kuomintang and proclaimed the People's Republic of China (PRC). Five days later Congress passed the Mutual Defense Assistance Program to finance the efforts of noncommunist countries "to safeguard basic rights and liberties and to protect their security and independence."[5]

The US government officially dropped its anticolonialism policy in December, after Mao's army drove the Kuomintang off the Chinese mainland. With nearly three-quarters of Asia now under communist rule, the Truman administration determined that the Truman Doctrine must be extended to Asia, to strengthen the region from communist advances whether by outside aggression *or internal subversion.* The National Security Council agreed that the United States must prepare itself "to help within our means to meet such threats by providing political, economic, and military assistance." Though Washington should continue to do what it could to satisfy legitimate nationalist demands, the NSC concluded, it must put more effort into "minimizing the strain on the colonial powers who are our Western allies."[6]

The American commitment to the French-Indochina War followed almost immediately. On January 19, 1950, Beijing recognized Ho Chi Minh's DRV government as "the only legal government of the Vietnamese people." Before two weeks were out, Moscow followed. Paris then saw its chance to get the financial help it had come to realize was necessary for victory over the Vietminh. On February 2 the French National Assembly granted Indochina extremely limited self-rule as the French Associated States of Vietnam, Laos, and Cambodia. The hollowness of the gesture was manifested by France's selection of the submissive Bao Dai as "independent" Vietnam's leader. Nevertheless, Truman deemed that France had taken a sufficient step toward freeing its colonies. The next day the United States and the United Kingdom formally recognized the Associated States. Within three months Washington declared the French-Indochina War to be part of the global struggle against Soviet imperialism and extended $10 million in economic and military aid to the Associated States.

Any residual qualms about taking sides in a colonial war were overcome in June, when communist North Korea invaded the Republic of Korea to the south. Less than five years after VE Day, the United States plunged back into war in Asia, fighting alongside France and Britain, against what its leaders believed was a major foe bent on world domination. The enemy was not North Korea but international communism. The front was any place that was threatened by communist expansion. Four days after the outbreak of the Korean War, Truman dispatched eight C-47 cargo planes to aid the French Union forces in Indochina.[7]

America and France had joined hands in prosecuting a war, but it was evident from the start that the two allies did not agree on the cause for which they were united. Paris's objectives were quite simply to return Indochina securely to the French Union fold and to regain some of the national dignity lost in World War II. Washington saw itself backing an anticommunist crusade. To encourage this vision, successive French governments took care always to portray the Indochina conflict in Cold War hues. But Paris revealed its true colors by insisting on wholly controlling the military effort, blocking any UN discussion of what France termed its "domestic dispute," and refusing to grant the Associated States any real autonomy. Aligning the French-Indochina War with the superpower struggle was simply a way of courting desperately needed American aid to prosecute the colonial war. France believed in the domino effect, but it was more concerned with its implications for the empire than for the free world.

It was with considerable reluctance that France had turned to the

United States for aid in fighting the war. Since before World War II, Washington had advocated decolonization of Southeast Asia. French officials feared that once the United States began to bankroll the war it would press more seriously for independence.[8] The decision to risk that unpleasant prospect revealed the despair of the French military command at its inability to produce what it originally thought would be an easy victory.

Using classical tactics that had worked impressively in pacifying France's North African colonies, French Union forces prosecuted the Indochina War by securing key cities, then attempting to radiate authority outward into the surrounding countryside. But the jungles of Southeast Asia were in no way analogous to the desolate plains of North Africa. While government troops quickly gained control of nearly all of Vietnam's urban centers, they were unable to use them effectively as bases from which to control the rest of the country. Hit-and-run guerrilla raids emanating from rural sanctuaries never ceased. When French Union troops moved on a jungle enclave, the Vietminh retreated to another hamlet. When the regulars withdrew, the Vietminh returned. By this method, the guerrillas succeeded in tying up a large number of French Union troops in a mammoth game of hide-and-seek.

As the years passed and Indochina sucked a seemingly endless flow of men and money from the already war-weary and financially strapped French nation, Paris gradually accepted that it must have help to win the war. The people of France wanted to keep their colonies, but they had dug about as deeply into their pockets as they were willing. The National Assembly would not even finance the final offensive it demanded. So, warily, the French government turned to the United States and its offer of "mutual defense" funds.

Despite France's apparent weakness in having to approach Washington hat-in-hand, the United States was not in a strong position for molding either the aims or the methods of the Indochina War. The "loss" of China, the outbreak of the Korean War, and, especially, the convergence of the two in the Chinese intervention into the Korean War in November 1950, severely shook America's Far Eastern security policy. The Truman administration feared that a communist victory in Indochina would knock down every other domino in Asia. However, with its own forces tied up in Korea, Japan, and Europe, the United States could not directly take on the burden of stopping the Vietminh. Washington depended on the French to fight the war in Indochina as much as Paris depended on American dollars to finance it.

After 1951, Paris wielded even greater leverage by holding up ratification of the European Defense Community Treaty. Though neglected by historians of early US policy toward Indochina, the EDC obsessed American policymakers in its time. If ratified, the treaty would create an integrated European defense force, including armed German units. The US government believed that only through combining all of its strength could Western Europe ward off a North Korean-style attack from the Soviet bloc. The French, however, could not stomach the thought of a newly militarized Germany so soon after World War II, no matter how hungry they were for assistance. In the aftermath of the Chinese intervention into the Korean War, which raised fears of an East German attack on West Germany, culminating in a third world war, Paris had signed the defense pact, but thereafter the treaty sat, unratified, nearly unmentionable, while all of the remaining powers enacted it into law. No French government would risk its political neck by submitting the treaty to the National Assembly for ratification. Only American pressure kept Paris from killing the plan outright.

Creating the EDC was still a matter of first importance to the US government when Eisenhower moved into the Oval Office, and it remained a major goal during his first year and a half in power. (Eisenhower had pressed actively for the EDC from the beginning, when he was the commander of NATO forces.) As will be seen, as long as Paris held the treaty hostage, promising to ensure either its passage or defeat depending on US cooperativeness in Indochina, it severely constrained United States policy toward the French-Indochina War.

The war remained thoroughly France's even as the US commitment to it grew steadily over the years. In the 1951 fiscal year Congress authorized nearly $450 million for the prosecution cf the war; the next year the figure climbed to nearly $550 million, 40 percent of the total bill. Still, France paid 60 percent. By January 1953 France's cumulative outlay on the Indochina War exceeded $3.5 billion—more than twice its income from the Marshall Plan. France had suffered more than 90,000 casualties to America's 1 killed.[9] Instead of making concessions to the Americans toward the freeing of the Indochinese colonies, French officials complained bitterly that France was bearing the brunt of the free world's defense of Southeast Asia. The colonial/communist dilemma confused Washington. The outlays grew, but, despite strategic statements like NSC 124/2, the nature and ultimate extent of the US commitment to France's war in Indochina remained unclear. In Dean Acheson's words, the US Indochina policy had become a "muddled hodgepodge," neither inspiring France to end its colonial control of Indochina nor going all out to help the French secure the area.[10]

The term "muddled hodgepodge" equally describes the French military position in Indochina. Constantly harassed by invisible Vietminh guerrillas, unable to win the loyalty of the rural population, and never sufficiently supported by French francs or reinforcements, the French Union forces were beginning their eighth year of fighting what was supposed to have been a "mopping-up action" when Eisenhower won the presidency. By then, the Korean War had stabilized, allowing the Chinese to channel more aid and advisers to the Vietminh. Guerrilla commander General Vo Nguyen Giap used these resources to turn his irregulars into a well-organized and fully equipped army. Vietminh troops inflicted heavy losses on the French, squeezing them into enclaves in the Red River Delta, central Vietnam, and the major cities in the south. Still, the French Union command refused to admit that the enemy had become a professional army. The colonial generals continued to plan their campaigns on the suicidal prejudice that the Vietminh could not win a direct confrontation. The run of defeats that resulted devastated French morale. As the Americans would twenty years later, France and its forces in Indochina lost the will to continue fighting.

During the first year of the Eisenhower presidency, the French position in Indochina eroded steadily. In April 1953 the Vietminh spread their military operations into Laos. A less direct, but ultimately more damaging blow struck the French Union army in mid-summer: the Korean War armistice of July 27 significantly widened the Chinese military supply line to the Vietminh.[11] Simultaneously, the negotiated settlement of the stalemated Korean conflict—a partition agreement that sanctioned the coexistence of North and South Korea (one communist, the other tentatively democratic and decidedly capitalistic) — convinced French officials that negotiations offered the best escape route from their Indochina quagmire.

The idea of negotiating peace, universally disparaged by the Western allies after the conspicuous failures of the Versailles, Locarno, and Munich settlements, was gaining respectability in Europe in 1953. The death of Soviet dictator Joseph Stalin in March seemed to many Europeans to augur the end of the Cold War. Even before Stalin's body had been lowered into the ground, his successor, Georgi Malenkov, called for a return to "peaceful coexistence." Those words struck an irresistible chord within the nation of France, worn out by a dozen years of war, occupation, and more war. There were colonialists, like Conservative Prime Minister Joseph Laniel, who might have been willing to press on to regain all of Indochina, but they lacked the political strength to do it. Laniel's goal became to salvage as much as he could through negotiations.

On October 27 the prime minister of France announced that he was willing to enter into talks with Ho Chi Minh and, if necessary, the leaders of communist China. "My government now stands ready to avail itself of every opportunity to make peace," he declared.[12] The next day the National Assembly returned Laniel's four-month-old government (the eighteenth French government in seven years) a vote of confidence of 330 to 260, a strong mandate by Fourth Republic standards.

France's call for peace anticipated the failure of yet another "end-of-the-war offensive" against the Vietminh: the Navarre Plan. Formulated in May 1953 by the newly appointed commander in chief of the French Union forces in Indochina, General Henri Navarre, the plan aimed to consolidate the French position in southern Vietnam by 1954 in preparation for a major offensive against the north in 1954–55. The cost of the operation would be high. Navarre called for 50,000 more French troops, 100,000 more Vietnamese troops, and $400 million from Washington. It was too high for all but the Americans. Congress approved $400 million for the Indochina War in July, and another $385 million two months later. But, despite the financial boost and the guarded optimism it created in Paris, the Navarre Plan could not get off the ground.

In the field, Navarre's strategy suffered from the wholly mistaken assumption that the Vietminh could not muster the strength or discipline to win major battles. At home, it ultimately failed because of the impossible demands it made on the Laniel government and the French people. France's volunteer army did not have anything approaching the 50,000 available reserves Navarre wanted transfused into Indochina. The government already had bled its European forces, especially the officer corps, until France's NATO units were dangerously understrength. To raise that number of fresh troops, France would have to resort to conscription—politically out of the question. So, Paris only belatedly and very partially answered Navarre's request for additional troops; and the government forewarned the general that the new units were not reinforcements but merely early replacements for his projected 1953 losses.[13]

The Laniel government replied even less agreeably to Navarre's request for additional native troops. A small number of Vietnamese, loyal to France or simply opposed to the communists, had fought under the French flag since the war's outbreak. However, the French command's refusal to promote more than a handful of Vietnamese to officer rank or to entrust them with responsible duties, dissuaded most Indochinese from signing up. The colonial military liked it that way; it had little trust of Vietnamese soldiers. When in 1952 the French government grudgingly determined it must build up the indiginous units in Indochina in order to win over the Vietnamese people to the notion that they were fighting their own war for freedom against communism, the effort mired in its own insincerity. The 100,000 more Vietnamese troops Navarre demanded exceeded by a full 50 percent the number enlisted thus far. Navarre acknowledged that the only way to attract that number of Vietnamese fighting men would be to surrender some of France's sovereignty over the colony. No French government could agree to that. The nation endured the sacrifices of war for the singular purpose of restoring the empire. If Indochina were to be set free, there was no more reason to continue the sacrifice. Navarre thought like a soldier; his goal was to win the war. But in making his plan to do so he lost sight of what his country was fighting for.

By November 1953 the Navarre Plan, touted by the ruling coalition only that summer as the vehicle for victory, was running out of gas. French disillusionment with the war hit a new low following passage of a declaration by an ad hoc Vietnamese National Congress, called by Emperor Bao Dai of all people, demanding complete independence and declaring that, once freed, Vietnam would pull out of the French Union. A stung Laniel growled in reply that France "has no reason to prolong its sacrifices if the very people for whom they are being made disdain these sacrifices and betray them."[14]

Ironically, the Chinese communists registered the greatest alarm at the spreading defection of the French. They feared that France would suddenly abandon Indochina, creating a vacuum that the United States would leap to fill. China had supported the Vietminh with tens of thousands of tons of weapons, food, and other military supplies and equipment. It had trained Vietminh fighters, sent in hundreds of military advisers, even massed 200,000 soldiers along the Chinese-Vietnamese border to scare back the French. But, when push came to shove, Mao Zedong's government vastly preferred a French colony to an American presence on China's border. And, so soon after the costly Korean War, Beijing would do what was necessary to keep the Americans at a distance without again having to resort to arms.

What was necessary included abandoning the Vietminh as it was on the verge of victory. Prime Minister Zhou Enlai informed Ho that he must respond favorably to Laniel's peace feelers or risk a severance of military aid (currently pouring in at about 6,000 tons a month). As if that were not enough, Moscow added its weight to the pressure for negotiations. The politburo did not share China's concern with power struggles in Southest Asia; it sacrificed the Vietminh to ease the threat to Russia from the West. Moscow hoped that it could use the Indochina peace forum to nudge the French into abandoning the EDC.

Though it could outfight the French Foreign Legion, the Vietminh was no match against the combined forces of its own allies. On November 26, Ho Chi Minh told a reporter from the Swedish newspaper *Expressen* that he, too, was ready to negotiate a peaceful settlement. On February 18, 1954, despite heavy countervailing pressure from the US State Department against negotiating with communists, Laniel agreed to a date. The Western allies formally placed the French-Indochina War settlement on the agenda of the five-power Geneva Conference on Far Eastern Problems, scheduled to begin April 26.

To put themselves into better bargaining positions for the conference, the two belligerents then launched their final campaigns. Navarre's strategy was to defeat an anticipated second, more serious Vietminh invasion of northern Laos and to lure Giap into a set-piece battle instead of the harassing war that had been so much to the Vietminh's advantage. His method was to airdrop 12,000 of his best troops into an isolated valley outpost in northwest Vietnam, a target he believed was "sufficiently tempting to pounce at, but sufficiently strong to resist the onslaught."[15] Giap happily accepted the challenge. More than 50,000 Vietminh soldiers began the arduous march north to meet the enemy. The world then waited for the battle that would decide the future of Vietnam, France, and perhaps all of Asia: the battle for Dien Bein Phu.

Dwight Eisenhower watched Dien Bien Phu with greater concern than most Americans. The first Republican president in a score of years, Eisenhower had entered office in January 1953 vowing both to stop the spread of communism and to cut back on government (largely military) spending. In essence, this committed his administration to defeating the communist insurgency in Indochina without a costly deployment of American troops. The problem lay in achieving a solution that would neither too seriously compromise the president's own convictions nor tip the delicate balance in his government between the champions of the conflicting causes—be they Asia-Firsters, Europe-Firsters, or budget balancers.

Theoretically, Eisenhower had enough authority, especially in foreign policy matters, to take the lead in Indochina and expect Congress and the American public to follow. He had won an impressive electoral mandate: 55 percent of the vote, outscoring his Democratic opponent by 6.5 million. His stature as a military leader was unparalleled. However, his overcautiousness in the political realm (evidenced by his timidity in dealing with Joseph McCarthy), exacerbated by (even as it contributed to) the bumptiousness of the 83rd Congress, inhibited Ike from exercising a strong leadership role.

Eisenhower maintained a light hold on the Republican party. His election was a landslide for the hero of World War II, not a ground swell of Republicanism. The general had only recently declared himself a Republican, after having worked amicably with both the Roosevelt and Truman administrations. He had gotten along so well with the previous administration that Truman had approached him to head the *Democratic* ticket. Many voters still perceived Ike in nonpartisan terms—a national rather than a party leader.[16] He at times shared that view. Revealing his alienation from and sense of oppression by the Republican hierarchy, Ike openly dreamed of starting a third, centrist party that he could more easily manage. He admitted to having run for president on the Republican ticket primarily to prevent the party's traditional, isolationist (from Europe) right wing from taking over. Though he fell firmly within the Republican camp on domestic matters, he saw himself generally as a middle-of-the-road outsider. He believed that to govern effectively, therefore, he must seek to appease the party's insiders.

Ike's inability to translate his popularity into votes for other Republican candidates further enfeebled his power over Congress. Despite his diligent campaigning for every possible congressional candidate his party offered up, the Republicans barely scraped a victory out of the election. Republicans topped Democrats by only eleven House seats and by a bare one-vote plurality in the Senate. (Within a year even that poor advantage was lost when Republican Senator Robert Taft died and a Democrat replaced him.) Ike thus claimed a tenuous lead over an unsubstantial majority. To realize any of his legislative goals, even relying on some Democratic crossover votes, he had to secure virtually the unanimous allegiance of the Republicans in Congress—a Herculean feat.

Even more than is usual in the American two-party system, the Republican party of the 1950s was an uneasy coalition in opposition to the Democrats rather than a unified political body. Its membership divided itself into two essentially irreconcilable wings: the traditional Eastern-establishment, internationalist, Europe-oriented bloc, led by Eisenhower; and the neo-isolationist, Mid- and Far-West dominated "Asia Firsters," led initially by Ohio Senator Robert Taft (Eisenhower's chief rival for the party's nomination), then, after Taft's death in late 1953, by his successor as majority leader, California Senator William F. Knowland. The two camps united only in their conservative fiscal philosophy. Although they agreed that Truman's "containment" foreign policy had failed in Asia and would eventually bankrupt the United States, they could reach no consensus on what should replace it. The Taft wing vehemently opposed enlarging

America's collective security commitments to Europe, tended to favor unilateralism in dealings with Asia, and stood solidly behind the "massive retaliation" concept of basing America's security primarily on the Strategic Air Command and the threat of a nuclear strike. Eisenhower, predictably, was committed just as firmly to collective security and multilateralism, and had considerably less faith in the ability of bombs alone to win wars. The clash between Taft's and Eisenhower's foreign policies had dominated the often bitter primary.

Once he won the party's nomination, Eisenhower showed himself willing to modify his positions in order to make peace with Taft and his followers. Without them, he believed, he would not have the votes to achieve any of his legislative goals. In his quest for compromise, he accepted in his platform a number of foreign policy clauses that offended his natural temperateness. These included the provocative vow to reverse "the negative, futile, and immoral policy of 'containment' which abandons countless human beings to despotism and Godless terrorism." (The main result of such defamatory rhetoric was to alienate the Democrats and imperil Eisenhower's ability to maintain bipartisanship in foreign affairs.) However reluctantly, he also allowed the platform to include a sentiment that would come back to haunt him at Dien Bien Phu: "we shall end neglect of the Far East which Stalin has long identified as the road to victory over the West. We shall make it clear that we have no intention to sacrifice the East to gain time for the West."[17]

Unfortunately for Eisenhower, neither the words nor the symbolic actions (like endorsing Republican candidates he detested) that he offered as sacrifices to party unity could appease the right wing. It was impatient to have its own way now that it finally had overturned the Democrats. The GOP of Eisenhower's first term remained split right down the middle. The 83rd Congress divided as evenly between Taft and Eisenhower Republicans as between Republicans and Democrats.[18]

The strain between the president and his party's legislators transcended ideology. The Republicans on the Hill had grown inflexible after calcifying for two decades on the political sidelines, where their job had been to denounce rather than to pass legislation. Not a single Republican senator and only fifteen GOP representatives had ever served under a president of their party. By the time they attained the chairmanships, the senior senators had developed a pattern of independence from, even antagonism to the White House. Eisenhower attempted to bring them into line by cajolery and compromise. But, try as he might, the president never achieved an easy working relationship with the congressional leadership.

Constant bickering between the executive and legislature, especially over foreign policy, marked Eisenhower's first year and a half in office. The Republicans in Congress tried hard to force the White House to repudiate the "secret agreements" made at Yalta and Potsdam. More seriously and concertedly, they fought to limit the president's treaty-making powers and assert greater congressional control over foreign policy via the Bricker Amendment. Fifty-eight times in 1953, proposals forwarded by Eisenhower to Congress passed thanks only to a large Democratic crossover.[19] In his 1954 State of the Union address the president called for a "bold new program" of foreign trade, mutual security, tax stimulation for economic growth, public housing, and social security liberalization. Instead, the Republican leadership made the passage of the Bricker Amendment—openly opposed by Eisenhower—its top priority.[20] In late January, the Army-McCarthy showdown grabbed the spotlight even from the Bricker Amendment, and the president's program faded from the House and Senate agendas entirely.

Ike fumed, but, except for his opposition to the Bricker Amendment, he avoided head-on battle. Eisenhower had built his impressive career on his talent for working with obdurate associates. To coax along the overblown egos of a Churchill or a Montgomery or a MacArthur, he had learned to submerge his own. He believed that the same technique would eventually win over the barons of Capitol Hill. Though by rights he should have become more overtly assertive once he attained the nation's highest office, he did not. Discomfort at being perceived as a military man running the civilian government may have actually increased his reticence. That and his deep respect for the separation of powers led Ike to defer to Congress more frequently than other post-Depression presidents. When he did oppose the legislature or the Republican leadership, he preferred persuasion to confrontation, manipulation to command. Except when he judged the stakes to be highest, the president calculated that the benefits of taking a strong lead could not compensate for the support that might cost him in his party or Congress. As he described it, "With such a line-up on Capitol Hill, I knew from the beginning that noisy, strong-armed tactics would accomplish nothing, even were I so inclined."[21]

Even had his party been more cooperative, Eisenhower still would have faced difficulties in turning the promises of his campaign into realities. The Republican party had won the presidency and its slim majority on the contrary platform of "No more Koreas" (land wars in Asia), "No more Chinas" (commuist victories in the Far East), and promises of a balanced budget and tax cuts (no more huge defense outlays). Beneath the rhetoric there was no concord on how these pledges were to be fulfilled.

Eisenhower's decision to accept a negotiated peace in Korea, restoring the *status quo ante bellum,* exposed the paradoxes of the Republicans' demands. Most of the nation and its politicians, though not delighted with the peace terms, supported them as the necessary price for ending the unpopular war. However, party hard-liners, among them House Speaker Joseph Martin and senior Senator William Jenner, denounced the armistice as a victory for the communists. China Lobbyists growled that if Truman had signed such a shameful "surrender" they would have demanded his impeachment. Even Dulles tried to dissuade the president from agreeing to a division of Korea. Nevertheless, Eisenhower would not renounce the peace compromise he knew the American people demanded and that he believed was in the nation's best interest. The majority of Republicans, who supported the armistice, were able to rationalize partition by shifting the blame for "losing" North Korea onto the Democrats. Truman had created a debacle by his failure to consult Congress and to prosecute the war fully in the first place, they said; Eisenhower had to bring it to an honorable, if imperfect, conclusion in order to unshackle his administration and its national defense policy from those Democratic-imposed bonds and to create a clear strategic perimeter.[22]

If the president could draw the ire of the Republican old guard by ending an extremely unpopular and debilitating stalemate that he could blame on his Democratic predecessor, how would he fare once he had established his "clear strategic perimeter"? Specifically, how could he prevent future communist victories while honoring his campaign pledges to reduce the standing army, balance the budget, and cut taxes?

His answer to the dilemma was the "New Look." As formulated in NSC 162/2 and approved by Eisenhower in October 1953, the New Look policy sought to prune the Truman administration's mushrooming defense outlays while continuing to nurture America's global commitments. Its device was to put more emphasis on training and equipping indigenous troops. Local armies would be the first line of defense in regional aggressions. US tactical air and sea forces, including nuclear forces, would act as conspicuous reserves, a sword of Damocles that would fall only if absolutely necessary. Supporters claimed that by deemphasizing conventional weapons, the New Look would allow a safe reduction of US troops by 25 percent and of military expenditures by 30 percent within three years. In immediate terms, Eisenhower reduced the active army from the FY 1954 level of twenty divisions to seventeen in FY 1955, while boosting outlays for continental air defense by a billion dollars.

Eisenhower fervently believed that a nation's security is based on its economic stability as much as on its military power. The "maximum strength" defense policy of the Truman administration he declared to be "pure rot" and "wildly irresponsible." "We must see, clearly and steadily, just exactly what is the danger before us," Eisenhower urged the House Air Force Appropriations Subcommittee.

It is more than merely a military threat. It has been coldly calculated by the Soviet leaders, for by their military threats they have hoped to force upon America and the free world an unbearable security burden leading to economic disaster. . . . Communist guns, in this sense, have been aiming at an economic target no less than a military target. . . .

[Our] defense must, first of all, be one which we can bear for a long— and indefinite—period of time. It cannot consist of sudden, blind responses to a series of fire-alarm emergencies. . . .

To watch vigilantly on the military front must never mean to be blind on the domestic front. . . . Prolonged inflation could be as destructive of a truly free economy as could a chemical attack against an army in the field.[23]

As he more bluntly put it some time later, "A bankrupt America is a defenseless America."[24]

While all in the Eisenhower administration agreed with the cost-cutting goal of the New Look, they did not agree on the proper means to achieve that end. NSC 162/2 could be and was read in many ways. Eisenhower interpreted the New Look primarily as a policy of strengthening other nations' economies, political structures, and home armies so that they could defend themselves if attacked, with America providing only a backup threat. He did not favor exclusive or even predominant reliance on nuclear weapons for world defense.[25] His secretary of state, on the other hand, tended to focus narrowly on the nuclear deterrent aspects of the philosophy. Promulgating what became known widely as the "massive retaliation" doctrine, Dulles defined the New Look in a major foreign policy address in January 1954 as reliance on the presumptive threat of America's "great capacity to retaliate instantly, by means and at places of our own choosing," in order not to spread American power too thin in an array of small conventional wars.[26] The chairman of the Joint Chiefs of Staff, Admiral Arthur Radford, took the doctrine an active step further: the New Look, he said, puts "maximum reliance on nuclear weapons *from the outset*" of a conflict (emphasis added).[27] To Radford the nuclear arsenal was not primarily a deterrent force, but a stockpile of very usable, superior weapons. The cost-conscious 83rd Congress, while opposed to the wide use of nuclear weapons in theory, in practice preferred whichever policy was the cheapest. The House voted to slash nearly a quarter off Eisenhower's FY 1954 mutual security request, even though the president warned that any cuts in funds to build up allied forces would undermine his entire New Look defense structure.

The New Look indulged such varying readings during Eisenhower's first year in office because no new foreign policy crisis had translated it from theory into action. Confined to words, the New Look glossed over the administration's internal differences and satisfied the Republican old guard without offending Ike's own moderate following. Once the plea of an ally about to be defeated by communists forced the president to put his policy into practice, however, the illusion of consensus would be divulged. Eisenhower, a self-confessed master equivocator, was alert to the risks of candor.

It is no longer shocking or even unorthodox to state that President Eisenhower was a skillful politician, as it was shortly after he left office, when former Vice President Richard Nixon told an incredulous world that Ike was "far more complex and devious than most people realized."[28] Nixon got it just right. As has been said, Eisenhower's genius lay not in decisive leadership, but in achieving his goals discreetly. Convinced that he could maintain his broad political appeal only if he satisfied the powerful forces on the right wing as he carefully played to the center, Eisenhower let others in his administration take the blame for unpopular stands and himself the credit for moderating them. To be the heavy was the role of his subordinates, ideologues like Radford, Secretary of the Treasury George Humphrey, and, especially, Dulles.

The debates over strategic doctrine and the Korean armistice were neither the first nor the last in which the president would take a more moderate line than his secretary of state. John Foster Dulles was far more doctrinaire a cold warrior than Ike. Though Eisenhower liked and respected his foreign policy chief, he occasionally grew exasperated at Dulles' mental rigidity and his tendency to be overly provocative. (Ike recalled, for example, how he had been forced to call Dulles onto the carpet during the campaign for failing to use the word "peaceful" in a speech advocating measures by the United States to liberate the "captive peoples" of Eastern Europe.)[29] More often, Eisenhower turned Dulles' verbal aggressiveness to his own advantage. In the words of a leading Eisenhower historian, Dulles became the president's "lightning rod, absorbing domestic criticisms and warding off attacks from the Right with his moralistic rhetoric."[30]

Dulles readily shielded the president from the considerable heat generated by US policymaking in the Cold War. He may have disagreed with Eisenhower's willingness to negotiate with communists, but he certainly did not want to see America's foreign policy hamstrung by isolationist Asia-Firsters. He was a smart enough politician to understand that, with the weak Republican majority divided as it was into equal blocs, Eisenhower's only hope of implementing his foreign policy agenda was by maintaining his popularity with the centrists of both parties. Moreover, the secretary of state never lost sight of from whom he derived his prestige and power of office.

Eisenhower gave Dulles almost complete rein in espousing, advising on, and even formulating foreign policy, but the decision on how to carry it out came from the Oval Office.[31] For his part, Dulles did not let his usually strong opinions on the direction foreign policy should take override his duty to carry out the wishes of the president.[32] He spoke bluntly at meetings, took a sharper tone than his boss in public, and liberally interpreted the president's orders; but he never repeated the professionally fatal mistake made by his uncle, Robert Lansing, secretary of state under Woodrow Wilson, who lost the president's confidence by pursuing too independent a course. Eisenhower rewarded his secretary's loyalty by always backing him up in public—even when he had made a mistake—and by letting the world believe that Dulles was the architect of the administration's foreign policy. But White House insiders had no misconceptions as to who was in command. Said General Lucius Clay, Eisenhower's friend and the man who first brought Dulles to his attention, Eisenhower "was very glad for Mr. Dulles to make everything but a major decision, as long as they were thinking alike."[33]

Dulles acted as Eisenhower's chief adviser in all areas of foreign policy except military strategy. On purely strategic matters he tended to defer to the military experts, chief among them the president himself.[34] However, in typical Eisenhower fashion, the public role of military strategist was played by a subordinate, JCS Chairman Admiral Radford. A Navy pilot who had once commanded the Pacific Fleet, Radford radiated the self-assuredness of the stereotypical airman, quickly eclipsing the nit-picking and equivocal secretary of defense, Charles Wilson. Radford had early caught Eisenhower's ear with his outspoken support of the cost-cutting goals of the New Look. With his reputation as a "ruthless partisan and outstanding bureaucratic infighter," Radford seemed just the man to wrestle the administration's budget cuts through the resistant defense establishment and its supporters in Congress.[35]

Unfortunately, the JCS chairman's definition of the New Look differed significantly from Eisenhower's. Radford, it will be recalled, favored a policy of reliance on a mobile strategic strike force in all varieties of international crises (the product, perhaps, of his training as a carrier pilot), whereas the president remained unconvinced that air power would be sufficient to wage war without ultimately having to call on ground forces. In this, Radford also conflicted with the Army and Navy chiefs of staff. And, though not so clearly, he was at odds with Dulles, with whom he shared a certain ideological kinship and for whom he thought he was a principal adviser.[36] The secretary of state agreed with Radford that the United States must take a hard line against communists, but he was far more cautious in advocating force than was the admiral, who rarely considered the larger ramifications of action.

Eisenhower himself, though firmly anticommunist, was a pragmatist in foreign affairs. He preferred to settle matters peacefully if possible, but he did not disdain the use of force when he judged it necessary. In those cases he favored quick, covert actions that promised fast results. He admired the deterrent aspect of massive retaliation, but he possessed no illusion that the threat or use of nuclear weapons would or should resolve all conflicts. His response to military threats depended on dozens of international, domestic, political, military, economic, even historical factors. That said, he did consistently operate on four basic principles: (1) if you appeal to force you must be willing to wield it to the limit necessary to ensure success; (2) power must be used selectively so as to conserve its strength; (3) you must keep control over the choice of weapons; and (4) a country's legal and moral positions and its retention of favorable world opinion are major sources of power.[37]

In his first year of office, Eisenhower frequently demonstrated his own brand of selective, controlled response. From his controversial order removing the US 7th Fleet from the Taiwan Strait and "unleashing" Chiang Kai-Shek's forces (intended to move the PRC toward a more conciliatory stance in the Korean truce talks), to his quick negotiation of the Korean armistice, to his approval of a covert CIA-sponsored coup in Iran, to his decision not to test the Republican party's "liberation" rhetoric during the June East German riots (which were rapidly suppressed by Soviet tanks), Eisenhower displayed his pragmatism. He judged each case for force on its merits and probable costs as defined by his four principles.

Among the most compelling foreign policy issues confronting Eisenhower in his first year and a half in the White House, the French-Indochina War stood out. It certainly ranked as one of the most complex ideologically. France's pleas for help in its continuing battle with the Vietminh raised the weighty issues of colonialism, the effectiveness of the New Look and massive retaliation doctrines, and the strength and dependability of the Western alliance system. The question of what action the administration should take would sharply divide the nation's decision-makers. However, this was not yet evident in 1953, when France limited its requests to material and verbal support.

Initially, like its Democratic predecessor, the Eisenhower administration focused its efforts on boosting the French will to win the war, while urging Paris to grant Indochina its independence. In keeping with the New Look doctrine, the administration put its military might implicitly behind the French by publicly warning on a number of occasions that Chinese or Soviet aggression would trigger an American response. As it took this united public stance, however, the administration privately impressed upon the French that the aid well would run dry unless they cooperated more fully with Washington: specifically, US Military Assistance Advisory Group (MAAG) personnel in Saigon must be let in on the details of the French Union forces' plans and operations; Paris must pledge firmly to expand the Vietnamese National Army; and, to realize that pledge, France must give the Vietnamese forces something to fight for—independence. In fact, Eisenhower had no more strength to force these concessions on the French than had Truman. America remained constrained by its reliance on its ally to defeat the Vietminh and by the rising priority it placed on France's ratification of the EDC. When all of the points were totaled, France continued to hold the stronger hand.

Eisenhower's commitment to the war in Indochina, therefore, climbed steadily, despite persistent French foot-dragging on broadening the war effort. The commitment stepped up all the more quickly as French enthusiasm for the war slipped away. Each sign of defeatism in Paris heightened fears in Washington that France would pull out of the war—a scenario that concluded with the equally odious alternatives of a Vietminh victory or United States intervention to replace France.[38] Thus, ironically, in trying to keep American troops out of Vietnam, the Eisenhower administration linked American prestige ever more closely to the colonial war.

The American commitment to the French-Indochina War swelled in the second half of 1953, with the suspension of hostilities in Korea. In July and September Congress voted to support the French Union forces with $785 million. Having eased France's financial worries, the administration then sought to calm Paris' and Saigon's fears that the Korean armistice would free China to intervene in the war in Indochina. "There is a risk that, as in Korea, China might send its own army into Indochina," Dulles warned in September 1953. "The Chinese Communist regime should realize that such aggression could not occur without grave consequences which might not be confined to Indochina."[39]

Despite all America's morale boosting, Prime Minister Laniel told the White House that summer that his government would collapse unless he put the Indochina War on the negotiating agenda of the Geneva Conference on Far East Problems, originally scheduled to tie up the loose ends remaining in the Korean settlement. Few within the Eisenhower administration had any confidence that negotiations stemming from France's military and political collapse in Vietnam would produce results favorable to the Indochinese people or to United States interests. Still, Eisenhower believed that, if he refused French demands for negotiating a settlement, he would morally oblige the United States to ensure France a victory in the field, no matter what the cost. The president felt also that he must accommodate Laniel, since "no succeeding government would take a stronger position than his [Laniel's] on the defense of Indochina, or in support of the European Defense Community."[40] So he agreed to add Indochina to the Geneva Conference agenda. In the contrary way of international politics, the peace initiative only hardened American military support of the French in Vietnam. Arguing that "negotiations with no other alternative usually end in capitulation," the administration tried rapidly to build up French morale and military might in preparation for Geneva.[41]

On January 7, 1954, Dulles declared before an executive session of the Senate Foreign Relations Committee that France was in the process of "perfecting" the independence of the Associated States. Given the indigenous population's "lack of political maturity," he asserted, independence was progressing as rapidly as the United States could ask.[42] (His words, intended to spread the message that America stood solidly behind France, did not signify a real change in the administration's policy on colonialism. However, they do testify that the Eisenhower government viewed the Indochina War primarily as a battle in the Cold War rather than as a war for liberation. Despite its insistence privately that "the key to victory [in Indochina] is the dedicated participation on the part of native (Vietnam) troops in the struggle," the White House publicly sacrificed—or, more precisely, ignored—Indochinese morale in order to boost that of the French.)[43]

The day after Dulles' Senate appearance, the National Security Council ordered the Defense Department and Central Intelligence Agency "urgently" to assess what steps the United States should take, *short of direct intervention,* to help ensure the success of the Navarre Plan.[44] For himself, the president formed a "Special Committee on Indochina" to come up with "an *area* plan, including the possible alternative lines of action to be taken in case of a reverse in Indo-China, or elsewhere in the area."[45] As his instructions to the Special Committee suggest, Eisenhower had not drawn a hard containment line on the China-Vietnam border. Despite the support he lent the French, Eisenhower was not optimistic that the Navarre Plan would be any more successful than previous French military plans for victory in Indochina.

Since before he became president, Eisenhower had criticized France's mode of conducting the war. His firecracker temper flared over Paris's unwillingness to develop the allegiance of the Vietnamese people or to construct an indigenous army with a native officer corps, and the outright refusal of the French military to give ears to American advice on how to counter guerrilla warfare. As president he assailed Navarre's decision to make his last stand before Geneva at Dien Bien Phu—a valley clearing surrounded on all sides by thick, camouflaging jungle, with no roads in or out for supply, reinforcement, or retreat. When Navarre stuck by his choice, despite Eisenhower's personal urgings that he reconsider, Ike was furious. "[T]he French wanted to run the war just exactly the way they decided," Ike recalled in his memoirs.

They wanted our help but wanted also our hands off of it. Well we didn't like this very much.

Finally, they came along with this Dien Bien Phu plan. As a soldier, I was horror-stricken. I just said, "My goodness, you don't pen troops in a fortress, and all history shows that they are just going to be cut to pieces. . . . I don't think anything of this scheme."[46]

Nevertheless, Navarre was committed to having his set-piece battle. And, once the pieces were in place, Eisenhower felt obliged to give him what support he could to prevent a total rout. Unfortunately, concluded the NSC at the dawn of 1954, "there is not in sight any desirable alternative" to backing Navarre.[47]

On January 29, 1954, Eisenhower's Special Committee on Indochina met to discuss "urgent French requests" for increased material assistance to wage the imminent battle of Dien Bien Phu. Assessing the requests were Radford, Director of Central Intelligence Allen Dulles (the secretary of state's brother), Undersecretary of State Walter Bedell Smith (Eisenhower's chief of staff in World War II and Allen Dulles' predecessor as CIA chief), Deputy Secretary of Defense Roger Kyes, and C. D. Jackson, the White House adviser on Cold War strategy.

The considerable shopping list before them included twenty-two B-26 bombers and four hundred Air Force mechanics to maintain them. If dispatched, the mechanics would become the first active American military presence in the French-Indochina War. (The few dozen MAAG officers assigned to Saigon were so circumscribed in their movements and access to information that they were not at the time, nor should they now be, considered active.)

Kyes and Allen Dulles opposed the requests. The deputy defense secretary voiced the apprehension that would prove uppermost in the minds of Congress, the JCS, and the public. To send uniformed technicians to assist the French Union Air Force in the field, he warned, could "so commit the United States to support of the French that we must be prepared eventually for complete intervention, including US combat forces." Allen Dulles' opposition was more conditional. He shared his brother's principal concern throughout the Dien Bien Phu crisis that the Eisenhower administration's "preoccupation with helping to win the battle at Dien Bien Phu" must not blind it to the need "to bargain with the French as we supplied their most urgent needs."[48]

The majority of the committee, however, decided that the urgency of the military siutation required a prompt, positive response. Kyes' and Allen Dulles' caveats elicited only a minor modification in the Special Committee's recommendation. The committee advised the president to send the technicians, but to reduce their number to two hundred and to obtain a promise from the French that they "be used only on air bases which were entirely free from capture." Smith and Radford added on record that, although they did not believe that sending the mechanics to Indochina would lead to military intervention, "if worse came to the worst [they] personally would favor intervention with United States air and naval—not ground forces."[49] Eisenhower approved the committee's recommendations (without comment on Smith's and Radford's addendum) and immediately signed the order dispatching the mechanics.

Congress, which learned of the technicians deal through a press leak, reacted violently, not only to the deal itself, but to its being made without congressional approval. To reduce tension, the president met personally with the top lawmakers in early February to explain why he had decided to send the mechanics to Indochina.[50] The meeting was fraught with tension and fear that troops would follow. Senate Majority Whip and Chairman of the Armed Services Committee Leverett Saltonstall led a vehement opposition, specifically to the sending of *noncivilian* mechanics. Eisenhower agreed that it was not the ideal course of action. He would prefer to send no Americans at all and to rely on indigenous troops, he said. However, that option was not available at present. The president said that sending the Air Force mechanics had the merit of being a "small project to serve a very large purpose—that is, to prevent all of Southeast Asia from falling to the Communists." By patience, persuasion, and compromise (the president vowed that the American technicians would remain only until they could train French mechanics and in no case past mid-June), Eisenhower eventually won the leaders' promise to support his decision on the Hill.[51] An outcry continued for several days to reverberate in the press and among the congressional rank and file; then it, too, faded away.

Eisenhower's handling of the mechanics controversy is illustrative. When he believed an action was a necessary and right one—especially when it involved a small, limited investment with a potentially big payoff—he decided on his own to go ahead. Afterwards, if need be, he met *personally* with key congressmen to persuade them to back him up. Both the sequence of events and the fact that he made a personal appeal are vital. Though, as has been said, he preferred to avoid direct confrontation, Eisenhower made exceptions when he felt the issue was particularly important and particularly imperiled. His sustained opposition to the Bricker Amendment is a prominent example. He came out of hiding during the mechanics controversy both because he believed his decision was the right one and one that must be implemented without delay, and because he wanted to mend fences with Congress after having acted unilaterally. In fact, Ike possessed considerable authority in military matters. Urged directly by the nation's foremost expert on war, even the normally independent 83rd Congress agreed to support a step its members feared could lead to US intervention in the French-Indochina War.

The congressional leaders' initial hostility to France's aid request served as a pointed reminder to Eisenhower, though he hardly needed one, that the nation's wounds were still fresh from the Korean War. If the legislature raised such fearsome objections to dispatching a couple of hundred mechanics to relatively low-risk areas in Indochina, it certainly would not sit passively while the president ordered bombing strikes or otherwise intervened in the war. Eisenhower's instinct was to steer clear of French Indochina. The hackles raised in Congress and the press by the mechanics deal reaffirmed his belief that Vietnam could not be won for the price Americans were willing to pay.

As soon as Congress passed the aid package, the president moved to calm the storm. "I cannot conceive of a greater tragedy for America than to get heavily involved in an all-out war in that area," he said in his February 10 press conference, when questioned about Indochina.[52] His conception was about to be put to the test.

II

The Ely Mission

The battle for Dien Bien Phu began on March 13, 1954. One week later, General Paul Ély, France's chief of staff, flew to Washington at Radford's invitation to brief the US defense establishment on the military situation in Indochina. Ély's mission would be the prime mover in the Dien Bien Phu drama, mostly because of the misunderstandings it created. These began even before Ély arrived. Radford thought that his French counterpart had come at last to listen to the Pentagon's suggestions for "strengthening and broadening" US assistance to the French Union forces.[1] In fact, Ély had been charged by his civilian superiors "to get the United States to align its position with our own"—in other words, to help prepare the ground for a negotiated settlement of the war.[2]

Though most American policymakers still clung to their vision of a total victory in Indochina won through the united efforts of French and Vietnamese soldiers and American money, advisers, technicians, and trainers, the French more than ever wanted out. Defense Minister René Pleven exposed the depths of France's battle fatigue in an "off-the-record" meeting with senior American newspaper correspondents in Paris just two days before Ély flew to America. He and Ély had returned recently from an extensive tour of the Indochina battle zone and had discussed their findings at length with the government in Paris. The judgment of the Laniel government was firm, Pleven told the newsmen. It no longer was interested in the Pentagon's optimistic assessments of France's potential for victory in Indochina; France was committed to achieving peace by negotiation and saving what it could through partition of Indochina. Ély had been ordered to Washington, said Pleven, for the "express purpose" of convincing the Joint Chiefs of Staff that, in pursuit of a favorable settlement, France did not need America's military presence, but rather its willingness to grant political concessions, including recognition, to communist China. He warned that if Washington withheld those concessions the Indochina peace talks would collapse, the Laniel government would fall, and the prospects for realizing the EDC and, perhaps, for any future Franco-American cooperation in the Atlantic Alliance would be buried.[3]

Pleven's words, duly reported to the White House, seemed clear enough. In reality, however, the differences between the positions taken by Paris and Washington were neither so clear nor even so extreme as Pleven implied. The defense minister himself confessed that his government would be dismayed if Eisenhower *openly* ruled out future US intervention in the war. The implied threat of action, he admitted, would be "one of the West's valuable cards" at Geneva.[4] Further muddying the picture, Ély's recollection of the orders given him by the Defense Committee, the foreign policy arm of the Laniel cabinet, made no mention of seeking American concessions toward China. And he never raised that issue during his visit. When he did bring up the subject of China with the Americans, it was to seek a promise to retaliate if Beijing directly intervened against the French.

Many of the mixed signals emanating from Paris can be traced to the incredible fragmentation of the French political structure at the time. Like all of its predecessors in the Fourth Republic, the Laniel government was a coalition. The most sensitive cabinet positions were filled by the leaders of competing parties, allied to Laniel's Conservatives only so long as it proved expedient, forever poised to jump ship if they thought it might win them their own command. Though the far-right Republican Independent (Conservative) party held the premier position, the top foreign policy posts went to allies on its left. Foreign Minister Georges Bidault led the Catholic, center-left Popular Republican Movement (MRP). Defense Secretary Pleven headed the right wing of the centrist Democratic and Socialist Union of the Resistance (USDR).

While the Conservatives, MRP, and USDR agreed on the broad themes of foreign policy (they all favored empire and, to varying degrees, European integration), their representatives in the cabinet backed different methods according to the rules of their perpetual competition for publicity and power. The rivalry was particularly intense and personal between Laniel and Bidault; the latter had come within a single vote of winning the premiership that eventually fell to Laniel. Pleven had no close shot at becoming premier, but he had a strong reason for wanting to affect the direction of the French-Indochina War. The author of the plan for the European Defense Community, Pleven wanted to settle the Indochina War without delay, so that France's attentions and military strength could return to Europe. The Americans could never be sure whether France's foreign policymakers were speaking for the government or their own constituency.

The entire Laniel cabinet shared a stultifying ambivalence toward mustering the military capacity of the United States, however, and this created still more inconsistency in their dealings with Washington. The French government balanced on the precariously thin line between its desire for a wholly believable threat of US intervention that would strengthen its bargaining position at the Geneva Conference and its fear that the United States might carry out that threat. Thus the Defense Committee told Ély he must persuade Washington to extend its material support of the French Union forces in Indochina and get "ironclad assurances of United States aerial intervention in the event of direct Chinese intervention," while at the same time convincing the Americans to abandon "the opinion that a military solution to the conflict was possible within a reasonable time."[5]

Ély's orders also reflected the Defense Committee's renewed confidence in Navarre's Dien Bien Phu plan. In February Ély and Pleven had toured the Indochina battlefront. The impressions they brought back, particularly of Dien Bien Phu, had been, in Ély's words, "rather comforting."[6] This does not mean that the French now believed they could win the war, but they did believe they could win the battle for Dien Bien Phu, giving France the upper hand at Geneva—all without having to call on, and answer to, the Americans for more direct support.

The Ely Mission

In the heart-shaped valley of Dien Bien Phu, about eight by twelve miles in size, Navarre had positioned twelve of his best fighting battalions. Eight strongpoints defended the outpost, four in the center and four on the peripheries. Supplies landed daily on the fortress's two airstrips. In the estimations of Ély and Pleven after their brief inspection, the garrison's artillery, ammunition, and aircraft, including six fighter-bombers, could more than sufficiently support the 13,000 defenders. The observers seemed to have based this conclusion not so much on what they saw as on what they heard. Their guide, General Navarre, infected the defense minister and chief of staff with his hubris. He estimated that it would require an enemy force of three times the size of the Dien Bien Phu garrison to break through the defense. Not only would Giap find it impossible to move so large an army with all its necessary equipment up the steep, jungly hills surrounding the valley, Navarre assured his superiors, but the effort would tie down the Vietminh's main battle force in a static battle on French terms. Once Giap took the bait and ordered his troops to attack in the open—as Navarre insisted the Vietminh general must do if he hoped to defeat the garrison—the defenders would slaughter them, clearing the way to a French victory at Geneva.[7]

Caught up in the optimism radiating from both the French Union command and the Dien Bien Phu defense force, even doubters like Pleven forgot their earlier objections to the battle site. The Pleven mission concluded that "despite the tactical disadvantages of its location it [Dien Bien Phu] appeared to be in an extremely strong position . . . with attack extremely likely to fail." Indeed, the garrison was "hoping and wishing for an attack and feared only one thing: that the enemy might give up his attempt to capture the place."[8]

The Dien Bien Phu garrison, Navarre, Pleven, Ély, and the Laniel government had disastrously misplaced their hopes. By March 20, when Ély presented his report to the Americans, the power of the first Vietminh thrust already had shattered the myth of the impregnability of Dien Bien Phu. The bombardment began on March 13. "Almost immediately," Foreign Minister Bidault recalls, "we discovered that the stronghold of Dien Bien Phu was a deadly trap."[9] In the first five days of battle, the Vietminh overran the fortress's three northern strongpoints, knocked out both airstrips (temporarily), and killed or wounded the equivalent of two French Union battalions. A third battalion deserted. CIA Director Allen Dulles reported to Eisenhower that agency estimates gave the defenders only a fifty-fifty chance of holding out.[10]

The Laniel government began a slide into panic and despair that would accelerate rapidly in the next several weeks. It had real cause for alarm. The ruling coalition faced the humiliating prospect of a major, highly publicized defeat that would surely bring down the government, and most likely would turn over the leadership of France to the parties on the left. On a higher level, the government saw the nation's peace strategy swept away by waves of Vietminh pouring over Dien Bien Phu. With the Geneva Conference set to open in just over a month, Paris had to do something immediately to reverse the tide of battle or see its power to secure a reasonable partition shipwrecked. The Laniel government impulsively, incrementally cast away its inhibitions and called out to the one ally who had the power and motivation to rescue its forces: the United States.

Ély was the first to raise seriously the question of US intervention into the Indochina War. He did not do so at the start of his visit to Washington, but only after days of encouragement by Admiral Radford and a spiraling succession of reports on the devastation at Dien Bien Phu. Under this powerful pressure, Ély gradually transformed his mission from a perfunctory briefing and shopping trip to a frenzied hunt for a way to save the besieged fortress and restore France's crumbling negotiating position. The urgency that overlay conversations between the French chief of staff and the JCS chairman would further cloud the already indistinct dialogue between the allies, as plans were improvised with little regard for their implications or for the positions of the actual decision-makers. One result would be to add another layer of confusion to the thick haze surrounding the position of the president himself.

On the evening of his arrival, Saturday, March 20, Ély dined at Radford's home with the JCS chairman, Army Chief of Staff General Matthew Ridgway, Vice President Nixon, and CIA Director Allen Dulles. The mood was agitated, the dinner guests shaken by the grim reports from Dien Bien Phu and the pessimistic French and American estimates of the garrison's hopes of survival. In view of the seriousness of the moment, the guests quickly dispensed with pleasantries.

Throughout the evening the conversation remained fixed on the ominous turn of events in Indochina.[11]

The four Americans grilled Ély on the latest news from the battlefront and the mood in Paris. The French chief of staff had few comforting words to offer on either. Like the CIA, Ély gave the fortress even odds of holding out. And he stressed that the loss of the battle would have grave political repercussions in Paris. But, having received no instructions to the contrary, he stuck by his government's earlier stated position that France saw no reason to widen the war. If Dien Bien Phu were to fall there would be even less hope or point in pursuing a military victory, he insisted; France's main concern must remain the creation of a strong overall position from which to negotiate a settlement. While he was not yet ready to write off Dien Bien Phu and he emphasized that his government would vastly prefer a victory there, Ély stressed that France could not become so obsessed with a single battle that it encouraged the world to lose sight of its military strength throughout Indochina.

To Radford's dismay, despite Ély's evident personal distress over the losses at Dien Bien Phu, the Frenchman did not request a "strengthening and broadening" of US military assistance. The Defense Committee sent him to seek material assistance and to that he limited himself. To the question, asked or implied, of what would happen to France's negotiating position if its best troops were publicly whipped by the Vietminh in a European-style battle, Ély replied that the allies must be ready to refocus the world's attention from Dien Bien Phu to France's military power elsewhere in the colony. For that strategy to succeed, he said, the United States must further insure the French Union Army's material strength. He handed his host the detailed list of equipment and supplies that Paris had determined the French Union forces required. Disappointed, Radford nevertheless promised to secure all of the items on Ély's list.

In fact, the JCS chairman already had begun to lay mental plans for providing far more than material aid to rescue the French. Guests at the Radford home that evening recall their host's alarm over the precariousness of Dien Bien Phu and his dramatic prediction that the French could lose the battle "within the next few days if not the next few hours."[12] Beset by the nightmares of the Asia-Firsters, Radford feared that Dien Bien Phu could be the domino whose fall would set

34

off the communist takeover of all Asia. That said, however, his display of exaggerated dread also had more calculated objectives. Radford long had sought a more active American role in the Indochina War, just as he hoped to find the right occasion to test his interpretation of the New Look—using nuclear weapons from the outset of a conflict as part of the conventional arsenal. If he could persuade the French, and his own government, of the overriding need for American airstrikes to save Dien Bien Phu, he would be closer than ever before to accomplishing these strategic goals. In short, he could kill three birds with one stone.

For the ostensible purpose of securing France's material requests, Radford arranged for Ély and himself to meet with the president on Monday. The JCS chairman apparently believed that Ély's briefing on the military position at Dien Bien Phu would persuade the president to offer military action to prevent a major communist victory in Asia, the first test of the Eisenhower administration's power to stop the spread of communism in Asia. Once again the admiral had miscalculated. Regardless of how he judged the merits of the case, the president was not about to be carried away into making rash commitments to a foreign power.

Eisenhower greeted Ély warmly, listened attentively to his report on the progress of the battle, expressed polite concern, but otherwise kept the conversation general and noncommittal. By his later admission, he did not share Radford's profound sympathy for Paris' predicament. Ike still smoldered over Navarre's and the Laniel government's decision to stage the French Union's central battle at Dien Bien Phu. Now he found it hard to reconcile Ély's distress with Navarre's earlier pronouncement that he was hoping to draw a major attack.[13] However, the president did not want to deny aid to an ally in dire straits, even if he believed it had willfully maneuvered itself there. And, despite the conviction he shared with his military advisers that the French could make little use of the additional weaponry they were requesting—including twenty-five B-26 bombers, twelve F-8F fighter jets, fourteen C-47 transport planes, twenty-four L-20 support planes, and twenty helicopters—he did not believe in haggling with a neighbor whose house was burning down. As Ély listened on through a translator, Eisenhower ordered Radford to see that the Defense Department filled the requests to the extent it was able.[14]

Eisenhower conscientiously had sought to help and encourage Ély and to acknowledge the gravity of France's situation, *without* committing the US government to *do* anything about it. In his own words, he had tried to appear "neutral."[15] However, Ély was so wrapped up in his own concerns, he heard something far different. Ély believed Eisenhower gave the Defense Department a carte blanche to do far more than fill a shopping list containing a hundred or so airplanes. The general's recollection of the meeting is that, after an admittedly casual discussion of the battle, the president ordered Radford to provide France, on a priority basis, with *whatever its government asked for to save Dien Bien Phu,* "seemingly," he adds, "without setting any limits whatsoever."[16]

Though, after the fall of Dien Bien Phu, Radford was to insist that the error was Ély's alone, evidence shows that the JCS chairman must accept considerable blame for abetting the Frenchman's misunderstanding. Ély testifies that Radford encouraged him to believe that, if asked formally by the French government, Eisenhower would authorize military action to save Dien Bien Phu. He claims that the admiral assured him that the president would support any recommendations he, Radford, made.[17] While Radford's own published account of this meeting naturally denies this, even it suggests that, in his enthusiasm for action, the admiral may have given a broad interpretation to the president's words. Admitting that "nothing serious was discussed" at the meeting, Radford adds nevertheless that Eisenhower "did tell me to give the French everything they asked for." As a result, Radford asserts, Ély understandably came away with "the wrong impression." The French chief of staff simply did not appreciate "the fact that the President was *not* meeting Ély with a view to discussing serious matters—that this was in the nature of a social call."[18] Radford's bitterness toward Eisenhower's casual treatment of a meeting that the JCS chairman regarded with the utmost gravity seeps through his words. The probable truth is that Radford himself did not appreciate the nature of the meeting until much later, after he had maneuvered himself into an extremely embarrassing position by, at the very least, hinting to the French that Eisenhower would grant a request for intervention.

With Radford chipping away at Ély's fatalism toward the outcome of the battle, assuring the Frenchman that he had the weight of the president behind him, Ély's resolve to seek no widening of the French-Indochina War began to crumble. Hoping to render it to dust and smooth a path for American entry into Indochina, Radford bombarded his guest with high-level meetings aimed at convincing him of the importance the American authorities placed on a victory at Dien Bien Phu and of the optimism they still held out. From the Oval Office, Radford took Ély to a conference with the congressional leadership. The French chief of staff listened with rising optimism as the JCS chairman told the gathering how United States forces could—and must—foil the Vietminh's push for military victory before the Geneva Conference.[19] Just as in happier times Navarre had convinced Ely against his better judgment to believe the French Union could win at Dien Bien Phu, now Radford finally converted him to his faith in victory through American air power.

To convert his own government, the admiral arranged some more meetings. The most important, with the secretary of state, he scheduled for the following day. Radford and Ély knew they had their work cut out for them if they hoped to persuade Dulles to join the supporters of action to save Dien Bien Phu. The secretary of state consistently had opposed Laniel's decision to seek a negotiated settlement of the war. Now that the Geneva peace talks were just weeks away, Dulles wanted nothing to do with an aid request intended primarily to secure France the best slice of a divided Vietnam, Laos, and Cambodia. He reaffirmed that position only hours before his meeting with Ély. Asked during a general press conference how the government would respond if a French defeat at Dien Bien Phu appeared imminent, Dulles stated outright that he would sanction no rescue action. Although the Eisenhower administration generally sought to downplay Dien Bien Phu so as to minimize the appearance of French weakness in Indochina, Dulles spoke in the press conference from his own convictions. Of all the nation's top officials, including the president, Dulles was the most opposed in the early days of the Dien Bien Phu battle to intervening to help the French. He strenuously objected to expending his nation's military strength to bolster the French while they made what he was convinced would be a limp-wristed deal at Geneva. Later, when it looked as if a defeat at Dien Bien Phu might trigger an immediate French disengagement from Indochina, Dulles would change his position. But under the conditions prevailing on

March 23 he considered a more active American role in Indochina to be out of the question.

In his press conference the secretary of state minimized the importance of the current battle within the greater war. The loss of a local skirmish or two would not result in a general communist victory in Indochina, he insisted; and the battle for Dien Bien Phu, stripped of all its emotionalism, was such a skirmish, engaging only a tiny 4 percent of the French Union forces. While he assured the press that the United States government held firm in its support of the French armed struggle in Indochina and to that end would provide the French Union forces with all the material assistance they needed to win the present engagement and the whole war, it had no intention of becoming militarily involved now simply to shore up France's short-term tactical position and increase its bargaining weight at Geneva. The Eisenhower administration remained unconvinced that negotiations with communists could achieve an equitable solution, Dulles emphasized. The United States wanted victory.

We have seen no reason to abandon the so-called Navarre Plan which was, broadly speaking, a two-year plan which anticipated, if not complete victory, at least decisive military results. . . .

As you recall, that Plan contemplated [that] . . . assuming there were no serious military reverses during the present fighting season, the upper hand could definitely be achieved in that area by the end of the next fighting season. There have been no such military reverses, and, as far as we can see, none are in prospect which would be of a character which would upset the broad timetable and strategy of the Navarre Plan.[20]

A few hours after Dulles gave his cool analysis of the French military position, Ély and Radford joined him in an uncomfortable meeting to find out how far the US would go to help out the French at Dien Bien Phu. As he had been ordered, Ély asked what help his government could expect from the United States if the Chinese bombed French positions in Indochina. (This question did not spring from any honest fear in the French military/foreign policy establishment that Chinese bombers were about to strike Indochina. Rather it was intended to secure a US military pledge that France could use to make itself appear more threatening during the Geneva talks—as Dulles was very much aware.) By the time Ély spoke with Dulles, however, the general had been moved by dire reports from the field and by his long conversations with Radford into believing that, to hold Dien Bien Phu, France would need much more than an arms delivery and a promise of retaliation against an implausible Chinese attack. Even as he limited his conversation to the Defense Committee's queries, Ély's thoughts raced toward how he could persuade his government to ask the Americans to intervene in the battle. He searched for evidence to bring to Paris that the Eisenhower administration would respond favorably. That may explain why he heard Dulles say something quite different from what Dulles himself reported to the president, what Radford recalled of the conversation, and what the secretary of state consistently advocated at the time.

According to Radford, the secretary gave away nothing. Were Paris formally to request US airstrikes in response to Chinese attacks, Dulles said, that request "would be received and studied in the light of the situation at the time."[21] Dulles' own account, written shortly after the meeting concluded, stressed Washington's unhappiness with the way the French were conducting the war, and made it clear that France would have to change its ways before the US government would even consider intervention.

> I said that if the French wanted our open participation in the Indochina war, I thought that they ought to consider that this might involve a greater degree of partnership than had prevailed up to the present time, notably in relation to independence for the Associated States and the training of indigenous forces.[22]

However, Ély was to insist he heard the secretary of state say that "the Free World would intervene in Indochina rather than let the situation deteriorate there through Chinese aid to the Vietminh"— a very different sentiment indeed. Ély interpreted that to be a promise that, *if the general French position in Indochina got too shaky,* the Americans would come in to prevent a collapse.[23]

Nevertheless, despite the broad interpretation he gave to Dulles' words, Ély was upset by what he heard. Dulles, he believed, had promised help if the Indochina situation got desperate, but when would that be? Dien Bien Phu verged on collapse, likely bringing down all hopes of a reasonable negotiated peace with it, yet the leader of the American foreign policy establishment did not find cause for immediate concern. Ély could not hide his frustration following the Dulles meeting. He felt Radford had betrayed him. The JCS chairman had encouraged him to set his hopes on an *immediate,* short-term US bombing mission to save Dien Bien Phu. And in allowing himself to be persuaded, Ély had put himself on a limb. He must go back to France and advocate a course of action that for years Paris had refused even to consider. The understanding upon which he mounted that limb was that the United States would cooperate. After speaking to the secretary of state he no longer felt sure.

Radford quickly revived Ély's wavering confidence. The admiral had worked determinedly to bring the French chief of staff over to his way of thinking. Now that he seemed on the verge of securing the more active Franco-American partnership in Indochina he had long desired, Radford did not intend to see his plans mired on State Department preconditions. Dulles could haggle over the political details *after* the United States had its foot in the door in Indochina. The JCS chairman apparently believed that the White House would agree with his logic. As they walked down the corridor of the State Department, Radford spoke reassuringly to his companion. Ély says that Radford "with a few spoken words gave me the impression, a personal impression only, that the position of President Eisenhower might be a little different from that of his secretary of state."[24]

Though there appeared to be a broad gulf between the secretary of state and the JCS chairman as they considered military action at Dien Bien Phu, they actually separated more on timing than substance. Dulles was not averse to intervening in the Indochina War, if such intervention were preceded by a full political settlement and had victory as its aim. He even would countenance unilateral intervention, if necessary. But he refused to be rushed into making any military commitments that merely would make it easier for France to strike a deal with the communists, turning over northern Vietnam. Radford, on the other hand, feared more that France would suffer a rout at Dien Bien Phu which, he believed, would precipitate a sudden and complete French abandonment of Southeast Asia, embolden international communism, and critically undermine the stability of the free world. Like Dulles, Radford desired a political settlement, but to his thinking it could follow efforts to deal with the more immediate military concerns.

The positions of the two foreign policy advisers were clarified in a telephone conversation they had on the morning of March 24, at Radford's instigation.[25] This was to be Ély's last full day in Washington. Only one more talk was scheduled, with the Joint Chiefs of Staff. Yet, Radford and Dulles agreed, almost nothing had been accomplished. Despite his display of urgency, Ély had the same basic attitude as his predecessors: he made big requests and offered nothing in return, political or military. (When Radford had pressed for France to give American officers a greater advisory, training, and planning role in Indochina, Ély replied with a lecture on the Americans' controlling and invading nature.)[26] On the other hand, Radford and Dulles also agreed, the United States could not sit by while communism spread into Indochina, Asia, and beyond. Where the admiral and secretary diverged was over *when* the United States should act to dam the spread.

Dulles quite simply was fed up with the French. Though once an ardent francophile, he had grown disenchanted by their "deplorable" conduct in Indochina, over Germany, and toward the EDC. He suggested angrily that the time may have come for Washington to divorce itself from its treaties with Paris. The United States must stop pleading with France, he told Radford, and strike out on its own. If America remained married to French policy, "[w]e could lose Europe, Asia and Africa all at once if we don't watch out." Dulles wanted the question of defeating communism in Indochina to be considered separately from French problems at Dien Bien Phu. According to the synopsized transcript of the telephone conversation made by Dulles' secretary (who, at Dulles' request, regularly listened in on an extension and took notes), "The Secretary said we must do some thinking on the premise that France is creating a vacuum in the world wherever she is. How can we fill that vacuum? . . . The decision in that regard is one of the most important the U.S. has made in a long time." It was not one that should be made in haste, Dulles insisted, though he assured Radford he was not advocating a policy of inaction. The United States could begin moving independently against the communist Chinese to keep them from aiding the Vietminh, he offered; "we might step up activities along the coast and from Formosa and also deal more directly with the Associated States." But the United States must act with its eyes on the future, even if that future did not include France.

While he raised no objections to Dulles' long-term strategy, Radford argued that the immediate, critical situation at Dien Bien Phu deserved first consideration. If the fortress fell to the Vietminh, the French might simply walk out of Indochina, he said. The admiral speculated that they could do that in two or three weeks, long before the United States could come up with a plan or the available forces to fill the vacuum. If that were to happen, he concluded, "we look bad here to our own people." Radford added the bite that he might have to give some embarrassing testimony at the congressional hearings that would surely follow. (The teeth to his implicit threat had a sharp edge. Radford had achieved notoriety before being named JCS chairman by leading the "revolt of the admirals," in which he testified before Congress against the policies of the Naval Department.) Dulles defanged the admiral by announcing that he had already talked to the president and, he implied, had received his full support.

At 8 AM, a full two hours before his conversation with Radford, Dulles had indeed met with Eisenhower to discuss three related foreign policy matters that pressed most heavily on the nation: Indochina, the EDC, and US policy toward the People's Republic of China. Throughout the Dien Bien Phu crisis Dulles remained constantly in touch with the Oval Office. His personal feelings as to how the United States should respond to the French pleas for help differed appreciably from the president's—both in the early stages, when Dulles more firmly opposed intervention, and especially later, when he made a 180-degree turn on airstrikes after Eisenhower had decided against them—and, in part, Dulles used these conferences to persuade. However, transcripts of their meetings reveal that Dulles' first concern was to ensure that he correctly carried out the president's orders, certainly the case in the March 24 meeting. Nevertheless, subtle and not-so-subtle differences remained.

As Dulles told Radford, Eisenhower agreed with him that the United States must have an independent policy toward Indochina and must not make any guarantees to the French to respond to Chinese intervention without first obtaining some political concessions (especially the future independence of the Associated States). But Eisenhower did not express, nor did he share, his secretary of state's readiness to abandon France altogether.[27] (Dulles' remark to Radford that "we may have to think of cutting loose on our treaties with France" over Indochina and the EDC is strikingly reminiscent of his unfortunate television statement in 1953 that if Europe did not cooperate on the EDC "it would be necessary to give a little rethinking to America's own foreign policy in relation to Western Europe." Eisenhower then had been forced secretly to disavow his secretary's words; he asked the chief of staff at NATO headquarters to pass the word to the European capitals that he was "amazed" that the members of the alliance believed that he would desert them.)[28]

Eisenhower's greater desire to continue to rely on the French to fight the Indochina war made him more willing than Dulles to consider limited US military intervention. According to Dulles' conversation memorandum,

The President said that he agreed *basically* that we should not get involved in fighting in Indochina unless there were the political preconditions necessary for a successful outcome. *He did not, however, wholly exclude the possibility of a single strike, if it were almost certain this would produce decisive results.* (emphasis added)[29]

This conversation is particularly noteworthy because it is one of two recorded occasions on which Eisenhower mentioned the possibility of ordering airstrikes to aid the French, without attaching prohibitive conditions in the same breath. Though arresting, however, it does not signify that the president favored intervention. Eisenhower followed a multistep decision-making process. He liked to think out loud with his advisers, to raise and discuss all possible options before winnowing them down to the one he would take. One very real option for resolving the Dien Bien Phu crisis was to order airstrikes to assist the French—though Ike's use of the qualifiers "not . . . wholly exclude . . . if it were almost certain . . . [to be] decisive" show that from the beginning he placed intervention on the very fringes of likelihood. Nevertheless, his musings make it clear that he had not yet decided, as had Dulles, to leave the French to clean up their own mess at Dien Bien Phu.

In fact, the previous week Eisenhower had told Chief of Naval Operations (CNO) Admiral Robert Carney to put the Pacific-based US 7th Fleet on alert. On March 18 Carney ordered the fleet's commander, Vice Admiral William K. Phillips, to ready his forces to defend Dien Bien Phu within twelve hours' notice. The CNO told Phillips to make full preparations to render military support to the French, if ordered, but to bear in mind that the steps were merely precautionary. "[T]here is no approved plan nor even any tentative plan for intervening," Carney stressed, however "authorities here, including Secretary Dulles, are aware of the potential critical military situation in Indochina and the possible implications of serious French reversals." Phillips' Attack Carrier Striking Group left Subic Bay headed for the Gulf of Tonkin on March 22, under cover of a routing training mission, not even letting the French know its true purpose. The day after dispatching the 7th Fleet to the waters off North Vietnam, Carney ordered Admiral Felix Stump, the Pacific Fleet commander in chief, to initiate with Navarre's staff in Saigon the necessary technical preparations for US naval-aerial intervention to aid Dien Bien Phu.[30]

Again, rather than this proving the president's intention to intervene in the French-Indochina War, Eisenhower's orders to Carney sought to hold all options open in order to respond to whatever situation arose. The presence of the US Pacific Fleet off the north coast of Indochina also posed the general threat Eisenhower so often used to sway an enemy, as he had used "discreet" hints of expanding the Korean War to bring the Chinese back to the negotiating table at Panmunjum. If nothing else, the sight of American carriers might persuade the Vietminh and its Chinese advisers to be more circumspect as they headed for Geneva.

Carney's specific reference to Dulles in his orders to Phillips unfortunately remains unclear. Most likely, Dulles proposed to Carney the same argument he advanced to Eisenhower and Radford: that the United States must prepare itself to launch its own anticommunist military policy in Indochina. It certainly was characteristic of Eisenhower and his foreign policy advisers to agree on the need to station carriers in the Tonkin Gulf and privately disagree as to why they wanted them there (to defend Dien Bien Phu, to harass independently the Vietnamese coastline, or to control the communists' greed at the conference table). And it was characteristic of Ike to indulge, if not to encourage, these multiple lines of thinking. As memorandum after transcript after diary entry reveal, he artfully dodged the most determined efforts to pin him down.

The March 24 meeting with Dulles is illustrative. Determined to block Radford's efforts to drag US forces into Dien Bien Phu, Dulles presented his position to the president frankly and unambiguously:

the United States must not get involved in the fighting without a prior political settlement; rather, the administration should consider taking independent action along the Vietnamese and Chinese coastlines. To only one of Dulles' suggestions did the president simply "agree." Instead he "agreed basically," "did not wholly exclude," or "indicated his concurrence with this general attitude." The only point to which he fully agreed was that Dulles should give a speech stating that the US government "could not look upon the loss to communism of that area [Southeast Asia] with indifference"—not even a precise verbal warning. Eisenhower did authorize the US ambassador to the Associated States, Donald Heath, to make efforts to build up the morale of local leaders if the French seemed to be about to disengage, but— always a but—he made it clear that he did not want Heath or anyone in his administration making an "explicit promise that we might not be able to live up to." Keeping pace with Eisenhower was not an easy job, as the president himself knew; Dulles must be forgiven, as Eisenhower invariably forgave him, for slipping up occasionally.

On Ély's last scheduled day in Washington he met with the Joint Chiefs of Staff, and received by far the iciest reception of his visit (perhaps contributing to his recollection of the Dulles meeting as relatively warm). Whereas Eisenhower had raised no objections to Paris' weapons shopping list, telling Radford simply to have the Defense Department fill it in so far as possible, the chiefs tortuously scrutinized every item. They cross-examined Ély relentlessly on how the French Union forces intended to use and maintain each plane. They castigated him for what they believed was the French military command's self-destructive pigheadedness. A few minutes into the inquest, Ély recalls with uncharacteristic understatement, "I sensed that the chiefs of staff did not much appreciate the way Navarre was conducting operations."[31]

The JCS deeply resented the French command's intractable refusal to enlarge the American role in military planning in conjunction with America's ballooning financial and material commitment. The chiefs told Ély that the US defense establishment's patience had nearly reached the bursting point at being consulted only when Navarre needed more planes or when his forces had gotten themselves into a bind from which they could not extricate themselves on their own. Both Ély and Navarre admitted that building up the VNA offered the French Union its only hope of matching strength with the Vietminh, Radford reminded his guest, so why not let US trainers help develop those forces? Ély bridled. Radford's words recalled to him what the United States had to gain in exchange for airstrikes over Dien Bien Phu and why Paris continued to pay the high human cost of fighting in Indochina rather than share the death toll with the Americans. The Frenchman accused the JCS of trying to take over France's war—perhaps even to supplant France's political and economic influence in Indochina.[32]

Nettled, the American military chiefs replied that they had not the least desire to get bogged down in Indochina; they just wanted to win the war. That's why the government was granting Ély virtually all of his material requests, they said.[33] They expected in return that France would use that aid to improve the military situation, which, they insisted, could be done only by properly training and equipping a dynamic Vietnamese Army, similar to the South Korean Army. A strong VNA would gradually relieve the French people from having to fight the war themselves, the chiefs argued. The American military optimistically estimated that its trainers could build up the VNA sufficiently to take over all of the fighting in Indochina within a maximum of two years—if the French Union had not already won the war by then.[34]

Two years might as well be two centuries, Ély shot back. He knew, as the Americans would learn for themselves in their war in Vietnam, that his nation had reached the limits of its capabilities, that its people did not have two more years to give. There could be no military victory, he said; a political solution was the only way out and it could not be delayed. As a gesture toward compromise he ultimately agreed to look informally into the possibility of creating some American role in training the VNA, but the French chief of staff would not budge from his determination to seek a negotiated peace at Geneva.

After Ély left the room, the joint chiefs discussed his requests for material in the light of what they believed should be America's future policy in Indochina. The position taken by Army Chief of Staff Ridgway formed the third standpoint inside the Eisenhower administration on how to respond to the growing military crisis. Responding specifically to Ély's requests for material aid, General Ridgway said that it would be a waste of the Defense Department's already strapped budget to support a war that was conducted only half-heartedly by the French and, therefore, that had no substantial prospect of decisive victory.[35] His objections to intervention far exceeded those of Dulles. As ensuing requests and deliberations would reveal, Ridgway opposed committing United States forces or funds to the Indochina War under *any* political conditions.

In his six months as Army Chief of Staff, Ridgway already had acquired a reputation for tenacious independence, surprising those who had backed the nomination of the former commander of both NATO and Pacific forces. Indeed, Ike had named Ridgway to the JCS especially because of the closed-mouth pliancy he had shown as MacArthur's replacement in the Korean War—a pliancy the president hoped would make it easier to slash the Army's budget and institute the New Look. However, Ridgway saw the duties of field commander and service chief as very different: the former followed orders; the latter acted as the Army's advocate and a watchdog over the security of the United States. Ridgway did not believe that Eisenhower's multibillion-dollar defense cuts (76 percent of the first year's coming out of Army coffers) were in the best interests of either.

The Radford mobile-strike-force strategy of relying on air power to defend US interests would lead the United States back "into that serious error that had placed us at such a grave disadvantage against an inferior foe in the first few months of the Korean war," Ridgway charged.[36] He clung to the traditional Army creed that the foot soldier was the key component in any victory. The 1954 budgetary retrenchment reduced those ground troops by more than 10 percent, however, despite the growth of America's worldwide defense commitments in Southeast Asia and elsewhere. Fearing that an understaffed and ill-equipped Army would be dragged into war in Indochina, General Ridgway concluded that the United States should withdraw its limited though rapidly escalating support from Southeast Asia altogether, and conserve its dwindling strength for other, more well-disposed enterprises.[37]

Whereas Ridgway maintained that the administration was throwing away money by aiding the lackluster French in Indochina, Radford argued just the opposite: that France's unwillingness to go all out to win the war was the very reason the United States must step in. Following the JCS meeting with Ély, Radford restated his conclusion in a memorandum to the president.

I am gravely fearful that the measures being taken by the French [in Indochina] will prove to be inadequate and initiated too late to prevent a progressive deterioration of the situation. The consequences can well lead to the loss of all of S.E. Asia to Communist domination. If this is to be avoided, I consider that *the U.S. must be prepared to act promptly and in force possibly to a frantic and belated request by the French for U.S. intervention.*[38] (emphasis added)

Shortly before Ély was to return to Paris on March 25, Radford asked him if he would postpone his departure for twenty-four hours. According to Ély, the JCS chairman said he was extremely concerned about French losses at Dien Bien Phu and would like to use the extra day to plan informally a possible United States air and naval action to rescue the fortress. Ély, who had grown more eager for a rescue plan with each cable he received on the tightening Vietminh noose around the camp, readily agreed to stay.[39]

From the start of Ély's stay in Washington, he and Radford had discussed various scenarios for US airstrikes in response to a Chinese aerial attack on French Indochina. The dialogue had become progressively more serious and detailed, culminating in Ély's suggestion, made near the end of his scheduled mission, that CINCPAC (the United States Pacific command) and the French-Indochina command begin drawing up *formal,* precise staff agreements on how to conduct such an intervention.[40]

Radford later claimed that he refused to go that far. Despite his anxiety over the fate of Dien Bien Phu and Indochina in general, he said, he steadfastly avoided saying or doing anything that might commit the United States to intervene militarily in the war, certainly not before extracting pledges from France to cooperate more fully with American military strategy. In a literal sense that is correct. The JCS chairman had no authority to commit US forces to anything, so he could not have made military commitments to Ély. Nevertheless, he certainly misled the Frenchman, especially in the extra day of talks.

Meeting in seclusion, the only other person present an interpreter, Radford asked Ély whether the Laniel government was prepared to make a formal request for United States airstrikes in the vicinity of Dien Bien Phu, "if the Communists intervened or if, *for other mili-*

tary reasons, the French needed more air power than they could muster" (emphasis added). The general replied that "since he had been instructed by the French Defense Minister to raise the question of American intervention, it was obvious that France contemplated making such a request if necessary to prevent a defeat."[41]

This was a generous interpretation of orders, justified by Ély on the basis that the success of the Vietminh attack on Dien Bien Phu had invalidated his original instructions, issued when the outpost still appeared impregnable. To keep up with the onrush of events, he determined, he must proceed not on the letter of his orders, but on their "spirit"—which he defined as a desire for an American military commitment that would back Laniel's Geneva strategy. Ély reasoned that a French Union defeat at Dien Bien Phu would destroy France's bargaining position and render meaningless any American guarantee against Chinese airstrikes. Therefore, he concluded, it was more in the spirit of his orders to secure an American guarantee against the fall of Dien Bien Phu.[42]

Ély says that Radford proceeded to lay before him a plan for US airstrikes around the periphery of Dien Bien Phu: Operation Vulture.[43] United States B-29 heavy bombers from Clark Air Force Base near Manila, covered and supported by naval fighter jets from the US 7th Fleet, would stage a number of bombing raids over one or several nights to disrupt enemy installations surrounding Dien Bien Phu and obliterate Vietminh communications, artillery, and antiaircraft defenses within Indochina. Ély records that the JCS chairman claimed that such an action would remain within the boundaries of the aid the United States already was providing French Indochina, since airstrikes by US jets were no more than a tit-for-tat response to the recent intensification of Chinese aid to the Vietminh. Moreover, Radford allegedly assured Ély that, since the action would remain confined to Indochina, it would not raise the threat of Chinese retaliation.[44]

Radford's recollection of what he told Ély in that meeting is much more restrained. The JCS chairman was to insist over and over in the weeks to come and years afterward that he made no offer of airstrikes nor did he even imply one. He merely told Ély, he said, that were Paris formally to request United States military assistance, *and were Washington to authorize that assistance,* he could guarantee the availability for action within two days of up to 350 carrier-based aircraft and a smaller number of medium bombers.[45]

The very mention of such an operation to a representative of the French government was unprecedented, however. Up to that point, all bilateral talk of a greater US role in Vietnam had centered around JCS efforts to widen the war (mostly through training local troops). Operation Vulture, on the other hand, contemplated a military action "limited in time and space" to relieving the siege at Dien Bien Phu. In Ély's estimation, by presenting the plan Radford showed that he had come around to accepting French rules. "The initiative in this project came from Admiral Radford," he was to recall. "But it might just as well have come from me, so natural a conclusion was such a proposal from our conversations and our analysis of the situation."[46]

One cannot entirely blame this misunderstanding on Ély's rattled nerves or his translator's skills. Radford had given a number of broad hints that Eisenhower would back an intervention plan. Indeed, recalls Ély, "Upon taking leave of Admiral Radford, I must say, I had the feeling that he thought I would have more difficulty in getting from my government the request for American support . . . than he himself would have in getting an affirmative decision from his." The poorly phrased minute by which Radford and Ély concluded their talks gave the general still another stroke of false comfort. It stated their agreement on "the desirability of anticipating such an intervention, of starting to prepare for it, and of going as far with this as possible in order to reduce the time for its *eventual execution*" (emphasis added).[47]

However, Ély also received from that closing minute a very strong signal that United States approval of a French request for airstrikes was not predetermined, no matter how sanguine Radford appeared. Radford submitted the draft agreement to Dulles for approval. The secretary okayed it, but only after excising a paragraph Ély had written and Radford had let stand:

There was complete agreement on the terms of . . . intervention by U.S. aircraft in Indochina in case of an emergency, it being understood that this intervention could be either by Naval or Air Force units as the need arises, depending on the development of the situation.

Dulles thus refused the inclusion of the one statement that implied a commitment.[48]

The Ely Mission

Once again, Ély closed his eyes to what he did not wish to see—no doubt aided by Radford's suggestions that Eisenhower, too, saw things differently from his secretary of state. From the deep depression in which he arrived in Washington, the French chief of staff departed on a crest of optimism. He reported to his government that he and Radford (and, by projection, the Eisenhower government) had reached "complete accord on all matters."[49]

III

United Action

At 10 AM on March 25, the day originally scheduled for Ély's departure from Washington, the US National Security Council gathered for its regular Thursday meeting.[1] As news of the battle for Dien Bien Phu overshadowed all meetings with the French chief of staff, the Indochina situation dominated the NSC session. Yet the discussants showed little sense of emergency. Word had arrived that the Vietminh had ended their first onslaught on Dien Bien Phu, giving the French Union forces a respite for repairing their defenses and airstrips and resupplying and reinforcing their troops. This raised hopes that Dien Bien Phu could hold out until the monsoons came in May, ending major fighting for the season and stabilizing the military background to the Geneva Conference. Even were those hopes to be dashed, however, Eisenhower and most of his advisers did not give the fall of Dien Bien Phu the overriding significance attributed to it by the French or the Asia-Firsters.

Eisenhower started off the discussion with a string of sardonic comments. He questioned why the French military had not been able to close the single road leading from Laos to Dien Bien Phu to prevent the 308th Vietminh division from returning to Vietnam to join the attack. He remarked that, if French forces could be moved only by air, perhaps the Vietnamese did not really want to be free of com-

53

munist domination. While he requested a Planning Board study on "the extent to which we should go in employing ground forces to save Indochina from the Communists," the President added that he "did not see how the United States or other free world nations could go all-out in support of the Associated States without UN approval and assistance"—and he was especially adamant that both the Vietnamese and the US Congress be behind any such move. Eisenhower remained committed to doing what he could to prevent the communists from toppling the first domino in Southeast Asia. However, he had not yet determined how to stop them, except that it must be a joint effort. He seemed willing to bide his time while he searched for a solution.

The most interesting aspect of this restrained meeting, which coincided with Radford's appeal to Ély to stay in Washington another day to discuss military solutions to what he believed was an impending crisis, is that no one on the NSC even raised the possibility of intervening to prevent the defeat of the French forces at Dien Bien Phu. Dulles even disagreed with the president's suggestion that it would be a provident to begin exploring how Congress would respond "in the event that it seemed desirable to intervene in Indochina." The secretary argued that "a lot more work needed to be done by the NSC on this problem before we were ready to take it up with Congress."

Dulles saw the problem facing the administration as political rather than military, centering on France not Indochina. Accordingly, he opposed bringing before the United Nations a charge of Chinese aggression against Indochina or even seriously discussing within the walls of the National Security Council forming a regional pact to secure Indochina and Southeast Asia. He worried especially about the repercussions on the EDC of making any *immediate* moves that were not wholly in concert with the French (though he believed that eventually "it would be necessary for the United States to beat the French into line, or else to accept a split with France"). The war would not be decided before the Geneva Conference, he insisted; there was time to prepare the political ground, perhaps even to get the EDC ratified, before the US moved independently to support the Indochinese.

One significant matter grew out of this otherwise fruitless meeting.

54

United Action

Eisenhower planted the seeds of what would eventually become the Southeast Asia Treaty Organization (SEATO). Responding indirectly to doubts raised by Dulles and others that the United Nations would be willing to intervene in the Indochina insurgency, the president suggested a second possible approach: the government of Vietnam could invite the free nations of Southeast Asia plus the US, Britain, and France to come to its aid through a series of defense treaties. That had the added advantage, he said, of avoiding "solely Occidental assistance to Vietnam." He left unmentioned the even more attractive advantages of freeing any US action in Southeast Asia from French control and the taint of French colonialism, while providing other proxies to do the fighting and help bear the costs.

The regional defense idea had still another benefit: it would take time to plan and even more to implement. (The government of Vietnam that Eisenhower foresaw sending out the invitations did not yet exist.) It required no immediate action or commitment. In other words, it gave the president a breathing space while events sorted themselves out in Indochina and Geneva—and allowed him to turn his attention to more pressing domestic troubles caused by Senator McCarthy's recent charges of communism within the US armed services. Eisenhower did not pin himself down to the regional pact scenario, however. He made no decisions at all, except to defer. As the meeting wound itself down, Eisenhower merely ordered yet another Planning Board study, this one to cover all conceivable options for preventing the "loss" of Indochina.

Thus it was left to Radford to stoke the fire for intervention on his own. He continued with vigor, as heedless of the lack of enthusiasm shown by the NSC as he had been of Dulles' antipathy. After seeing Ély off, the admiral was due to brief a joint meeting of the JCS and State Department on his week of talks. He turned it into an arm-twisting session to get the backing he needed for Operation Vulture.[2] Radford projected the desperate position of the French Union forces at Dien Bien Phu, their imminent defeat, the evacuation that would follow, and the resulting boost to communism throughout Asia. His audience of military and foreign policy advisers listened intently. They too feared a communist victory in Southeast Asia, which Radford's scenario placed just around the corner. However, when the JCS chairman read out the text of his March 24 memorandum

55

to the president ("the U.S. must act promptly and in force possibly to a frantic and belated request by the French for U.S. intervention"), General Ridgway broke the spell.

The Army chief of staff bitterly opposed Radford's efforts to commit US forces to the French-Indochina War, which he believed would result in a war of attrition more costly in American lives and dollars than the Korean Conflict had been.[3] Even more, he was outraged at what he saw as yet another attempt by the JCS chairman to appear falsely to Eisenhower to be speaking for all the chiefs (a practice that had first raised Ridgway's rancor during the negotiations over the military budget). This time (unlike that earlier incident), Ridgway would not give Radford the benefit of the doubt. Demanding the convening of an executive session of the Joint Chiefs of Staff at once, the ACOS presented his dissenting position with a clarity that left no room for misunderstanding.

I made the point, with respect to Admiral Radford's final paragraph and particularly the last sentence [of his March 24 memorandum to the president, quoted above], that while I recognized that this was put forward as his personal view, it would be very easy for either the President or others into whose hands it might fall, to misconstrue this as the official expression of the corporate views of the Joint Chiefs, and even to interpret it as advocating U.S. armed intervention.
The JCS must not, I added, advocate any such course.[4]

From the breach between Radford's and Ridgway's positions that had opened discreetly during the March 24 meeting with Ély erupted a volcano. Previously, during the 1954 military budget quarrel, Ridgway had kept his peace too long, waiting in vain for Radford to present the Army's position along with his own. He eventually did speak up, after he realized that the JCS chairman had no intention of revealing dissent from the New Look, but by then the budget had passed. This time Ridgway was determined to press his views forcefully from the start, if necessary side-stepping an obstructing chain of command.[5]

He decided that if he could reveal to the nation's decision-makers the tremendous costs of intervening in the Indochina War, he would convince them of its folly. Soon after this meeting Ridgway organized a team of battlefield experts on Indochina to evaluate the conditions there and to forecast the price of a US victory over the Vietminh. They would leave for Indochina on May 31, reporting back to Ridgway on July 12 that Vietnam did not have sufficient resources and infra-structure to sustain a ground war fought by US troops.[6] Ridgway would immediately present the Army's detailed findings to the president. It was a brilliant report, striking for its exceptional fore-thought, but Ridgway erred in believing that it "played a consider-able, perhaps decisive part in persuading our government not to embark on that tragic adventure" in Indochina.[7] Though he was impressed by the Ridgway report, Eisenhower had made up his mind not to intervene in the war before the Army team had left for Vietnam. Fu-ture presidents and generals, tragically, would pay its conclusions no mind.

The less formal objections hammered upon by Ridgway beginning just after the Ély mission did have a perceptible impact, however, especially on the US Congress and the British government and mili-tary—and especially as the other service chiefs joined Ridgway's side.

The president's civilian advisers also took sides on how to answer the questions raised by the approaching Geneva Conference and the French crisis over Dien Bien Phu. Their positions were not so rigid as the military chiefs', partly because they did not view the American role in the Indochina conflict with the intense inward gaze of men concerned with its effect on line items and service strength. More important, though, they had developed a pattern of deferring to Sec-retary of State Dulles on foreign policy matters and to Eisenhower on military policy.

Since taking the foreign policy helm, Dulles, with Eisenhower's blessing, had steered America's Indochina policy toward two goals: independence for the Associated States and the eradication of the Vietminh. While the war groaned along inconclusively, he pursued these objectives by applying slowly graduating pressure on the French in exchange for money and supplies. Fifteen months of exhortations and mild threats had brought them no closer to realization. Never-theless, Dulles remained confident that, as Paris became increasingly dependent on outside aid, it eventually would be forced to drop its hard line against Vietnamese, Cambodian, and Laotian independence and American military advice—and would come to a more agreeable political understanding with Washington on the EDC. He therefore approached the Dien Bien Phu problem gingerly. Radford's feverish activities on behalf of intervention alarmed him. Precipitate action could release the pressure he had been pumping hard for more than a year to build up. Similarly, Dulles was loath to release his control over Indochina policy to the military unless absolutely necessary. Saving French face at Dien Bien Phu, he believed, did not constitute such a necessity.

Dulles reiterated this in the strongest terms at the March 26 cabinet meeting.[8] The battle for Dien Bien Phu was only of the slightest military importance, he insisted. Projections of battle casualties revealed that a communist victory would be so costly to the Vietminh that they would gain no significant advantage even if they took the fortress. The administration must not fall into the trap, he said, of letting a minor skirmish blind its eyes to the overall picture. Indochina, not Dien Bien Phu, should be the focus of Washington's concern. Once one adjusted that focus, Dulles concluded, it became clear that the problem in Indochina was not primarily a military one, but rather a long-building Vietnamese reaction to the disintegration of France's colonial ties. Therefore, no attempted solution that failed to resolve the colonial issue would have any reasonable chance of success. Victory on the battlefield would be won not by American bombs, but by building up indigenous forces and giving them a nation of their own to fight for; then the Vietnamese themselves would let loose an all-out, nationwide offensive to annihilate the communists. In other words, Dulles stood by the Navarre Plan.

Dulles did not disregard the considerable psychological effect a defeat at Dien Bien Phu would have on the French. He had considered it as carefully as Admiral Radford had, he told the cabinet. But, whereas the JCS chairman had concluded that Paris's high state of emotion would imperil US policy by forcing Laniel to withdraw French troops if Dien Bien Phu fell, the secretary of state thought that the situation and mood actually might act to Washington's advantage. Navarre's and Laniel's deep desire to avoid a humiliating defeat could provide the grease that finally would enable the US to push through its demands for Indochinese independence and an American role in planning strategy and training troops. If the Eisenhower administration grasped the opportunity by offering to help the French win the war, Dulles believed, France would be induced to remain fighting past the fall of Dien Bien Phu and the Geneva Conference all the way to victory.

This was the crux of Dulles' argument: the United States must help France *win* in Indochina—not partition, withdraw, or continue its stalemate. Otherwise the communists would conquer Southeast Asia and "cut our defenses in half." The United States may be required to take "fairly strong action" carrying definite risks, he predicted, "but these risks will be less if we take them now rather than waiting for several years." By "now" he meant once the French agreed to Washington's conditions: independence for the Associated States, cooperation with American military advisers, and a promise to keep fighting until they won the war. (Dulles apparently believed that tremendous domestic pressure to avoid military defeat would soon force Laniel to acquiesce to these conditions, though the virtual unanimity in France for a negotiated peace regardless of the cost makes it surprising that he could think so.) In other words, the secretary of state argued *for* intervention by the United States into the French-Indochina War and for making the *conditional* offer to Laniel at once; he opposed only *immediate, unqualified action* to save Dien Bien Phu.

Unlike Dulles, Eisenhower rarely is quoted in the minutes of this meeting. Throughout the cabinet's lengthy discussion of Dien Bien Phu, Eisenhower made only a few remarks, preferring to listen to what his advisers had to offer him. This was typical of his behavior in cabinet meetings, quite different from that in discussions with the NSC. When meeting with his National Security Council, Eisenhower was more in his milieu as a general; he spoke his mind freely, probed for facts, encouraged argument. In the cabinet he tended to be more circumspect, perhaps out of respect for his belief in cabinet government, perhaps out of concern that in this civilian setting anything he said on a military issue might squelch all dissent. However, even in the few brief remarks he made in the March 26 meeting, the president revealed a pessimism about the chance for victory in Indochina.

When UN Ambassador Henry Cabot Lodge compared the French-Indochina War to the Greek civil war which had spawned the Truman Doctrine, Eisenhower emerged from his shell of silence like a pugnacious tortoise. The situations were incomparable, he snapped. The Greeks were sturdy folk, fighting for their political freedom with all of their might; the Vietnamese, on the other hand, were "backward people" who had to depend on the French for their freedom and who had lost all faith in Paris' sincerity in promising it. "France presents difficult questions everywhere you look," he grumbled. The conversation moved on, but the president clearly continued to be bothered by the problems of working with the French. Some time later he mused aloud, "If we could sit down and talk to them, man to man, like we can the British when things get tough. But not the French. It sure takes a lot of patience." Patience, however, was Ike's stock in trade.

As March drew to a close, the war in Indochina took up an increasing but still not dominant portion of President Eisenhower's calendar. Senator McCarthy's attack on the Army had spread to the White House. That battle commanded the attention of the media, Capitol Hill, and even the Oval Office as much as if not more than the one fought by the French and Vietnamese halfway around the world. Much of the last days of March were given over by Eisenhower's staff to writing the president's "fear speech," a countervolley against McCarthyism in which he would warn against the dangers of excessive fear ("fear of Kremlin, fear of Communism, fear of investigation, fear of depression, etc.").[9] For Ike personally this speech stood in the forefront of concerns.

Dulles kept the administration's watch on Dien Bien Phu, briefing Eisenhower daily or when special problems arose. The secretary of state was working hard to prepare a major speech of his own on Indochina: "a paraphrase of the Monroe address that the freedom of the Southeast Asia area was important from the standpoint of our peace, security and happiness, and that we could not look upon the loss to Communism of that area with indifference," as he described it to the president.[10] With the unfortunate irony that so often marred Eisenhower's boldest initiatives, Dulles' Indochina address, which Ike approved from first concept through final draft, carried the opposite message from the president's "fear speech." While Eisenhower's address sought to calm the wave of fear of Kremlin and communism convulsing the nation, Dulles' warned of the worldwide calamity that would follow upon a communist victory in Indochina. The specific canceled out the general. Dulles' clarion call reverberated around the world long after Eisenhower's sober phrases were forgotten.

The occasion for the secretary's speech was a long-scheduled engagement before the Overseas Press Club of America on March 29. Dulles surmised that the meeting of media correspondents in New

York would provide both a timely and particularly effective forum for issuing an open warning to the Vietminh and their Chinese supporters, marshaling domestic opinion behind possible future action, and casting the lure that he hoped would entice the French to abandon plans for negotiating themselves out of the Indochina War. Once again, though, the secretary's shot exceeded his aim. His attempt to address the broad issue of stopping the spread of communism in Southeast Asia succeeded only in focusing the world's attention on Dien Bien Phu, the battle he was trying hard to downplay. After Dulles' March 20 "united action" speech, Dien Bien Phu became a constant front-page story and a household name.

Using apocalyptic phrases reminiscent of the Truman Doctrine speech, Dulles opened his address with a grim prediction of what would follow even a partial Vietminh victory.[11]

If the Communist forces won uncontested control over Indochina or any substantial part thereof, they would surely resume the same pattern of aggression against other free peoples in the area.

The propagandists of Red China and Russia make it apparent that their purpose is to dominate all of Southeast Asia.

Southeast Asia is the so-called "rice bowl" which helps to feed the densely populated region that extends from India to Japan. It is rich in many raw materials, such as tin, oil, rubber, and iron ore. It offers industrial Japan potentially important markets and sources of raw materials.

The area has great strategic value. Southeast Asia is astride the most direct and best developed sea and air route between the Pacific and South Asia. It has major naval and air bases. Communist control of Southeast Asia would carry a grave threat to the Philippines, Australia, and New Zealand, with whom we have treaties of mutual assistance. The entire Western Pacific area, including the so-called "offshore island chain," would be strategically threatened.

The threat to the free world was even more serious, he continued, because Vietminh victories in Indochina were won through the indirect intervention of the People's Republic of China. Chinese agitators whipped up violent and misguided Vietnamese nationalism; Chinese military instructors trained Ho Chi Minh's forces; the PRC and USSR provided the insurgents with most of their supplies and weapons; nearly 2,000 communist Chinese had infiltrated Vietnam to support, train, and even direct Vietminh troops. In other words, he concluded, although the "Chinese Communists have, in fact, avoided the direct use of their own Red armies in open aggression against Indochina, . . . they promote that aggression by all means short of open invasion."

Perhaps, Dulles suggested, Beijing acted on the incorrect assumption that if it only refrained from open invasion it would not test the Eisenhower administration's recent declarations that communist aggression anywhere would bring a swift response at places and by means of its own choosing. This was a dangerous gamble.

Under the conditions of today, the imposition on Southeast Asia of the political system of Communist Russia and its Chinese Communist ally, *by whatever means,* would be a grave threat to the whole free community. The United States feels that that possibility should not be passively accepted, but should be met by united action. This might involve serious risks. But these risks are far less than those that will face us a few years from now, if we dare not be resolute today.

The free nations want peace. However, peace is not had merely for wanting it. Peace has to be worked for and planned for. Sometimes it is necessary in war to take risks to win victory. The chances for peace are usually bettered by letting a potential aggressor know in advance where his aggression could lead him. [emphasis added]

Dulles had fired a powerful salvo. His speech was far more than a warning shot directed at the Chinese lest they attempt to step up aid to the Vietminh on the eve of the Geneva Conference. In underscoring the importance of Southeast Asia to United States interests, Dulles by implication drew the danger line at *any* communist takeover in Indochina—whether it be a total battlefield victory or a compromise division of territory parceled out at the negotiating table; whether it be achieved through the direct or indirect participation of the PRC or solely by the Vietminh. By giving him the go-ahead on his speech, Eisenhower had allowed his secretary of state to create a broad trip-wire for "united action." A Vietminh surrender appeared to be the only option that would avoid it. No one believed that was even a remote possibility. The alternative was that the administration was preparing the nation for war.

Several aspects of the speech led to this conclusion. Dulles laid considerable stress on Indochina's vital importance to the security of the United States. Communist domination over "any substantial part" of Indochina, he forewarned darkly, could lead to the swallowing up of the entire Western Pacific. Less than a decade after World War II, his words reawakened the American public's memory of Japan's establishment across the same region of the "Greater East Asian Co-Prosperity Sphere," the resource pool from which it fueled its attack on Pearl Harbor. Dulles sharpened the analogy by attributing the menace to Indochina to a major power bent on world domination. The Vietminh were merely puppets, he charged; the real enemy was China and, behind it, Russia. Ho Chi Minh himself, Dulles continued, was a Russian-indoctrinated, international revolutionary who, only after helping "bring China into the Soviet orbit, . . . transferred his activities to Indochina." Beijing provided the Vietminh's supplies, weapons, and propaganda.

Having laid the ideological groundwork for American intervention into what once had been deemed a French colonial war, Dulles then called, obliquely, for "united action." He never defined the term. However, he clearly meant to imply military action. Dulles charged that the PRC had close to 2,000 troops in Indochina, only a step short of actual invasion. To combat this virtual intervention, Dulles declared, the United States government and public must be willing to take "serious risks" (another allusive phrase he had used in executive meetings and private conversations on Indochina). Though imprecise, this term connoted far more than the costs of increasing material aid. Some of this might have been, in the popular phrase of the time, "brinksmanship": a warning to the Chinese to keep themselves and the Vietminh in line up to and during the Geneva Conference.[12] However, supporting evidence shows that Dulles' remarks, to the extent that they were aimed at foreign powers, were aimed as much at the French and British as at the enemy; and to the extent that they concerned Geneva were intended to torpedo the negotiations.

Secretary Dulles' principal concern, as it had been since Laniel had announced his willingness to discuss a settlement of the French-Indochina War at the upcoming Conference on Far Eastern Problems, was to prevent the French from negotiating away to the communists all or part of Indochina. If United States military assistance would steel the French against accepting anything short of victory, he would advocate such an action.

He spelled this out to his staff when they went over the draft of his speech. The State Department's director of policy planning, Robert Bowie, argued against taking such a hard line. The American people were not ready for another war, he cautioned; it would be more realistic to accept a compromise settlement in Vietnam. Dulles replied testily that the United States would never promote appeasement. "Neither policy is popular," he glowered, "we better take the one that is right."[13] Congratulated on his tough stand by Senate Leader Knowland the day after his "united action" speech, Dulles again conjured up the image of Chamberlain and the events leading up to World War II. He realized his speech had elicited quite negative responses from Paris and London, he told the senator, but "he had to puncture the sentiment for appeasement before Geneva."[14]

Eisenhower shared much of this sentiment, except that he was more willing than his secretary of state to give peace talks a chance. Though it is not clear how much specific input Eisenhower had into the "united action" speech, Dulles fastidiously had kept the president informed of what he would say, showing him drafts, gaining his approval. The choice of words and the evangelistic style bore Dulles' mark. However, the overarching principles—the importance of Indochina to US defense, falling dominoes, the willingness to draw on force when necessary—were as much Eisenhower's as Dulles'. And the concept of "united action" was a modification of the president's proposal for a regional defense initiative.

Dulles' speech strayed from the Eisenhower line principally in its tone, which carried its own deep implications. He exaggerated the danger of communist rule over even part of Indochina, ensuring that any negotiated partition would cause either a split between the United States and its principal European allies or a loss of face for Eisenhower. Dulles was willing to accept the former; the president was not, so he eventually would be forced to accept the latter. Dulles also overstated (or overimplied) the administration's willingness to take military risks to prevent that victory. Eisenhower had used general threats in the past to impress recalcitrant enemies. He often gave his cabinet secretaries leave to make extreme statements that he could then qualify, thus striking the intended target while keeping the peace generally. The "united action" speech, though, was so direct that it upset the American public (not to mention the British) every bit as much as it did the Chinese. While it may have had its intended effect on the communists, domestically it set off a walloping anti-intervention reaction that would make it impossible for the president to use the quiet diplomacy at which he excelled.

Most significantly, Dulles' "united action" speech transformed Eisenhower's idea of a regional defense coalition with Vietnam at the center into a joint Franco-American effort to prevent the fall of Dien Bien Phu, if only because that was on everybody's mind at the time. Neither the secretary of state nor the president had foreseen this reaction. Dulles had aimed to strike short of offering the French unilateral assistance: to raise the possibility of US action to encourage the French at least to keep fighting up to and beyond the Geneva Conference, at best to satisfy Washington's long-ignored list of demands. A case could be made that he did help to achieve the smaller goal. In any event, though, the cost proved inordinate. The unfortunate effects were, first, to convince the Laniel cabinet that Ely's estimation was correct, that the Americans were ready to save Dien Bien Phu, thus exacerbating the pernicious misunderstandings that were alienating the allies; and, second, to scare off potential members of the Southeast Asian coalition, who feared that they would be bamboozled into plunging into the French-Indochina War before Geneva. This time, taking foreign policy to the rhetorical brink landed it on its head.

Few in the Eisenhower administration were prepared for the range, the direction, and the decibel level of the response to the Overseas Press Club speech. Instead of mobilizing the nation, the call for "united action" paralyzed it in confusion. The *New York Times* reported simultaneously that Dulles' words were intended merely to warn the PRC and boost the spirits of the French and loyal Vietnamese as they entered into their difficult negotiations, that they signaled that the Eisenhower administration was "prepared to risk war to help [France] to victory in Indochina," and even that they might mean that the United States was willing to join forces with South Korea and Taiwan to drive the communists out of Southeast Asia. Covering all bases, White House watcher William S. White "authoritatively reported" that "united action" was "such action as might become necessary, in the United Nations or out of it, as circumstances indicated."[15]

Capitol Hill groped just as helplessly in the dark. Listening to his fellow senators debate US policy toward the Indochina War and bandy about the merits of "united action," Democrat John Stennis threw up his hands in despair. "I followed Secretary Dulles' speech very closely, and I have not been able to decide exactly what he means by 'united action,'" he declared. "Exactly what is meant by 'united action' and what is the necessity or the case for it?" No one answered.[16]

A week later the Senate still was going back and forth, trying to divine the secretary of state's meaning. Montana Democrat Mike Mansfield fumed over the administration's lack of communication with the legislature. Mansfield had led a study mission to Indochina in 1953 that had concluded that "American aid . . . should not involve the commitment of combat forces [to Indochina].[17] Now he suspected that the White House was leading the nation to just such a commitment behind Congress' back. The administration must say what it means by "united action," he demanded.

[W]hen we refer to "united action" we do not know what the Secretary of State is speaking about, except as we read by the press reports this morning to the effect that the Government has asked for conferences with Great Britain, Australia, and New Zealand. Is this to be the extent of "united action"?

Turning to his junior colleague, Seantor John F. Kennedy, who had initiated the debate, Mansfield asked him in a prearranged question what he thought Dulles "had in mind when he was making the Overseas Press Club speech. . . ."

The Massachusetts Democrat replied, "There is every indication that what he meant was that the United States will take the ultimate step."

"And what is that?" Mansfield asked.

"It is war."[18]

The governments of the world, especially those of nations allied to the United States, shared the Senate's confusion and concern. Ambassador G. L. Mehta of India, a nonaligned country in the British Commonwealth, called on Secretary Dulles the day after the press club address to seek an explanation of "united action." He came away having failed to get a precise definition, but with the "personal view" that it meant military action.[19] (Dulles no doubt encouraged Mehta to believe this, expecting him to pass a warning to the Chinese. The Eisenhower administration frequently used India as the channel for messages it wanted to send to Beijing, with whom Washington was not on direct speaking terms. Eisenhower and Dulles credited similar warnings they had made to the Indian ambassador during the Korean War with bringing the Chinese to the negotiating table and to a quick settlement.)

Less propitiously, British Foreign Secretary Sir Anthony Eden, who earlier had obtained Dulles' promise that his speech would contain no implication that the allies would take part in any joint military action, was aghast to hear precisely that implication.[20] Like Mehta, he believed that the United States was preparing to intervene in the French-Indochina War and, worse, that Washington intended to try to drag Britain in as well. Moreover, he agreed with American anti-interventionists like Ridgway that military action in Indochina could not be contained. (He noted that Dulles had placed no limits on "united action.") Was the speech, he worried, a repudiation by the Eisenhower administration of the pledge Undersecretary of State Walter Bedell Smith had made to the Churchill government in February that the United States would never commit land troops to the French-Indochina War?

Fearing half-correctly that Dulles intended to draw France away from the Geneva Conference with hollow promises of winning the war through quick, limited intervention, Eden on April 1 sent the secretary of state his government's reply to the Overseas Press Club speech, transmitted through British Ambassador to the United States Sir Roger Makins. The message included a stern warning to its ally against taking any action or making any further public statements without regard to London's views. "[A]fter earnest study of military and political factors," Eden wrote,

we feel it would be unrealistic not to face the possibility that the conditions for a favourable solution in Indochina may no longer exist. Failure to consider this possibility now is likely to increase the difficulty of reaching tripartite agreement should we be forced at Geneva to accept a policy of compromise with the Communists in Indochina.

Makins added verbally that, in light of the French Union's current position on the battlefield, London considered partition the solution least damaging to the interest of France, the Associated States, and the entire free world.[21]

The French, too, defined "united action" to be United States military intervention into the Indochina War. To their considerable relief, they specifically heard Dulles announce the US government's decision to defend Dien Bien Phu if called upon. The straitened Laniel government had nurtured faith in deliverance from Dien Bien Phu since receiving Ély's report on his mission to Washington, two days before the Overseas Press Club speech. The secretary of state's words appeared to confirm Ély's account of his tantalizing conversations with Radford and Eisenhower and validate the chief of staff's "very clear impression . . . that the intervention of American heavy bombers can be obtained from the United States if the government of France asks the United States government"—that Washington was ready to make "a firm offer."[22] Confident that the United States was now ready to make that offer, Laniel and his cabinet trained their thoughts on how much they should ask for.

The deliberations of the Laniel government over whether to risk widening the war by asking for American airstrikes began shortly before Dulles' address. On the afternoon of March 29 an ad hoc executive War Committee entered into session to hear Ély's account of his conversations with the US leadership and to decide on a response to Radford's feelers.[23] The committee's mood vacillated between desire and prudence. Of the thirteen government, party, and military leaders debating whether to gamble to Operation Vulture, only Laniel and Ély initially were keen to lay the wager. Though he too had rigorously opposed American meddling in French Indochina, Laniel argued, he now faced the unfortunate truth that US airstrikes were "the weapon of last resort left to us" to prevent a rout at Dien Bien Phu. He echoed Ély's judgment that a short-term, limited action by United States air and naval forces carried little risk of provoking a military response by China or otherwise unalterably widening the war.

The other deliberators agreed with Laniel and Ély that the likelihood of a PRC counteraction was slim, as long as American forces confined themselves to bombing targets in Indochina; but Ély had not convinced them that an American "gesture" limited to airstrikes was somehow less than direct US intervention in the war or that it would not merely be the first step on the road to full-scale superpower involvement. The great majority of the War Committee had serious qualms about Operation Vulture. They feared that it would destroy the Geneva peace process (to which they remained unanimously committed, despite Dulles' enticements), that it would deepen and prolong the war, and that it would end in the domination of the French-Indochina War, economy, and political system by the American colossus. Nevertheless, they ultimately decided that they must take those risks *if* General Navarre determined that he needed US airstrikes to hold Dien Bien Phu. To receive that judgment, they dispatched General Staff Officer Colonel Raymond Brohon to Saigon.

While the Laniel government waited to hear General Navarre's decision, Admiral Radford campaigned vigorously to ensure that his government would respond favorably to the French appeal for airstrikes that he fully anticipated. On March 29 he passed along to the President's Special Committee on Indochina his memorandum on his conversations with Ély, in which he had called for "prompt and forceful intervention by the United States" into the French-Indochina War as the only way to prevent the communist takeover of all of Southeast Asia. He knew, however, that the lack of support from the other military chiefs crippled his efforts.

Radford needed a JCS consensus (unanimity was out of the question because of Ridgway's obduracy) if he hoped to build a momentum for intervention; and he believed he could get it. The Air Force and Navy chiefs had been as brusque to Ély and his shopping list as had Ridgway, but that was because the French refused to accept military advice in return. That would not be an issue with airstrikes, Radford thought, because they would be controlled by the US military. A few American bombs might even obliterate France's resistance to American advice and assistance. The Air Force and Navy also stood to gain institutionally by Operation Vulture: if effective it would prove that America could defend its interests through air power (either land- or carrier-based), and those two services would benefit substantially in prestige and dollars. The commandant of the Marine Corps could be expected to join Ridgway in opposing the action, but that would still leave a majority in favor. (Besides, the commandant's vote carried lighter weight than the chiefs' since the Marine Corps was not an independent service and the commandant was not a statutory member of the Joint Chiefs of Staff.)

His hopes high, Radford called a JCS special executive session into order March 31. After a brief restatement of his own position, he asked the Joint Chiefs of Staff to join him in signing a statement he had drafted advising the president to make an "immediate offer" of US aerial intervention to "assist" the French in their war in Indochina. To the chairman's frustration, not one of his colleagues took out his pen. One by one every service chief voted against advising limited intervention at that time. Radford remained completely alone.[24]

The most surprising "no" vote came from Air Force Chief General Nathan Twining. Everything in Twining's background and current interests indicated that he would support an aerial intervention plan to stop communism in Asia. He had served as an air commander in the Pacific (he commanded the unit that dropped the first atomic bomb), and from that experience had developed an abiding faith in air power and in the importance of Asia to American security. The Air Force also had the most to gain from a successful test of the New Look. Under slightly different circumstances, Twining probably would have seconded the chairman's proposal. However, one word in Radford's draft prohibited him, and that word Radford would not change: "immediate."

While he would likely have endorsed US Air Force and Navy action in Indochina *after* his planning staff had the opportunity to examine the logistics of the requested strikes and he had received satisfactory political and military concessions from Paris and Saigon, Twining balked at making a hasty, unilateral commitment. To toss France a life raft at its first cries for help, without demanding anything in return, he told Radford, would be to throw away the chance of achieving what the Pentagon ahd been demanding vainly for years. Twining let it be known that he might be persuaded to change his vote. He told Radford that he would support US action if France would agree that the American units to be engaged would remain under their regular command, if Navarre would place the training and advising of Vietnamese troops under US leadership, and if Paris would grant "true sovereignty" to the Associated States.[25] Though this seemed to leave the door to intervention open a crack, in fact the second and third conditions slammed shut any possibility that Twining would cross over.

Admiral Carney repeated all of Twining's objections to the timing of Radford's proposal. As expected, he also could see some attractions to offering France airstrikes, though he was more dubious than either Radford or Twining of their ability to win the war. Carney thought that bombing would "improve the French tactical situation" at Dien Bien Phu. However, as a former fleet commander (not, like Radford, an airman), the Navy chief remained dubious that air power, especially in the jungles of Vietnam, could be "decisive"—certainly not if called upon before a complete assessment had been made of US Navy and Air Force deployment capabilities in the region. Moreover, while agreeing that Indochina was strategically important to the West and that its loss "should be averted if possible," the chief of naval operations hesitated to advocate committing American forces and prestige to another Asian war so soon after Korea. The "potential tactical advantage" of United States intervention to save Dien Bien Phu, he warned, "must be weighed against the potential consequences of this US involvement in the Indochina War." Having placed the question on his own scales, the CNO added his "no" vote to Vulture.[26]

More forcefully, Shepherd, the Marine Corps commandant, denounced Radford's scheme for winning the Indochina War by bombing the jungle. Having devoted his career to building up America's amphibious forces, Shepherd opposed on grounds of both strategic dogma and professional obligation an action designed to prove the singular effectiveness of air power, especially in guerrilla war—the Marine Corps' specialty. Shepherd's veto protested the New Look as much as it did Operation Vulture. In explaining his position, he wrote:

If I could convince myself that such intervention—on any scale now available to us—would turn the tide of military victory in favor of the French, I would hold an entirely different opinion despite the hazards and uncertainties attending upon such a course. But I feel that we can expect no significant military results from an improvised air offensive against the guerrilla forces. They simply do not offer us a target which our air forces will find remunerative. . . .

The inevitable result would be the necessity of either admitting a fresh military failure on our part or intervening further with ground forces in an effort to recoup our fortunes. We can ill afford the first. I do not believe the other is a matter which we should even consider under present circumstances.

The weight of America's failure to decisively win the Korean War hung heavily on Shepherd's words. Like the chiefs of the Army and Navy, the Marine commandant did not want to risk having to pull the Air Force's irons out of the fire and take the blame for another military "failure," more humiliating than Korea, given Indochina's jungle terrain and the French Union's poor morale. "For us to participate in a defeat cannot be accounted as a means either of combatting Communism effectively, or of enhancing our position in the eyes of the Asiatics," he concluded dryly.[27]

That left only Ridgway. His reply seared the pages on which he wrote. Not only was the airstrike plan an exercise in the greatest folly, he charged, but, thanks to the New Look, the United States no longer was militarily capable of winning an Asian war by any means. In his memorandum of the executive meeting, Ridgway wrote that his reply to Radford's request that the chiefs advise Eisenhower to offer France airstrikes, was "an emphatic and immediate 'No'."

From the military viewpoint, the United States capability for effective intervention in the Dien Bien Phu operation was altogether disproportionate to the liability it would incur.

From the military viewpoint, the outcome of the Dien Bien Phu operation, which ever way it might go, would not in itself decisively effect the military situation there.

If recommended and executed, intervention by United States armed forces would greatly increase the risk of general war. If the United States, by its own act, were deliberately to risk provoking such possible reaction, it must first materially increase its readiness to accept the consequences.

The general hammered on the phrase "from the military viewpoint" to drive home a point. In addition to condemning Radford's proposal on its military merits, Radford castigated the JCS chairman for overstepping his limits as a military counsellor and meddling in matters constitutionally restricted to Congress and the White House. Neither Radford nor any of the chiefs had any business gratuitously profering political advice on the president, Ridgway charged.

Unless the question [of US aerial intervention in Indochina] emanated from proper authority, any such recommended action—for or against—was clearly outside the proper scope of authority of the JCS. This body was not charged with formulating foreign policy, nor of advocating it, unless its advice was specifically sought by the President, or the Secretary of Defense. To do so otherwise would be to involve the JCS inevitably in politics.

In a closing slap at Radford, who had warned both the president and his Special Committee on Indochina that if the United States failed to act to prevent a French defeat in Indochina "the consequences can well lead to the loss of all S.E. Asia to Communist domination," Ridgway admonished that

[i]n my opinion, the JCS should limit themselves to stating US military capabilities for rendering assistance in Indo-China; . . . the military consequences as the JCS view them, in the event of the rendering of assistance of United States armed forces, should be directed by proper authority.[28]

Most men would have been given pause by the overwhelmingly negative response Radford received from the Joint Chiefs of Staff, but Radford was too determined to have his way to so much as slow down. In a brief memorandum to the secretary of defense, he stated simply that while the service chiefs and the Marine Corps commandant had all recommended against offering France US airstrikes at the present time, "the Chairman is of the opinion that such an offer should be made."[29]

On March 24, midway through Ély's stay in Washington, two competing factions within the Eisenhower administration had taken positions in response to the crisis at Dien Bien Phu. Radford, supported by Nixon and, more significantly, Assistant Secretary of State Smith, favored intervention by US air and naval forces to prevent a communist victory over the French. Dulles, backed by his brother the CIA director, and Deputy Secretary of Defense Kyes, opposed any action that would subordinate America's military to French policy. At that point the two camps were of roughly equal strength. A week later the forces had altered dramatically. The noninterventionists outnumbered the war hawks by more than two to one and outgunned them by even greater odds. To the man, the chiefs of staff of the United States Army, Navy, and Air Force, and the commandant of the Marine Corps, turned thumbs down to Radford's plea for airstrikes against the Vietminh forces besieging Dien Bien Phu.

Still, the question of US military intervention into the French-Indochina war remained unsettled. Two of the joint chiefs appeared willing to withdraw their opposition in less pressing circumstances. From the State Department, Secretary Dulles lobbied to secure public and congressional support for a long-term, carefully planned, allied intervention, designed to prevent a "sell-out" at the Geneva Conference and ultimately to see the war through to victory. And the focus

United Action

of all the attention, France, hoped both to secure an American promise of aid *and* to negotiate a settlement at Geneva. The biggest question mark of all concerned the position of President Eisenhower. In the wake of the Overseas Press Club speech the world turned to him for the answer.

IV

Three Conditions

Despite all of the position papers, meetings, and informal discussions, the president had not yet made up his mind what to do about French Indochina. He had considered a number of options for preventing a communist victory there—ranging from an appeal to the United Nations to an American (nonnuclear) bomb drop near Dien Bien Phu—but none of them satisfied him. The problem was that politically, strategically, even emotionally, the French-Indochina War appeared to Eisenhower as a two-headed monster. One side threatened communist victory in Vietnam, setting off a tidal wave across Southeast Asia, eventually engulfing all of the Eastern hemisphere, and destroying the Eisenhower administration and the Republican party in its wake. The other, interventionist side menaced a broad array of principles and political goals that Ike held dear: anticolonialism, military discretion, a balanced budget, peace itself. Moreover, Eisenhower could not shake a nagging doubt that intervention could produce any better results than negotiations.

Eisenhower blamed the French for most of the problems they faced in their war in Indochina. In part because he shared France's racial bias, Ike attributed French defeats not so much to Vietminh prowess as to France's colonial policy, its refusal to listen to the advice of American strategists, capped by Navarre's stubborn insistence on Dien

Three Conditions

Bien Phu as his principal defense site. But Eisenhower also understood that, no matter how well or wisely that French Union fought, geopolitics doomed it to defeat just as surely as it had doomed MacArthur in North Korea. Long before Paris considered throwing in the towel, then-General Eisenhower mused on the hopelessness of the French struggle for Indochina:

[I]f they [the French] quit and Indochina falls to the Commies, it is easily possible that the entire of Southeast Asia and Indonesia will go, soon to be followed by India. That prospect makes the whole problem one of interest to all. I'd favor heavy reinforcements to get the thing over at once; but *I'm convinced that no military victory is possible in that kind of theater.* Even if Indochina were completely cleared of Communists, *right across the border is China with inexhaustible manpower.*[1] [emphasis added]

Three years later, in 1954, the inability of the French to come any nearer to victory, even with vastly increased material and financial aid, gave credence to Eisenhower's estimation. And by then the French Union forces were in a far worse position to achieve that victory. Troops were demoralized. Their pipeline of supplies and replacements narrowed. The Vietnamese had ceased listening to French promises. On the Vietminh side, the manpower and firepower coming from China flowed more freely than ever, no longer syphoned off by the war in Korea. The impossible military situation offered Eisenhower the most convincing argument why he should want to keep American forces out of the Indochina War—at least until the political situation in the Associated States improved sufficiently to develop an anticommunist fighting spirit among the Vietnamese. Ultimately, it convinced him that no limited bombing action could turn the war around for the French.

However, a president could not say "no" with the impunity of a military officer speaking only to his diary. First, he must be careful to say nothing to damage the morale of France or the Associated States. The president's advisers warned repeatedly that if defeatism spread too thickly across France and French Indochina, Navarre could surrender all or most of Vietnam to the communists even before the Geneva Conference. More realistic than his secretary of state, Eisenhower accepted that, one way or another, the French were going to extricate themselves from Indochina at the peace conference and that would entail some measure of victory for the Vietminh. He concentrated on ways to minimize the loss and secure what remained: principally by encouraging Paris to turn over its governments in Vietnam, Cambodia, and Laos gradually to local democratic leaders, preferably remaining in an advisory and defense assistance capacity until the new governments were secure, rather than merely walking out and leaving Indochina to whomever could grab it first; and by encouraging the democratic forces in the Associated States to unite to take over the reins of government and to motivate their people to fight for their own freedom from communism. Though Ike retained his conviction that no purely military victory was possible in the Indochina theater, he felt just as strongly that a long-term political solution was attainable, if all the democratic players acted together. Therefore, as a key supporting player, Eisenhower must say or do nothing to imply that he was not fully behind—and ready to help— the noncommunist forces in Vietnam.

Domestic politics and Ike's presidential style composed the second big reason that the president could not simply announce that the French were on their own in Dien Bien Phu. Presiding over the nation at the nadir of its internal war against communist subversion, over a party torn between internationalists and isolationists, Europe and Asia, guns and butter, Eisenhower tried to maintain a steady course by dodging controversy. Whether it be judged a weakness or a strength, he held together his pluralistic congregation of allies, advisers, and supporters by appearing to agree in spirit with every one of them. Thus Radford had complete faith that the president's position on Dien Bien Phu accorded with his own; so he assured Ély that Eisenhower would be willing to give France air support. Thus Dulles told his assistant secretary for public affairs, Carl McCardle, that Eisenhower agreed with him that the United States must stand strong against the pressure for giving in to communist demands at Geneva (although, far more perceptive a man than Radford, Dulles added cautiously that the president was not as critical of negotiations as he was).[2] Even when events forced Ike to declare his true position, he normally tried to do it in a way that would offend no one. The result, as when he finally spoke out on "united action," was often (and intentionally) unmemorable.

Three Conditions

At his weekly press conference on March 31, two days after the Overseas Press Club speech, the president made his first public statement on Indochina since the Dien Bien Phu crisis came to a head.[3] Immediately hit with a barrage of questions on the likelihood of American military intervention into the war, Eisenhower fended off the attack with the skill of years of practice at evasion. He was in "complete agreement" with Secretary Dulles on United States policy in Indochina, he said. But when asked if he would endorse and amplify on the various points raised in the State Department chief's speech, the president swiftly disengaged himself. "The speech must stand by itself," he said unhelpfully. He seconded Dulles' call for "united action," but with a few simple adjectives he recast its meaning back to his original intent. "[I]t is in the united action of all nations and peoples and countries affected in that region [Southeast Asia] that we can successfully oppose the encroachment of communism." This carried a far different *connotation* from Dulles' unqualified phrase, though it was not really any clearer—nor was the amplification he offered in response to a reporter's direct question whether he advocated military action by United States forces:

I have said time and time again that I can conceive of no greater disadvantage to America than to be employing its own ground forces, or any other kind of forces, in great numbers around the world, meeting each little situation as it arises.

What we are trying to do is make our friends strong enough to take care of local situations by themselves, with the financial, the moral, the political and, certainly, only where our own vital interests demand, any military help.

In the president's words, "united action" still had a military component, but that was just one aspect. While continuing to stress the need to stop the spread of communism in Indochina, Eisenhower downplayed the cruciality of the current problem ("each little situation") and placed greater emphasis on the need for self-help by the nations concerned. In other words, he reiterated his definition of the New Look: a mutual security policy by which United States funds would underwrite allied nations' defense, with military forces available as a last resort. He offered hope of succor to the Indochinese and the French and retained the threat aimed at the Chinese and Vietminh against becoming greedy at the bargaining table, but, in keeping with the retaliation aspect of the New Look, he left wide open the question of whether or not he would call on US force. (Dulles' stronger words had implied that the question had been decided.) When the assembled journalists demanded clarification of what "vital interests" would demand US military action, Eisenhower said, obliquely and with notable lack of dramatic tension, that every local situation had "its own degree of risk and danger" and each would be judged on its own merits. (It is interesting to note how Eisenhower adopted the most highly charged words and phrases from Dulles' speech— e.g., "united action," "risk"—then sapped them of their power.)

In assessing his presidency at the end of his first year in office, Eisenhower wrote in his diary that his preeminent achievement had been to end the fighting and casualties in Korea.[4] His guarded comments to the press on March 31 reemphasized that he did not want another Korea, this time in Indochina, next time in some other "local situation." But he had not *ruled out* US intervention, nor would he. To do so would bring him no benefit. (Secretary of State Acheson had publicly ruled out US defense of South Korea a few months before the communists invaded there, and not only did he have to swallow his words, but he had to bear accusations that his speech had encouraged the North Koreans to attack.) So, as Eisenhower closed the door on Dien Bien Phu, he carefully left a window or two open.

What was the effect of Eisenhower's modification of Dulles' "united action" speech? Virtually nothing. The Laniel cabinet continued to cleave to Radford's assurances that the president would order airstrikes. Radford himself continued to press for them. Most weekly news and commentary periodicals did not even carry reports on the press conference. One that did, *The New Republic,* charged that, since the president had neither denounced Dulles' speech nor wholly excluded the possibility that United States forces might be committed to the fighting in Indochina, his words held only one possible meaning: "the Administration has decided to do whatever is needed to win in Southeast Asia—if necessary it will commit US ground forces."[5]

In fact, the administration remained in a quandary over what do do. Eisenhower, Dulles, and the rest of the cabinet and NSC had their inclinations, often strong ones, but each day news came in that changed the situation, forcing them to consider the pros and cons of intervention all over again. A "no" spoken in the belief that the battle position would hold essentially stable until the Indochina portion of the Geneva Conference convened began to shake when a battlefield disaster loomed. When the NSC met on March 25, Dien Bien Phu was quiet, the French garrison resupplying; so the Americans could treat the battle as a side show, while turning their full gaze on long-term, large-scale solutions to the war. They could no longer take the long view by the next meeting, one week later, however.

Once again, the Vietminh had stormed the periphery of Dien Bien Phu, striking so forceful a blow it rocked even those who thought least of the French defense. In the first day's attack, on March 30, the garrison lost all but a fragment of two of its remaining five positions (though in a counterattack the next day it recaptured part of one) and between one and a half to two battalions, bringing the total French Union dead to near 1,300. In addition the Vietminh captured a huge amount of critical weaponry, six out of twelve artillery pieces on one strongpoint alone. Bad weather and Vietminh antiaircraft fire prevented French reinforcements from parachuting into the fortress; half of the airdrops of ammunition and resupply landed in enemy hands. It looked as if Radford was right. Dien Bien Phu could not hold out until the monsoons came. US Ambassador Donald Heath cabled from Saigon on April 1 that the French commissioner general for Indochina, Maurice Dejean, had told him "that the issue now depends upon hours and days." Dejean, Heath reported, put his hopes on a miracle.[6]

Radford's ceaseless activities to create concern for Dien Bien Phu also contributed to the greater tension at the April 1 NSC meeting, especially since his prediction of an imminent Vietminh conquest appeared to be materializing. Determined to make the NCS face the crisis at Dien Bien Phu this time around, Radford brought in a Navy intelligence expert to brief the council on the battle situation. After a brisk question-and-answer period, Radford summed up: without early reinforcement, the Dien Bien Phu garrison was finished. This time no one argued otherwise.[7]

Events now threatened to overtake Eisenhower unless he quit holding his options open and decided what to do about Dien Bien Phu.

Three Conditions

He accepted his fate grudgingly, fuming at France for forcing the unhappy decision upon him. "Why had the French ever committed forces to a remote area where these forces could not be reinforced?" he raged. "Nevertheless," he admitted, "the plight of the French certainly raised the question whether the United States ought now to consider any kind of intervention to help save Dien Bien Phu." He confirmed with Radford that he alone among the Joint Chiefs of Staff favored US airstrikes. Still withholding his final judgment, the president made it clear that he shared their concerns. An aerial operation was neither as simple in its execution nor as predictable in its results as Radford and other proponents made it sound; Eisenhower "could see a thousand variants in the equation and very terrible risks." But, he said, in what must rank as one of history's most half-hearted preambles to a decision for or against war, "there was no reason for the Council to avoid considering the intervention issue."

Dulles already had begun reconsidering intervention. Reports coming in from Paris and Saigon led him to revise his earlier dismissal of Dien Bien Phu. An extremely literal man, Dulles took longer than most in the administration to understand that the battle had acquired colossal symbolic dimensions that dwarfed the size and strategic value of the actual territory contested. The secretary of state began to fear that Radford's warnings would materialize: the fall of Dien Bien Phu could set off an immediate French withdrawal from Indochina, before any of the international machinery was in place for resecuring it. Now even the methodical secretary of state started to think in terms of early action—*not to save Dien Bien Phu, but to save Vietnam if the French bolted.*

Dulles manifested his newly acquired apprehensiveness in a cable he drafted and sent to Ambassador Heath in Saigon a few hours after the NSC meeting, in which he referred to the situation in Indochina as both critical and urgent. He advised the ambassador to prepare himself to respond to instructions from Washington to meet whatever contingencies may arise. He described only one:

Without wishing to adopt alarmist attitude, one of these contingencies, remote I hope, would be one in which French decided to abandon struggle under conditions which confronted local Governments, especially that of Vietnam, with hard decision of either capitulating to Communists or of continuing struggle alone. I would not wish that decision to be taken unless US given opportunity of examining situation and determining extent to which by positive action we can insure continuance of struggle under favorable conditions.[8]

Despite his conversion from temporization to the belief that the United States must quickly ready itself for the day of reckoning that was closing in on Indochina, the secretary of state remained unshaken in his opposition to intervening to help the French without prior political and military agreements. During the NSC meeting he stood pat against Radford's entreaties for airstrikes at Dien Bien Phu. Inverting Radford's insistence that the fortress could hold out for only a few days at most, Dulles asked the JCS chairman whether the United States could do anything in that short time to rescue the French Union forces. That was the question Radford had been waiting for. His reply called for an end to all further delays and evasions: US forces could be launched as early as the next morning, "If the decision were made."

Unfortunately, here the page goes blank. After Radford's declaration, Eisenhower ended the NSC discussion—the decision, he said, was one for "statesmen" to make—and asked for a few top advisers to join him after the meeting to talk privately in his office. The minutes to the extraordinary meeting were either lost or destroyed. No record has been uncovered of the arguments made by the president or his advisers. From several related records, however, we do know the conclusion: Eisenhower ordered Radford and Dulles to go ahead with the suggestion he had made at the previous NSC session and explore whether and under what circumstances Congress would approve US aerial action in Indochina.[9]

According to the most popular account of the resulting meeting, Ike's decision to place the Dien Bien Phu question before the congressional leadership offers incontrovertible evidence that the JCS chairman had won the president's support for his bombing plan.[10] In fact, as Radford himself half-suspected even then, Eisenhower had merely found another way to delay and evade responsibility for the uncongenial decision of saying no. The president would not attend the congressional briefing. He already had decided to let history take its course unaided at Dien Bien Phu. Rather than announcing that controversial decision, though, he would leave it to time—and Congress—to settle.

Dulles called the congressional leaders' meeting for Saturday, April 3. Radford wanted an earlier meeting, on the 2nd. "[T]ime is the question," he emphasized to Dulles. "[I]f there is a disaster the President might be criticized for not doing something." With his own focus not on Dien Bien Phu but immediately beyond, however, Dulles successfully held out for the later date. Saturday was a better day for keeping things low key and out of the press, he persuaded Radford.[11] An extra day would also give the secretary of state more time to prepare his case and consult with Eisenhower. Dulles no longer procrastinated as he had a week before, though. He was worried. When the director for foreign operations, Harold Stassen, called him later in the day on another matter, to suggest that in some testimony he would be presenting to Congress the secretary should point out that no territory had fallen to communism during Eisenhower's administration, Dulles warned Stassen to "watch out . . . Indochina might go under."[12]

Early the next morning, April 2, Dulles, Radford, Defense Secretary Wilson, and NSC chief Cutler met with the president to outline the points Dulles and Radford should raise at the congressional leaders' briefing.[13] Dulles hoped also to establish where each of the top administration officials stood on the question of intervening in the French-Indochina War. Particularly, he was determined to clarify the difference between the intervention he was prepared to support and the form advocated by Admiral Radford, which Dulles found unacceptable; and he wanted to make sure that his understanding of the conditions under which the United States might intervene in the war agreed with the president's. This two-part hidden agenda underlay virtually everything Dulles said at the meeting.

The secretary of state first showed Eisenhower a proposed congressional resolution on Indochina that he had drafted in preparation for the meeting with the congressmen. The resolution authorized the president,

in the event that he determines that such action is required to protect and defend the safety and security of the United States, to employ Naval and Air

Forces of the United States to assist the forces which are resisting aggression in Southeast Asia, to prevent the extension and expansion of that aggression, and to protect and defend the safety and security of the United States.[14]

Dulles prepared the resolution to expedite legislative approval of US intervention into Indochina in the event that the French took flight or the Eisenhower adminstration entered into a military coalition with France and the Associated States. Failing that, he could at least use it to gauge the president's position: was Eisenhower willing to make what amounted to a public military commitment to Indochina at this time?[15] Unfortunately for Dulles, the draft resolution failed to attain either of its objectives. Eisenhower read the proposal, told Dulles it was fine, but barred him from submitting it to the congressmen. It would be a poor move tactically, he explained. Rather than thrust on the legislators a position which they must then either accept or reject, Eisenhower preferred that Dulles find out what the congressmen themselves thought would be the proper response to the troubles in Indochina. In other words, Eisenhower successfully tucked his own position behind the banner of separation of powers.

Redirecting his approach, Dulles said that he had not intended to show the draft to the legislative leaders, but "had put the matter down at this point in resolution form so as to be sure that we ourselves know what it was that we thought was desirable." At best, this was half true. Dulles' telephone conversation records for the previous day leave no doubt that he *had* intended to submit the draft to the congressmen. (He told Attorney General Brownell over the phone that he was preparing "something to show" the congressional leaders at the April 3 meeting.)[16] However, the secretary of state was most sincere in emphasizing the importance he placed on having everyone—especially the president—lay his cards on the table. Nevertheless, Ike again eluded him. According to Dulles' memorandum of the meeting, Eisenhower replied that "he quite agreed with the importance of having our own minds clarified," but apparently not enough to get him to reveal his own thoughts. Indeed, the president spoke not another word that Dulles considered worth noting.

Receiving no signal from Eisenhower to guide him into more adventuresome territory, Dulles took a step back toward the center. He dropped his recent recommendation that the United States ready itself to replace France in Indochina and produced instead a combi-

nation of Eisenhower's coalition idea and his own long-standing goal
of pressuring the French to stand pat at Geneva. He had designed his
draft resolution, he said, to give the Eisenhower administration the
authority it would need to create "a strong position with which to
develop strength in the [Indochina] area by association not merely
with France and the Associated States," but also with the other regional powers. He agreed with Defense Secretary Wilson's interpretation that "the proposed congressional authority was designed to
'fill our hand' so that we would be stronger to negotiate with France,
the UK and others." He would be talking with the ambassadors of
those countries in the next few days, he said. He believed along with
the president that it was very important that the neighboring countries join in any defensive effort.

Dulles aimed the last statement directly at Radford. Closing in on
the JCS chairman and his Dien Bien Phu intervention plan, Dulles
records himself as suggesting to the others that "Perhaps Admiral
Radford looked upon this authority as something to be immediately
used in some 'strike' and irrespective of any prior development of an
adequate measure of allied unity." No, came Radford's surprising
reply, that was no longer the case. The JCS chairman was not fooled
by Eisenhower's prevaricating tactics. When the president refused even
to allow Dulles to show the draft resolution to Congress, Radford
saw that Eisenhower had no intention of acting swiftly to save Dien
Bien Phu. Believing the battle lost, Radford retreated. Though he had
once considered using airstrikes to rescue the French at Dien Bien
Phu, he said, he had since abandoned that option, as the battle "would
be determined within a matter of hours," and there was no longer
anything United States forces could do to change things. However,
Radford was not as willing to abandon his airstrike plan as he first
appeared. The French position in Indochina could take a turn for the
worse after the Dien Bien Phu fortress fell, he warned. In that case
there might be a need for "more active U.S. intervention." But for
the moment, he said, he had nothing specific in mind.[18]

From this meeting Radford emerged empty-handed, Dulles con-
tented himself with half a loaf (he had stifled Radford's clamor for
immediate airstrikes, but he failed to get the clarification he wanted
from Ike), and Eisenhower got everything he wanted. The president
managed to defer his way out of going to the aid of Dien Bien Phu,

without having to bear the burden of saying no. He wriggled out of making what was generally believed to be a "no longer avoidable" decision on US intervention, by seeking the uninfluenced thoughts of the congressional leadership. And he redirected Dulles' urge to do something into putting together the Southeast Asian coalition Eisenhower envisaged for the long-term security of the region. If Dulles succeeded in forming the coalition *before* the Geneva Conference settled the fate of Indochina, Eisenhower could reconsider then how far he wanted to go (if at all) to influence negotiations. If Dulles failed, his efforts would at least bolster the French to deal from strength at Geneva and perhaps convince the communists to settle for a poorer bargain; they would lay the groundwork for a post-Geneva regional security system; and they would quiet those forces in Congress who were waiting for their chance to accuse Eisenhower of "losing" Indochina by nonaction. In either case the president remained free to follow his own dictates, despite all the pressure of people and events to bind him to one policy or another. By slight of hand, Eisenhower invisibly controlled the situation.[19]

As soon as Dulles left the meeting with the president he set off in search of the allied support he believed was the first step on the road to American intervention to keep Indochina in the Western camp. At 3 PM the secretary of state and his principal deputies met with British Ambassador Makins and pleaded for the creation of a "solid front to stiffen the French attitude at Geneva."[20] Typically, Dulles wasted neither time nor words. Once the ambassador sat down, Dulles plunged into the heart of the Indochina problem as he saw it. "The situation in Indochina had reached a serious stage," he told Makins, as recorded by one of the attending State Department officals.

There was a threat of a French collapse or of a French desire to reach a settlement on terms which would result in the loss of Indochina and the rest of Southeast Asia to the Communists. There was a need, therefore, to encourage the French and to keep them from reaching a settlement at Geneva or elsewhere which would be disastrous to the French and the free world. . . . Even now the situation in Dien Bien Phu was critical and the possibility existed that the French defenders would be overwhelmed, bringing in its train possibly serious repercussions in France, including a public demand to withdraw from the war. Even if Dien Bien Phu could be held and the French were able to maintain the present military situation until the monsoon rains came, when there would be an abatement of military operations, the possibility existed that the French would go to Geneva to seek a settlement either through the Conference or directly which would lead to the loss of Southeast Asia. The U.S. Government had of late been giving serious consideration to this matter and had come to the conclusion that we could not stand by passively and let Southeast Asia go by default to the Communists.

Barely pausing for breath, Dulles rattled off all of Britain's colonial and commonwealth interests in Southeast Asia. The UK and other democracies in the region must accept responsibility for checkmating communist advances there, he said. They must take preventative measures now; three or four years later communism may have grown so strong that to resist it then could result in a world war. In particular, said Dulles, the United States and United Kingdom must act together to "encourage the French not to engage in a sell-out of Indochina," and simultaneously to lead a consideration of "some broader collective security arrangements which could be utilized to keep Southeast Asia out of the hands of the Communists irrespective of what position the French might finally adopt."

Makins did not reply directly. Instead he read aloud Eden's April 1 reply to Dulles' Overseas Press Club speech, in which the foreign secretary argued that a military solution was no longer feasible in Indochina and called for allied unity in seeking a *good negotiated compromise*. On his government's instructions, Makins added that partition was the solution toward which London believed the allies should aim.

Dulles had smacked into a brick wall at the very start of his quest for "united action." He was shaken, but not so badly as he would have been had he struck it wholly unexpectedly. The secretary of state had been at odds with the British over the French-Indochina War since the Berlin Conference earlier that year, where Dulles felt Eden had washed his hands of the future of Southeast Asia. Dulles believed that Eden had taken the attitude that Britain was an uninterested bystander in the Indochina conflict and thus had convinced the French that the only way out of their predicament was through negotiated withdrawal. From that time on, Dulles considered the Churchill government to be both an undependable ally and a myopic one, since it failed to recognize that the communist takeover of Indochina would pose a direct threat to Malaya, Australia, New Zea-

land, Hong Kong, and the free world in general. Now it seemed to
Dulles that Eden intended to compound his uncooperativeness and
defeatism by actually aiding the enemy—by encouraging a settlement
that would result in a communist victory in Indochina—despite the
Eisenhower administration's agreement to attend the Geneva Conference only on condition that France and Britain promise not to
negotiate "any solution of any kind which directly or indirectly in
the near future or over a period of time could lead to the loss of
Indochina to Communists." Dulles believed partition would lead directly to the complete takeover of Indochina by the Vietminh and so
was prohibited by the allied agreement. Undersecretary Smith said as
much to Makins.

The ambassador replied, diplomatically, that he shared Dulles' view
that the Indochina problem deserved further consideration and he
would be pleased to put the secretary of state's arguments to his government. But first, he asked Dulles, just what did the Eisenhower
administration have in mind in regard to "united action"? The true
answer, of course, was nothing—at least nothing agreed to, nothing
approved of by the president. Dulles told Makins that the plan "was
under active study at this time" and he was not free to discuss it in
detail. However, he said, the general idea was that the free governments of Southeast Asia would "band together in some kind of common defense" of the region. He suggested directing the coalition's
deterrence power against the PRC.

Despite his well-deserved reputation for insensitivity, Dulles tried
to handle the British delicately. In conversations with associates, he
spoke of a "wave of hysteria" in Britain over nuclear war and warned
them against saying anything to encourage the impression growing
in the UK that the Americans were preparing to start one.[21] Yet in
this meeting with Makins, Dulles did just that. Ironically, he was
trying to prove that "united action" offered the best chance for peace
in Asia. He hoped thereby to create a compelling reason why the
Churchill government—bogged down in the mire of a despondent
economy, distracted by its own troubles in Iran, confronted by a public up in arms over a recent American hydrogen bomb test that had
radiated a boatload of Japanese fishermen, and committed since the
death of Stalin to easing world tension through negotiating peace

with the communist bloc—should enter a coalition to fight communism in French Indochina.

Dropping all talk of stopping the French from negotiating peace at Geneva or of creating a multinational army to finish the war with the Vietminh, Dulles turned to the Chinese side of his "united action" triangle. A Southeast Asian coalition could convince the communist Chinese that "stepped-up activities on their part in Southeast Asia could lead to disastrous retaliation on our part by sea and air, [so that] perhaps they could be persuaded to refrain from adventures in that area," he told Makins. "If so, Southeast Asia could be saved from communism and probably a world wide conflict avoided." A scrupulously honest man, Dulles admitted that there would be risks in raising the threat of massive retaliation. However, he said, "the alternative of sitting by and letting the Communist overrun Southeast Asia, was . . . likely to lead to greater risks and disasters in the long run." At this point honesty or enthusiasm or his powerful sense of logic overbalanced the secretary of state's resolved sensitivity to London's nuclear fear. He explained to Makins that "the atomic balance, which is now advantageous to us, might decline over the next four years." The ambassador gingerly replied that Dulles' argument "had merit" and that he would pass it along to his government. When Dulles concluded with the hope that his proposals could begin to be put into action before the Geneva Conference, Makins drew back still further. He repeated that he would tell Eden of their conversation, adding with studied reserve that he "hoped to be able to transmit the views of his Government at some later date."[22]

The threat of nuclear war weighed so heavily on the minds of those in the Churchill government it would have become a factor in the "united action" debate even had Dulles not specifically mentioned it. Dulles' gaffe merely demonstrates how ill-fated was his quest for "united action." The minute he ventured beyond the vaguest words, agreement ended. If those within the same governing administration of the same country could not agree on its proper meaning and how far they were willing to go to carry it out, it was senseless to imagine that all of the separately focused allies could do better.

Dulles rejected the single action Makins favored: ordering the British military liaison officers in Washington to confer at once with the

Three Conditions

US Joint Chiefs of Staff on the military situation in Indochina and to explore whether "united action" could be a useful deterrent against Chinese aid to the Vietminh in the few weeks remaining before the Geneva Conference. This time the Englishman was moving too fast for the American. Dulles had yet completely to silence Radford, Ridgway was making threatening noises of another sort, and the JCS had fallen into disharmony over Indochina. This discord, Dulles feared, could put the British off "united action" entirely. Dulles also did not want "united action" perceived as primarily a military matter. Political arrangements must come first, he told Makins; military details could be discussed later (Dulles suggested the end of the next week).[23]

On its own, however, the United States military machine continued to gear itself to intervene in the war, if ordered. Following Carney's March 19 order to Phillips, reconnaissance air units from the US 7th Fleet had been studying southern Chinese air fields, supply depots, transport roads leading into Indochina, and the condition of the northern Vietnam communist strongholds of Lang Son, Cao Bang, and Lao Kay. Phillips' aircraft carrier group moved into the Tonkin Gulf to about 125 miles off of Haiphong Harbor. Not part of the bluff, these forces maintained the strictest secrecy. The Eisenhower administration told neither the British, the French, the Vietnamese, nor the US Congress anything of the maneuvers.[24]

At 9:30 in the morning of Saturday, April 3, Secretary of State Dulles, Admiral Radford, State and Defense Undersecretaries Smith and Kyes (Wilson was out of town), Navy Secretary Robert Anderson, and State Department congressional liaison Thruston Morton sat down around a conference table in the State Department building in Foggy Bottom with eight leading congressmen: Senators Knowland and Eugene Milliken of the Republican party, Democratic Senators Lyndon Johnson (minority leader), Earle Clements (minority whip), and Richard Russell, and Representatives Joseph Martin (House speaker), John McCormack (minority whip), and James Priest (Democrat). The meeting had been called at the president's request, Dulles told the gathering, to organize a response to the crisis in Southeast Asia.[25]

Admiral Radford gave the legislators a comprehensive rundown of the military situation in Indochina, particularly at Dien Bien Phu. The position was desperate, he concluded; the French garrison could fall any day, if it had not surrendered already. Fully supporting Radford's strategic analysis, Dulles followed it with a prognosis of the political repercussions. The secretary of state said that a defeat at Dien Bien Phu could set off a general French rout and lead to the communist capture of all Indochina, striking a fatal blow to America's defense line in Asia. If nothing were done to save Indochina, "it was only a question of time until all of Southeast Asia falls along with Indonesia. . . ." To prevent that from happening, he urged Congress to give the president its backing "so that he could use air and seapower in the area if he felt it necessary in the interest of national security."[26]

Only Knowland offered his immediate, unqualified support (and he later withdrew it to side with his colleagues). The congressmen balked at what seemed to them to be a request for unilateral intervention. "We want no more Koreas with the United States furnishing 90% of the manpower," they insisted.[27] Both Dulles and Radford argued that the action they contemplated would be on a much more limited scale than the US effort in Korea had been, since French and Vietnamese troops, not Americans, would fight the ground war. But the lawmakers did not trust France to maintain its share of the war burden. Once the United States flag was committed, it would be impossible to limit action to air and sea, they countered. By acclamation the eight congressmen voted their reply to Dulles' request: before they would ask the House and Senate to support any commitment of US military forces, they must be assured that it would be part of a multinational effort. Could the secretary of state offer that assurance, they asked.

Dulles said that he had talked already to the representatives of Britain and the Philippines and would meet with the French ambasssador in a short while. However, he was caught up in a paradox. He could not ask foreign governments to commit themselves to the coalition until he could assure them that his own government was committed. So he could not get the promises of allied support the congressmen demanded as a precondition for their support, without having their support in advance. Dulles tried to satisfy the assembled legislators by assuring them that Australia, New Zealand, Thailand, and the Philippines had expressed unofficial, preliminary willingness to contribute troops to a defense coalition. However, according to notes taken at the meeting by Senator Russell, when pressed on the likelihood of a British commitment Dulles admitted that he was "unenthusiastic."[28]

The legislators turned back to Admiral Radford and asked whether an immediate congressonal approval of airstrikes would save the day for the French forces at Dien Bien Phu. No, he replied, it was too late to win that battle. If the United States had committed its air forces three weeks earlier they could have rescued the French position and sent the communists packing, he said, but now the aim of US military efforts would be to help the French pick up the pieces after the lost battle and go on to win the war.[29] The congressmen asked the JCS chairman whether the service chiefs agreed with his assessment that US airstrikes launched now with no ground support could defeat the Vietminh. Radford confessed that they did not. By one account he added the objection, "I have spent more time in the Far East then any of them and I understand the situation better."[30]

The JCS opposition reinforced the legislative leaders' apprehension that a US commitment to the French-Indochina War could not be limited to a few bombing raids. Yet they were not ready to abandon Southeast Asia to communism or to shoulder the blame for doing so. Therefore, just as Eisenhower had passed the buck to them, they passed it on to Britain and France (and back to Dulles who would have to negotiate with the allies). They said that they would support a resolution to authorize the president to comit US military forces to the war in Indochina on three conditions: that Dulles secure "definite commitments of a political and military nature" from the UK and other allies to join the coalition; that the government of France guarantee that its forces would remain in the fight until the allies won the war; and, to prove that the Americans were fighting to protect the people of Indochina from communist tyranny, *not* to keep them under colonial domination, Paris must promise to accelerate the independence of the Associated States.

Since political columnist Chalmers Roberts wrote his famous account of this meeting in September 1954, based on information supplied him by Congressman McCormack, April 3, 1954, has gone down in history as "the day we didn't go to war."[31] According to Roberts, the conditions set at the April 3 meeting prevented Eisenhower from ordering airstrikes over Dien Bien Phu, which the president, Dulles, and Radford were willing, even eager, to do to prevent a communist victory there. The principal competing assessment of the meeting, developed some fifteen years later, is that it was a forum staged by Dulles to reassert control over foreign policy toward Indochina after Radford had snatched the lead by devising Operation Vulture. In the view of historians Robert Randle and Townsend Hoopes, the two most prominent proponents of this interpretation, Dulles planned the congressional leaders' meeting precisely to court the Hill's negative reaction to a Dien Bien Phu rescue attempt and thereby kill the JCS chairman's airstrike plan; Eisenhower himself neither favored nor opposed military intervention, though after the congressmen set out their conditions he felt constrained by them.[32] Both popular interpretations thus portray Eisenhower as a passive witness to decision-making on April 3 and the meek executor of the legislators' decision against war at Dien Bien Phu thereafter.

However, recently opened documents on this meeting support neither of those conclusions. The discrepancies between popular tradition and fact are significant. Foremost is that the April 3 meeting, as has been shown, was *not* concerned with the rescue of the Dien Bien Phu garrison. The administration's only active senior-level proponent of Operation Vulture was Radford—and he had thrown in the towel on Dien Bien Phu the day before. Therefore, the secretary of state had no need to set up the JCS chairman and his airstrike plan for congressional interdiction. On the contrary, Dulles and Radford now were in substantial accord. Both supported a New Look response to the French-Indochina War. Dulles and Radford came to the meeting together hoping to secure the legislature's backing for a fully negotiated US naval-aerial action with which to buck up the French, frighten the communists, and win the war in Indochina.

The other principal error was that Eisenhower was either gung-ho for action or passively waiting on the golf course while his secretary of state took care of foreign policy. Eisenhower indeed was playing golf at Camp David during the conference, but he acted with the forced calm of a general who stands back while subordinates carry out his strategy. Eisenhower, after all, set up the meeting (over Dulles' initial objections), went over the agenda ahead of time, and set strict limits on how strongly Dulles could push for action. His only apparent act of passivity was to leave the job of doing the asking to his advisers—and that was not passivity at all, but rather a pointed, nonverbal statement.

Though he used it sparingly, conserving it for matters of most importance, Eisenhower knew how much weight he pulled on the Hill when it came to foreign, especially military policy. That is why he personally explained to the congressional leadership his decision to send US Air Force technicians to Indochina back in January. That is why he carried out a massive telephone and public appearance campaign to defeat the Bricker Amendment, regardless of the overwhelming popularity of the bill and the long odds everyone gave him of succeeding. The amendment had the backing of virtually every influential political and professional body in the country, from the American Bar Association to the Veterans of Foreign Wars; it was co-sponsored by 63 senators, 46 of them Republicans. Still, for more than a year Eisenhower fought it, hauling out every piece of ammunition in his arsenal. The amendment failed by a single vote to win the necessary two-thirds support of the Senate in February 1954. Meanwhile, the president kept up a continuous battle with Congress for more funding for his Mutual Security Program. Just two days after the April 3 legislative leaders meeting on military intervention in Indochina, which Ike saw fit neither to attend nor to sway in any way, he appeared before the Legislative Conference to plead for his 1955 fund package, about one-third of which was earmarked for material aid to Indochina. Clearly, the president was more interested in obtaining material support than airstrikes for the French Union forces in Indochina. (It is worth noting that once he announced his final decision *against* intervening in the French-Indochina War, Ike straightway called a meeting with key legislators to tell them why face-to-face.)

Conversely, when Eisenhower thought that getting congressional authorization for a military action would be a problem, either because of the time it would take or the publicity it would generate, he did not hesitate to go behind Congress' back and make his explanations later (as he did with the technicians for Indochina and with the covert operation in Iran in 1954 and as he would do in Guatemala just a month after the fall of Dien Bien Phu). The day before the congressional leaders' meeting he agreed unhesitatingly to provide airlift for two French paratroop battalions from North Africa to the Indochina battlefield, without informing anyone outside of the executive branch.[33] The conclusion one must draw is that Eisenhower did not want to send American forces into the French-Indochina War, elsewise he personally would have asked Congress for its authorization—or refrained from asking at all and explained his reasons later.

The president *knew* that the legislators would raise difficulties. The bare defeat of the Bricker Amendment, designed to curb the executive's independence in foreign policy, signified that Congress would not spontaneously write a blank check for presidentially decreed action in Indochina. The *Congressional Record* of February and March reveals serious qualms on Capitol Hill about the American role in Indochina.[34] Yet Eisenhower sent Dulles and Radford to talk to the legislators alone, made no supporting phone calls, even refused to let Dulles submit his draft resolution. From his interviews with the eight lawmakers attending the meeting as well as several others, Chalmers Roberts concluded that, had the president asked forcefully for authorization to intervene, Congress would have granted it.[35] Eisenhower must have known, at least suspected, as much. He invited a public rejection of military action. He gave the congressional leaders a free hand to construct barriers to intervention that he could then display mournfully to the French and to American jingoes ready to pounce on the creator of another "loss" in Asia. If anyone bears the guilt of cynically staging the April 3 legislators meeting, it was not Dulles, but the man golfing at Camp David.

The congressional meeting had not gone as Dulles had hoped. The congressmen's thinking actually did not differ dramatically from the secretary of state's, but he had wanted the legislators to give him the go-ahead, leaving it up to the administration to decide what constituted French moves toward granting Indochina independence or, especially, who would participate in an allied coalition. In either of the uses of "united action" that he envisioned—as a carrot to dangle before the French as they headed into Geneva or as a stick to wield against the Vietminh if the French "sold out"—speed was of preeminent importance. Dulles might be willing to relax his own set of political preconditions in order to save Vietnam from imminent communist takeover and so, he thought, might the president. However, without a congressional mandate that option did not exist. He had nothing absolute that he could show other possible coalition members, much less the French.

The legislators' insistence that Britain must commit itself politically and militarily to the coalition, if seconded by the White House, posed the most serious obstacle to creating preemptive "united action." Dulles had no illusion hat he could convince the Churchill government to do anything before the Geneva Conference that might be considered provocative. Though ideally Dulles, too, preferred British participation in the coalition, he would press on without it if need be, moving forward independently with Australia and New Zealand through the ANZUS mechanism. Forcibly tied to Britain his coalition had little chance of getting off the ground. Nevertheless, Dulles strained to raise it.

Shortly after the congressional leaders' meeting, Dulles held his prearrange conference with French Ambassador Bonnet to discuss "united action." It had been over a week since Ély departed Washington, leaving Radford with the firm impression that the Laniel government soon would be asking for United States aerial intervention to save the Dien Bien Phu outpost. Since then Paris had kepts its own council, while awaiting Navarre's word. Though he did not know what Radford and Ély had been planning, Dulles found the Laniel government's general silence over Dien Bien Phu worrisome. He was haunted by the thought that France was quietly preparing to bail out of Vietnam. If that were to happen, he feared, the US military might have to jump in to fill the gap, without sufficient political prearrangements—Korea all over again; or helplessly watch Vietnam go down the drain—another China. Yet, because of his failure to get a mandate from the congressional leadership, Dulles had nothing to offer the French ambassador to deter his government from giving up, except hope.

Bonnet entered Dulles' State Department office at 12:30 PM and remained there for an hour, listening to the secretary's offer, probing to establish its full dimensions.[36] The arguments the secretary of state laid before the Frenchman resembled those he had offered Makins (a negotiated peace would be surrender; partition equaled defeat), although he deleted all references to a French "sell-out" and put greater emphasis on saving France's prestige. The waning glory of France formed a powerful undercurrent in the secretary's stream of argument. He mentioned North Africa and France's relative standing in Europe. "[T]he future of France as a great power [is] at stake," he warned.

Would the government of France be willing to consider internationalizing the war, the secretary of state asked. Bonnet seemed very interested, though not precisely in the way Dulles had hoped. Dulles spoke of a coalition; Bonnet ignored his lead and returned to the question of US intervention. He asked whether Congress would sanction US military action in Indochina. Dulles said it would if such action were part of a coalition of regional powers, including Britain, and with France's active participation. Bonnet pressed him on whether he honestly believed he could get British participation. Dulles confessed that he was doubtful. So, continued Bonnet, if the British would not enter the coalition, what then? Were the United States government and Congress prepard to "go it alone"?

Pressed against the wall, still trying to persuade the French to stand firm at Geneva, Dulles put the case as hopefully as he could. "The difficulties would be greatly increased—although he would not say it was impossible—if the British would not agree," he told Bonnet, according to Dulles' own synopsis of the conversation. Then he moved on to another subject, spoke of strategies for the Geneva Conference, said that the regional coalition offered the only alternative to defeat at Geneva. But Bonnet had already absorbed the impression that the Eisenhower administration would be willing to "go it alone" in Indochina. Dulles had implied that Britain's participation in the coalition was expendable; taken to its ultimate conclusion, so must be that of the lesser powers. This confirmed the interpretation Bonnet had given Dulles' Overseas Press Club speech.

Requesting permission to speak personally, the ambassador told Dulles that the alternative to negotiated withdrawal could be found not in a regional coalition, but in Dulles' "united action" speech and its warning that the United States would not allow Indochina to fall under communist control. That speech had created the strong impression in Paris and elsewhere that the United States was prepared to intervene militarily in the region, by itself if necessary. This is what the communists feared and France needed, he said. The only value of a coalition would be to make it easier for the American government to explain intervention to its own people.

The blunt truth of the ambassador's words irritated Dulles (perhaps aware of his own role in demeaning the coalition he now sought to create). He replied sharply to Bonnet that all of the allies in the region had a stake in Indochina, not merely the United States. "If our Allies held back there would be grave repercussions here on our relations with our Allies around the world," he warned. He ended the conversation by reminding the ambassador that the United States had always given the French the help they urgently requested. "[T]his fact was fully known and appreciated in France," Bonnet replied.

Dulles felt a bit better after the meeting. He had not moved an inch toward his goal of "united action," but, if Bonnet's response was a fair measure, he believed he had stimulated Paris' interest enough to head off an immediate withdrawal from Indochina. That gave him the space he needed to continue trying to build a coalition. He pressed on relentlessly. Minutes after Bonnet departed, the secretary called the president to report that the meeting with the congressional leaders had gone "pretty well" and that he already had scheduled a meeting with the ANZUS ambassadors for Monday to follow it up.[37] As Saturday afternoon ticked by with no progress, however, Monday began to seem too long a wait. Back on the phone, Dulles arranged for the ambassadors to come to his home on Sunday afternoon, April 4.[38]

Dulles hoped his meeting with Australian Ambassador Sir Percy Spender and New Zealand's Leslie Knox Munro would lead to their countries' membership in the "united action" coalition and that he could enlist them to pressure London into joining too. He had reason for optimism. Neighboring Southeast Asia, the Oceanic powers had a greater concern in the fate of Indochina than did their mother country tucked away in the corner of Europe. Both Spender and Munro personally favored military action to defeat the communists in Indochina and they expressed the belief that their governments would too, given a suitable period for planning, negotiations, and taking care of domestic matters. As it had been for many in Washington, the sticking point was time. The Australian national elections were less than two months away. Military action by Australia before that time might give the election to the challengers (whose policies were "contrary to our long-term aims" in Southeast Asia), said Ambassador Spender. Ambassador Munro said that while he foresaw no immediate election problems in New Zealand, he too was pessimistic that his government would approve immediate action. Dulles had put the cart before the horse; New Zealand would consider military action only if Britain supported it.

Dulles, on the other hand, quite specifically sought an *immediate* force (though he hoped it would not be required to go into action immediately). When Sir Percy asked what type of military assistance the Eisenhower administration expected of his country, Radford, whom Dulles had invited to participate in the meeting, suggested that Australia could contribute an aircraft carrier and air support and New Zealand could supply naval assistance "comparable to its contribution in Korea." Dulles backed him up. The level of action contemplated would not in his opinion trigger a Chinese response, he said, "but if it does it should be possible to knock out their airfields and engage in certain activities along the South China coast." He stressed again the importance of acting before the Geneva Conference. If the coalition were not at least openly in the works by them, he said, "he could not guarantee that the United States Government and Congress would go along." Spender and Munro said they would discuss the matter immediately with their governments.

Armed only with a limp, unreliable congressional mandate, Dulles and Radford returned to the president to seek his blessing for "united action" before the Geneva Conference. At 8:20, Sunday evening, just back from Camp David, Eisenhower met at the White House with Dulles, Radford, Smith, State Department Counsel Douglas MacArthur II, and Deputy Defense Secretary Kyes.[39] Their discussion centered on the three conditions set by the congressional leaders the previous day. This was the first time Eisenhower had heard the complete list (an indication of the low level of urgency he felt toward the Indochina problem as compared to that shown by his top advisers). As Eisenhower had anticipated, the conditions were sufficiently stringent that, if not completely unrealizable, they would require lengthy negotiations to satisfy. If he had aimed for the *appearance* of impending intervention to encourage and help the French to secure the best possible terms of Geneva, Ike could not have fared better. Nor could the congressional leaders have been more obliging in taking onto their shoulders the burden for the possible "loss" of Vietnam. Eisenhower was quite content to follow the legislators' lead. "There was nothing in these preconditions or in the congressional viewpoint with which I could disagree," he later recalled. "My judgment entirely coincided with theirs."[40]

The president then delineated his own three preconditions to US intervention. While seeming to follow the legislators' blueprint for action, Eisenhower's demands erected an even sturdier barrier against such action ever taking place—and protecting the White House from blame when it did not. First, he said, to satisfy Congress any action by United States military forces would have to be as part of coalition with active participation by Britain, Australia, and New Zealand, *including troops,* and, if possible, participating units from Thailand, the Philippines, and other states in the region. Second, he issued the rather vague demand that Dulles first secure a "full political understanding with France and the other countries." This stipulation has been interpreted as generally including the legislative leaders' second and third conditions—that France accelerate the independence of the Associated States and agree to remain in the war until its conclusion. In fact, Eisenhower had worded in it such a way that he could define it as he wanted depending on the situation. (He would use it in practice to stiffen the conditions demanded of France.) Finally, the president insisted that any intervention by US forces would require the *advance* approval of Congress. It would not be sufficient merely to satisfy the leaders' April 3 conditions; Congress as a whole must vote for action, a time-consuming process at best.

Eisenhower assured his advisers that if his conditions were met and he judged the military situation sufficiently serious, he would dispatch US military forces into Indochina. For the present, he said, Dulles had enough of a base "to feel perfectly able to talk to other nations and tell them that if they would go along with our proposals we would be ready to participate in a regional grouping."[41]

By convincingly dispatching Dulles on a quest for "united action," Eisenhower had diverted the activist secretary of state and the interventionists within his administration for the period leading up to the Geneva Conference, provided a deterrent against the communists demanding too favorable terms at that conference, and deflected criticim away from his administration for not aiding the French or preventing a negotiated settlement. The only price he would pay would be an increase in the volume of accusations that he could not control his own government, a price he had born willingly before in other instances and would bear again as he found it convenient.

In portraying a president prevented from the action that he ardently desired, by a cool response (not the uncompromising opposition) of a bipartisan group of eight congressmen, Chalmers Roberts and his followers fell into the trap Eisenhower had laid. Their error is not only in misjudging Eisenhower's position before the legislative leaders' meeting, but, more critically, in failing to perceive the president's high level of control over the ultimate decision. Had Eisenhower been sufficiently keen on pressing his suit for intervention, he stood a good chance of securing Congress' support. Its concern over Indochina was never very deep and was more often focused on the issue of executive openness with the legislature than on the question of military intervention and who must participate.[42] Dulles told French Ambassador Bonnet after the congressional leaders' meeting that if Britain refused to join "united action" it would still be possible to form a military coalition. That was before he consulted the president. It was Ike's insistence on a British troop commitment that killed "united action." Asked whether he believed the congressmen had influenced the intervention decision, Thruston Morton, a participant in the April 3 meeting, said:

> No, I don't think so. Their negative approaches didn't affect Dulles too much. The fact that the President had reservations is what stopped it. Hell, if he had let Raddy go he would have been in there with the whole carrier fleet. Eisenhower put the quietus on that. . . . Raddy had it all figured out, how he could get carriers in the area and bomb the hell out of them and knock them out of this high ground. . . . *Dulles accepted Raddy's estimate of the situation, but Eisenhower didn't,* and that was the end of it so far as Dulles was concerned.[43] [emphasis added]

The significant event in the Dien Bien Phu decision against war was not the April 3 congressional leaders' meeting, but the April 4 meeting at the White House at which Eisenhower for the first time explicitly set out his position on and the conditions for intervention. By doing so, he prevented Dulles and Radford from speaking or acting too rashly in the future. In historian Townsend Hoopes' view,

Three Conditions

Eisenhower at that meeting "reasserted control" over American policy in Indochina.[44] More correctly, he reminded his strong-willed subordinates of the control he had never relinquished. He then gave them just enough rope to weave a deterrent and a cloak of righteousness to insulate the Oval Office from accusations of defeatism.

V

"Resigned To Do Nothing"

At the very moment Operation Vulture was being buried in Washington under the crushing weight of unfulfillable conditions, General Navarre cabled Paris to request United States airstrikes to save the outpost at Dien Bien Phu. The appeal by the commander in chief of the French Union forces in Indochina marked a major, abrupt change in French-Indochinese military policy and in Navarre's own thinking. Less than three months before, the general had flatly opposed even the stationing of an American military liaison team in the war zone, on the grounds that it would undermine his control over Vietnamese troops. In late February he had termed active American military support "absolutely unthinkable."[1] Indeed, just the day before he sent the cable calling for US aerial assistance, Navarre told Colonel Brohon to reply to the War Committee's query that he could not approve Operation Vulture. United States intervention, no matter how limited, carried too great a risk of provoking a Chinese response, he said.[2] After Brohon had departed Saigon to take the hopeless news back to his government, however, Navarre reversed himself. He cabled General Ély on April 3 (April 4, Paris time): "It is my opinion that the intervention Colonel Brohon discussed with me can have a decisive effect, especially if it takes place before the [final] Viet Minh assault."[3]

"Resigned To Do Nothing"

Navarre's change of heart coincided with the climax of the Viet-minh's second offensive, a devastating five-night attack on Dien Bien Phu. During the two-week lull in fighting, the communists had advanced their antiaircraft and artillery batteries into the foothold in the camp's defenses they had carved during their first assault. The weakened defenders, on the other hand, had been unable to use the time to do little more than rest. Even during the fortnight of relative calm, enemy fire had so steadily harrassed Dien Bien Phu's single remaining airstrip that no planes could land. Supply reinforcements were limited to those that could be parachuted in; the French could not even evacuate their wounded. The eastern side of the defensive line remained shrunken and vulnerable. Then came the renewal of heavy fighting on March 30. By the night of April 2, the fourth straight night of all-out attack, Navarre was forced to reconsider the reply he had given Brohon in the quiet of daylight. With its defenders reeling under the one-two punch of Vietminh artillery barrages and heavy clouds that prevented French supply drops and effective bombing, the fortress could not stand much more punishment.

In desperation—it would have required nothing short of that—Navarre decided he had no choice but to gamble everything on Operation Vulture. His hope was that United States intervention could be limited to a one-shot, localized bombing mission to knock out enemy artillery and antiaircraft guns around Dien Bien Phu, allowing the garrison to resupply and stabilize its defenses, in turn enabling the French Union forces to retake control and beat off their attackers without further assistance. Navarre also gambled that, since the air-strikes would be limited to Vietnamese territory, the Chinese would not retaliate across the border.[4]

As soon as he received Navarre's cable (the evening of April 4, Paris time), Ély rushed to Premier Laniel's office. The government must request United States aerial intervention to cut the noose tight-ening on Dien Bien Phu, the chief of staff demanded. Laniel agreed and called an immediate meeting of the War Council. Before mid-night the council had reached a decision: the government of France would request that the United States intervene in the Indochina War; Operation Vulture must take wing.[5]

In the last remaining moments of the day, Laniel and Foreign Minister Bidault placed their request before US Ambassador Douglas Dillon.[6] The Vietminh had neared the end of its supply line, Laniel assured Dillon, but that still outmatched the pitiful stores of the defenders, as well as anything the French could drop to them through the solid cloud cover. At present, the communists were pressing their short-term advantage forcefully, yet it would take only a "relatively minor" effort by the Americans to turn the advantage to the French side. Laniel insisted, however, that the effort would succeed only if it were made immediately, *before the end of the week*. Otherwise the communists would turn their momentary advantage into a major victory over the free world. To make intervention easier for the Americans, Laniel claimed that French intelligence had gathered evidence of accelerating Chinese participation in the war. (In fact, the War Council's concerns went no farther than Dien Bien Phu and the Vietminh soldiers who were attacking it.) The premier then asked for a series of airstrikes on enemy installations around the fortress by US heavy bombers from the American carrier fleet. "Only this operation," he recalls telling Dillon, "can save the garrison at Dien Bien Phu."[7]

Like Navarre, the French government relied on the possibility that the garrison could be saved by a limited American airstrike—or even the open threat of a strike. Even in its trough of despair, therefore, Paris specifically limited its request to *American* intervention. In an attempt to head off more grandiose plans for "united action," Bidault told Dillon that he had received Dulles' proposal for forming a regional defense coalition, but that he would not be able to respond to it until his cabinet had a chance to meet and consider the offer later in the week (a significant delay, given the French insistence on intervention by week's end—and, considering the speed at which Laniel's War Council had met and voted for airstrikes, a disingenuous one). To Dillon's objections, Bidault sternly replied that his government based its request for unilateral American action on specific assurances given Ély by Admiral Radford that the JCS chairman would help to secure such support.

Once again, the French government not only withstood the pressure directed at it by its more powerful ally, but countered with even greater pressure. If the Americans allowed Dien Bien Phu to fall, Bidault darkly insinuated, France would make whatever peace it could at Geneva, regardless of Washington's concerns. Reporting back to Washington, Dillon recalled the foreign minister's threatening words:

Bidault closed by saying that for good or evil the fate of Southeast Asia now rested on Dien Bien Phu. He said that Geneva would be won or lost depending on outcome at Dien Bien Phu. This was reason for French request for this very serious action on our part.[8]

MacArthur at the Department of State picked up Dillon's report of Laniel's and Bidault's request for US airstrikes at 10:15 PM, April 4 (EDT), and immediately passed it on to Dulles and Radford. Simultaneously, Ély sent a cable of his own to General Jean Valluy, head of the French Military Mission to the United States. Ély worried that, since Dillon had not been privy to his conversations with Radford, he might transmit the message poorly—or it might get waylayed by Dillon's boss, Dulles. He instructed Valluy to tell Radford that the War Council had approved Operation Vulture and to ask the JCS chairman to transmit the request for the bombing mission personally to Eisenhower.[9]

Dulles beat Radford to the punch. He telephoned the Oval Office first thing Monday morning to tell the president of Laniel's conversation with Dillon and of his petition for US airstrikes at Dien Bien Phu.[10] Even in the flat language of a tepehone conversation memorandum, it is evident that Eisenhower took the news badly. Laniel's request was an embarrasing inconvenience—coming just when Ike thought he had detoured the intervention issue toward a coalition quest—but the revelation of Radford's unauthorized assurances to Ély was far worse than that. Eisenhower's delaying action would have no effect on boosting French morale if the Laniel government believed that he could override Congress and authorize airstrikes if he wanted. And his Geneva strategy would collapse if Paris' low morale, exacerbated by anger over America's refusal to bomb the periphery of Dien Bien Phu, caused it to adopt a defeatist attitude at the conference or pull out of Indochina altogether before the conference.

What Laniel desired was impossible, exclaimed the president. Without a prior political arrangement that would satisfy Congress, it would be "completely unconstitutional and indefensible" for the president to order any form of military intervention. Radford had done a grave disservice by implying otherwise. The JCS chairman "should never have told a foreign country that he would do his best because they then start putting pressure on us," Eisenhower fumed.

"Resigned To Do Nothing"

The responsibility for the fate of Dien Bien Phu, which the president had allowed Congress to place on French and British shoulders, now threatened to be dumped again onto his lap because of Radford's rash words. This revived all of Ike's anger over the French handling of the war and of American aid, about French "whims" and the expectation that the United States would satisfy every one.[11]

Dulles seemed to be taken aback by Eisenhower's anger. He had been delineating the level of Chinese communist intervention on the side of the Vietminh as revealed in Dillon's cable and was voicing his own worry that it was accelerating, when Eisenhower burst out against Radford's folly. Although Dulles must have been appalled as well by the admiral's incaution, he jumped to his defense in an effort to calm tempers and keep "united action" on track. He assured the president that, in his talks with Ély, Radford had clearly emphasized that the United States would not take part in any military action until the political aspects had been cleared up. He said that he had spoken to Radford earlier that morning and that the admiral had no intention of recommending a Dien Bien Phu rescue mission; he is "quite reconciled to [the] fact that it is [a] political impossibility at present time." Eisenhower did not appear mollified. When the independent action of his advisers became embarrassing and potentially damaging to White House strategy, it ceased to be politically useful.[12] Ambiguity had to end. The president closed the conversation without any of his usual equivocation. He suggested that Dulles look into some other way the United States could help the French, but, he said, "we cannot engage in active war."

This four-minute conversation was an epiphany for Dulles. Until then he had not percieved the extent of Eisenhower's reservations about the war in Indochina; now his eyes opened. According to the simultaneous summary made of the conversation by a secretary listening on the extension, the president expressed no interest in Dulles' estimate of the level of PRC activity in Vietnam and gave no indication he was even considering US intervention. He referred to the request for airstrikes as just one in a line of *French* "whims." "[W]e cannot engage in active war," he had said, in the fortright words of anger. It was the anger that seemed to shake Dulles into alertness. After this conversation, the secretary of state's tone changed. He continued to press for the fulfillment of the conditions that would enable the United States to intervene in the war, but thereafter his statements contained a note of cautiousness. (This change was observed by his contemporaries. Radford recorded in his memoirs that, after this conversation with the president, Dulles gave up his earlier effort to obtain United States intervention and limited his energies to pumping up French morale in preparation for Geneva.)[13]

An hour after speaking to the president, Dulles cabled to Dillon the administration's reply to Laniel's request. Here one can readily detect the change of tone. It was not forty-eight hours since Dulles' long conference with Bonnet. Then, despite his knowledge of the congressional leaders' terms for intervention, he had pursued the Southeast Asian military coalition with unqualified zeal, ignoring the most divisive condition of independence for the Associated States and implying that the participation of Great Britain was not absolutely necessary. However, in his cable to Dillon, which Dulles drafted personally after his telephone conversation with Eisenhower, the qualifications smothered his former enthusiasm.

As I personally explained to Ély in the presence of Radford, it is not possible for US to commit belligerent acts in Indochina without full political understanding with France and other countries. In addition, Congressional action would be required. After conference at highest level, I must confirm this position. US is doing everything possible . . . to prepare public, Congressional and Constitutional basis for united action in Indochina. However, such action is impossible except on coalition basis with active British Commonwealth participation. Meanwhile US prepared, as has been demonstrated, to do everything short of belligerency.[14]

In a personal aside to the ambassador, Dulles emphasized that there could be no coalition without the UK and its regional associates. The United States, he said, "cannot and will not be put in position of alone salvaging British Commonwealth interests in Malaya, Australia and New Zealand." He told Dillon that the question was currently under discussion between Washington and London at the highest level.[15]

The discussion he referred to was actually a cable Eisenhower had sent Churchill the night before, at Dulles' request, asking his government to join the United States in a pre-Geneva Southeast Asian coalition.[16] Written in much stronger terms than the president employed when discussing the French-Indochina War in private, the message leaves one questioning its intent: could it have been an attempt by Ike to establish an alibi against accusations that he had not done everything he could to "save" Indochina? Certain passages suggest that. Adopting a metaphor favored by Dulles (the State Department drafted the message), Eisenhower told the prime minister that a negotiated settlement to the Indochina War would be nothing more than a face-saving measure to cover either a French or a Chinese surrender, and the American government would never accept the former because of its disastrous implications for the rest of the region. (Yet, not two days later, before receiving Churchill's reply and without any appreciable change in the political or military status quo, Ike would tell his National Security Council that the loss of even all of Indochina need not inexorably lead to the loss of Southeast Asia.) In his cable to Churchill, the president said that the ad hoc coalition "must be willing to join the fight if necessary" (again Dulles' phrase) and even implied that the effort might require some use of ground forces. That compares with what Eisenhower told Dulles in response to Laniel's request for airstrikes—"we cannot engage in active war"— a determination which at the April 6 NSC meeting he made doubly clear applied not just to the Dien Bien Phu operation.[17] One is forced to the conclusion that when Eisenhower sent his message to Churchill, he was still playing his game of political hot potato. However, he grew more circumspect when Laniel's request threatened to burn the president's fingers badly.

By the morning of April 6, the Dien Bien Phu crisis had become a Washington crisis. A cable arrived from Dillon advising that, far from finding its discouraging, the French had interpreted Dulles' message of April 5 as offering them what they needed. Again, they had latched onto a single phrase, this time Dulles' abstract pledge "to do everything short of belligerency." After a discussion by the full French cabinet, Bidault called Ambassador Dillon to his office to say that, since intervention was not immediately available, the government of France would settle for a loan of ten to twenty US B-29 bombers, operating from American bases in the Philippines, and maintained by American personnel.[18] Except that French servicemen would supply the flight crews, it was Operation Vulture. Showing his concern that events were moving beyond control, Eisenhower made a rare exception to established procedure and called an emergency meeting of the NSC for that evening. Press Secretary James Hagerty told the immediately inquisitive media that it was simply the regular meeting held two days early for the sake of convenience.[19]

Adding to the sense of climax, the NSC Planning Board and the president's Special Committee on Indochina announced that they had completed their studies on whether or not the United States should intervene in the French-Indochina War. Neither, however, had reached a decision, other than the Planning Board's feeble recommendation that the administration settle the question "now."[20] Chairman Cutler opened the meeting by reading the Planning Board's conclusions, then turned over the debate to the full gathering. With one critical exception, they too believed that the Indochina intervention decision could no longer be delayed.[21]

While the Security Council as a whole shared the Planning Board's indecision on whether the United States should send its armed forces to Indochina (the NSC's Intelligence Advisory Committee split over whether military intervention, if sufficient to defeat the Vietminh, would bring on a Chinese response), the president's top military advisers saw no alternative to intervention but a Vietminh victory. Action had slackened off at Dien Bien Phu, but the CIA reported that 20,000 more Vietminh troops were on their way to join the siege and the combined enemy force could be expected to renew the attack within ten days. Admiral Radford added, from his intelligence sources, that the French garrison had no more than three days' supply of food and five days' of ammunition; he could not give precise figures because the defenders' radio had been out of commission for two and a half days. As it had been for the last few weeks, Dien Bien Phu appeared to be just a gun crack away from total collapse. The defense secretary, the JCS chairman, and the CIA chief agreed that the anticipated loss of Dien Bien Phu meant that a military decision on all of Indochina was imminent.

Eisenhower strongly disagreed. A defeat at Dien Bien Phu, given the huge price paid for it by the Vietminh (their estimated casualties already reached between ten and twenty thousand), *should* not lead to a general military defeat for the French, he said; it *would* not do so were it not for the French Union army's inexplicable failure to press its powerful advantages elsewhere. According to the NSC minutes, the president said "with great emphasis" that as far as he was concerned,

there was no possibility whatever of U.S. unilateral intervention in Indochina, and we had best face that fact. Even if we tried such a course, we would have to take it to Congress and fight for it like dogs, with very little hope of success. At the very least, also, we would have to be invited in by the Vietnamese. [emphasis added]

Later, he indicated that he also doubted the likelihood of multinational intervention in the French war. After a long report by Dulles on his efforts to organize a regional defense coalition to force the communists' hand at the Geneva Conference, Eisenhower made the surprising statement that he was hostile to the notion that the loss of Indochina would necessarily lead to the loss of all of Southeast Asia—an about-face from the domino theory he had earlier espoused. The regional coalition as he conceived it, the president said with feeling, would be intended *not for emergency military action, but to defend Southeast Asia even if Indochina should be lost.* This was Ike's first explicit statement that, if need be, he would accept the partition or even forfeiture of French Indochina.

Several of the president's top advisers expressed alarm at the new direction toward which the administration seemed to be veering. How would a regional coalition stop internal communist subversion, especially if Indochina were allowed to go communist and thus could send thousands of revolutionists across its borders, Vice President Nixon asked. Dulles replied that he had issued his "united action" speech as a warning that indirect rather than direct aggression posed the greatest peril to Southeast Asia. "Yes, indeed," burst in Wilson, "you point out that it's a very great danger, but still you do not know what to do about it, and we have the same problem to face in Italy, in France, and in other areas outside of Asia." Like Nixon, Wilson had grown frustrated by his administration's practice of speaking loudly and wielding nothing.

Stassen asked if there were not a middle course that the United States could take between accepting the communist takeover of Indochina and intervening to push the Vietminh beyond the Chinese border. Could the US not take measures to hold southern Indochina while forming a regional grouping to defend the remaining states in the region? Before he could complete his thought, the president broke in. "[W]e certainly could not intervene in Indochina and become the colonial power which succeeded France," he said vehemently. Stassen ventured that the administration could send US forces to Thailand, freeing the Thais to help hold southern Indochina. Again Eisenhower interrupted him. If the French and the Associated States agreed to join a regional coalition, there would be no need to lose Indochina, he said. (From the other end of the spectrum, Wilson, Nixon, and Radford also rejected Stassen's suggestion on the grounds that any loss to communism was too great and would surely lead to the fall of all of Southeast Asia and Japan.)

Eisenhower held his ground against intervention, but it gave him no sense of victory. He opposed the circumstances of battle, not the cause for which it was waged. He saw the wisdom in waiting to see how things shook themselves out at Geneva (despite the risk that France may turn over all Indochina to the Vietminh), so that he could build his Southeast Asian defense coalition upon a settled foundation rather than basing America's prestige in the region on an unstable, "decadent" (his word), and extremely difficult colonial ally. At the same time, politically and emotionally, he hated to bear the responsibility for turning over millions of people to communist "enslavement." Thus, he lashed out at Treasury Secretary Humphrey for advocating a policy of nonintervention on the basis that the United States should not take upon itself the responsibility for policing all of the governments of the world. That was not his reason, Eisenhower insisted; he believed wholeheartedly in containment.[22] For a few minutes, as he distanced himself from Humphrey, he sounded as if he might support intervention into Indochina, even unilateral. But the mood passed. (At an NSC meeting three weeks later, Eisenhower would passionaltely argue much the same point as Humphrey's, without even blushing.)[23]

When the conversation turned back to the details of forming the coalition and of preparing for military intervention, Eisenhower again became the reluctant dragon. He restated that he would propose US participation to Congress only *after* an ad hoc coalition had been established. Asked whether he thought that would take days or weeks or months, he answered, "whatever time it took, it was a matter of the highest urgency." Nixon, a perceptive judge of the president's character, saw that Eisenhower was creating a smoke screen. He tried to cut through it by reminding the council of the abilities of the president, secretary of state, and military advisers to get Congress to agree to whatever they said was in the national interest. "Congress would do what the National Security Council felt was necessary," Nixon insisted. As an example he pointed out how easily and quickly Eisenhower had got the legislature to support the dispatch of the American airplane technicians to Indochina. The president responded,

if that were the case, then let's commence tomorrow to ask Congress to agree to the prompt dispatch of additional technicians and maintenance crews to Indochina. We should tell Congress that if more technicians can be sent at once the whole situation may be saved.

That is not what Nixon had intended.

Eisenhower ended the meeting by postponing once again the decision on whether or not the US should intervene in the war. The NSC voted to turn down Bidault's request for B-29s (all of the military advisers agreed that the French were incapable of flying them effectively). The only positive actions approved by Eisenhower were (1) to continue efforts to form a regional organization for the defense of *Southeast Asia,* and (2) for the deputy defense secretary and JCS chairman (not the president) to seek congressional support for more US aircraft maintenance technicians for Indochina.[24]

Disillusioned, Nixon wrote in his diary after the meeting,

From the conversation . . . it was quite apparent that the President had backed down considerably from the strong position he had taken on Indochina in the latter part of the previous week. He seemed resigned to doing nothing at all unless we could get the allies and the country to go along with whatever was suggested and he did not seem inclined to put much pressure on to get them to come along.[25]

Eisenhower could safely "back down" from intervention because, since the latter part of the previous week, he had come under the protection of the congressional leaders' conditions. It was almost too good a cover. Ike's apparent capitulation to Congress convinced many that the president was tractable on Indochina. Nixon seems to have followed that to the conclusion that, if the president had been pressured to change his mind once, with proper inducement he could do so again; if the weight of political opinion triggered the first switch, the crush of popular opinion would force a second.

"Resigned To Do Nothing"

Following the NSC's instructions, Dulles returned to his efforts to organize the coalition, though it no longer had so clearcut a purpose. He made the last of his initial contacts with potential coalition members when he met with the representatives of Canada and the Associated States on April 7. He had spoken to the ambassadors of Thailand and the Philippines on April 5 and they had given him tentative assurances that they were on board, though both stressed that they could bring very little in the way of material support with them. The others reserved their answers until they could confer with their governments.

The only *government* that had replied to Dulles' enquiries was Laniel's (though unofficially), and not in a way that the secretary of state found encouraging. Paris continued to refuse to discuss anything but unilateral intervention by US aerial forces. "[T]he time for formulating coalitions has passed as the fate of Indochina will be decided in the next ten days at Dien-Bien-Phu," Bidault said impatiently to Dillon on April 5. In the next two days, rather than becoming more cooperative, the French foreign secretary's message grew threatening. In an early morning meeting with Dillon on April 7, Bidault said that, although he personally understood Eisenhower's desire for congressional support and allied unity, French public opinion and (a new twist) Vietnamese morale would not. Dillon cabled to Washington that Bidault had warned that if Dien Bien Phu fell, "it would be most unlikely that either Associated States or France would be willing to continue war even with full American military support."[26]

Behind Bidault's hard line, encouraging him to hold firm, stood Ély, who insisted that Washington would come through with the airstrikes if Paris exerted sufficient pressure. The general based his conclusion on a report he had received from General Valluy in Washington that the US government, despite all of its talk of joint action, was poised to implement the bombing plan.[27] Valluy, in turn, derived this misconception from a statement Dulles had made to the House Foreign Affairs Committee on April 5, in which he recounted verbatim French intelligence allegations of Chinese incursions into Vietnam.[28] The level of Chinese assistance to the Vietminh, Dulles told the congressmen, indicated that the PRC teetered on the brink of open aggression—"they save themselves from the charge only by technicalities"—which could bring on a major American retaliatory response.[29] The prevailing attitude of the entire French War Council upon receiving Valluy's report was that Dulles was preparing the United States for military intervention.[30]

In reality, Dulles' brandishing of massive retaliation was not a preparation for anything; the threat *was* the administration's action in response to the Dien Bien Phu crisis. Dulles had decided to issue the charges of active Chinese involvement in the French-Indochina War following a telephone conversation with Eisenhower earlier that morning, which had ended with the president telling the secretary of state to do what he could to influence the military situation, "but we cannot engage in active war." Dulles immediately had phoned Radford to tell him of the president's decision and to ask the admiral if he could think of any useful alternative to military intervention.[31] Did he think it would be all right to publicize France's intelligence about Chinese intervention, during his scheduled appearance on the Hill later that afternoon, he asked. Radford had answered that it could do no particular harm. Once again, Radford's prediction missed the mark, as was shown by Bidault's April 7 message to Dulles through Dillon.

Dulles shot back a stinging reply to Dillon's cables of the past several days conveying the Laniel government's request for B-29s for Indochina and Bidault's warning that the time for coalitions had passed and that France would probably hand over Indochina to the communists if the United States did not prevent a French defeat at Dien Bien Phu. "I am deeply disturbed by character of these latest requests from French as well as their tone," Dulles wrote Dillon.

Not only do they seem to have been hastily advanced without having been thought through as to their military or political feasibility but there are overtones which suggest French may be preparing to place upon us responsibility if Dien Bien Phu should fall which are all too reminiscent of desperate and indeed hysterical appeals which Reynaud addressed to US in June 1940. . . .

Finally, Bidault's reaction . . . to serious and far-reaching suggestion for a coalition is even more disturbing. It involves in essence a proposal that US should become a war ally even though not itself directly involved or threatened. Responsible persons do not treat such momentous proposals as reported. I sincerely trust that it was merely preliminary and hasty reflex of a deeply harassed man. If his first rection becomes fixed, it will appear to us here as a loss of perspective and understanding on his part which however understandable in light of pressures he is enduring hardly reflects a frame of mind conducive [to] effective collaboration between our two governments in this difficult period.

Dulles ended his communication by exhorting Dillon to turn all of his efforts toward building up Bidault's and other French leaders' courage and perspective.[32]

"United action" was proving to be far more difficult a proposition than Dulles had suspected when he raised the idea before the Overseas Press Club. Eisenhower had limited it to a moral boosting mechanism, at least until the Geneva Conference ran its course, but the French refused to have their morale boosted, except by American bombs. Meanwhile, British hesitation prevented Dulles from forming even a moral force.

As adamantly as Bidault, Foreign Secretary Eden wanted no part in an arrangement that he believed was intended to prevent France from negotiating peace at Geneva.[33] (Already tipped as the next leader of the Conservative party and thus prime minster, Eden, rather than the aged and declining Churchill, was principal architect of the UK's foreign policy.) On the other hand, he could reason that to reject Washington's plan too abruptly would rend the Atlantic Alliance when its strength and unity were most needed, just before the Geneva Conference, imperiling hopes of negotiating a peace settlement acceptable to the French and favorable to the interest of the Western democracies, and perhaps even leading the Americans to take unilateral action in Indochina.

Taking the same road Eisenhower had followed, Eden delayed announcing any decision for as long as possible. In response to Dulles' urgent request, seconded by President Eisenhower, that the secretary of state immediately fly to London to discuss the formation of a coalition prevent the "loss" of Indochina, Eden said that he would first have to consult with Churchill, the cabinet, and the British military chiefs. Only then, he said would he be able to judge whether a trip to London would be a profitable investment of time. Adding that he felt the urgency with which Dulles was pressing for a coalition was based on excessively gloomy military reports, Eden reflected dryly that the "French cannot lose the war between now and the coming of the rainy season however badly they may conduct it."[34]

Eden's level assessment of the military situation in Indochina bore no resemblance to the analysis being circulated by the State Department. In a massive public relations blitz (Washington columnist Richard Rovere dubbed it "one of the boldest campaigns of political suasion ever undertaken by an American statesman") Dulles and his deputies hosted lectures for hundreds of political figures and media representatives. An imminent crisis threatened all of Asia, they stressed at each gathering. Rovere, a guest at one of the briefings, vividly recalls the picture painted of the brewing storm:

> The somber word-portraits of the diplomats show Communist influence radiating in a semicircle from Indochina to Burma, Malaya, and Thailand, and then across the South China Sea to the islands of Indonesia. They show Soviet Russia and Communist China economically and militarily strengthened by the strategic raw materials available to them in that region, and the United States and other anti-Communist powers correspondingly weakened by the loss of these materials. They show Nehru's India impressed more deeply than ever by Communist power and no longer offering any sort of resistance to Communist infiltration, and they concurrently show Pakistan, the Philippine Republic, South Korea, Formosa and Japan disheartened and discouraged by an American failure to succor a threatened Asiatic people. Even Australia, Mr. Dulles's lieutenants argue, would find its security threatened by a Viet Minh victory.

"Hearing this analysis," Rovere concluded, "one gets the impression that they have grave doubts whether the United States would survive the establishment of Communist power in Indochina." The columnist predicted that, while the campaign would prove quite effective at persuading public opinion leaders of the seriousness of the American stake in Indochina, it would not be able to erase the national memory of the Korean War sufficently to create a mandate for intervention.[35]

The congressional debate of April 6 refuted Rovere's conclusion. In a discussion of the French-Indochina War and America's response to it, again led by Kennedy, the Senate stressed its reluctance to order American forces into a colonial war or to take any action except as part of a coalition of equally committed allies; however, like the legislative leaders canvassed by Dulles and Radford, the senators indicated that they would give their approval to military action if those prerequisites were filled and, most important, if the White House promised to bring Congress more into its confidence in Indochina decision-making. The painful lessons of past experiences in which Congress had followed a president blindly dominated the senators' speeches.

Kennedy led the charge that the executive branch had not dealt openly and honestly with the legislature, by reading a chonology of White House, State Department, and Pentagon misstatements predicting an imminent solution to the Indochina problem. In sum, he said,

> Every year we are given three sets of assurances: first that the independence of the Associated States is complete; second, that the independence of the Associated States will soon be completed under steps "now" being undertaken; and third, that military victory for the French Union forces in Indochina is assured, or is just around the corner, or lies two years off.[36]

The senators also voiced concern that, under the guise of such vague terms as "united action" and "defense coalition" the effort the administration wanted Congress to support might turn into another Korean War, with the United States bearing nine-tenths of the free world's burden. This was a scenario feared and denounced by Democrats and Republicans alike. Even Senator Knowland, a leading China Lobbyist and Asia-Firster who during the leaders' meeting initially had voiced unqualified approval of intervention in the French-Indochina War, spoke out now against unilateral (or unequal) action. The United States people, he said, are "not in a position time and time again to assume the overwhelming share of the burden as they did in Korea. . . . I do not believe the Korean experience should be allowed to stand as a precedent." He hedged his position by saying he would feel compelled to back up a presidential decision to intervene if it were in response to Chinese intervention "in force." But, he added paradoxically, since such action would be in the interest of all the Western world, it must be taken as part of a collective effort by the leading western powers.[37]

The Senate debate encouraged all interventionists but the most ardent unilateralists. Although the senators did not welcome another Asian conflict so soon after the Korean War, they appeared willing to go to war in Indochina if it were a multilateral effort. They even seemed ready to forego or at least compromise on the demand for decolonization.[38] Not one participant in the April 6 debate voiced opposition to intervention if the established conditions were first met. Since the president already had adopted Congress' conditions as his own, Dulles could rightly count the debate as one of the few favorable responses to "united action." The full senate at least had put no new obstacles in his path. Eisenhower, however, had even more reason to be pleased. The senators' loud insistence that the president remember that they, not he, held the power to declare war, merely helped to secure his cover. Congress would set the conditions for intervention, so Congress (or the allies it insisted upon) would bear the responsibility for the failure to intervene to save Dien Bien Phu.

Publicly protected by Congress' conditions, Eisenhower could now sound off threateningly against communist expansion in Indochina. In a sharp departure from past practice, he voluntarily raised the subject of the French-Indochina War in his April 7 news conference.[39] The possible consequences to the free world of the "loss" of Indochina were incalculable because of the "falling domino principle," he said. Though the domino concept was neither new nor original to the Eisenhower administration, this was the first time it had been used before the public. The phrase immediately captured the popular imagination and would become the symbol of an era in United States foreign policy. To his listeners at the time, Eisenhower's explanation of how a communist victory in Indochina would set off a chain reaction that would topple the entire anticommunist bulwark in Asia had the ring of impending war.

The call to arm seemed to resonate ever more clearly in the second part of the president's statement. His public words sounded more like the sentiments of Dulles or even Radford than the thoughts he had spoken, frequently with passion and conviction, in the privacy of the White House. Eisenhower insisted that United States security could not afford any more losses to communism. He downgraded the likelihood that the Geneva Conference would be able to achieve an acceptable peace settlement. He implied that the independence of the Associated States was not a condition for United States intervention. (He told reporters, outrageously, that he was unsure if the Indochinese nations themselves really wanted to be independent.) Finally, the president refused to comment on a reporter's question whether, as a last resort, the administration would "go it alone" in Indochina.

The judgment of the press was unanimous: "The U.S. has picked

Indochina as the place to stop Communism in Southeast Asia, even if it means war for Americans," announced *U.S. News and World Report.* "[T]he U.S. is putting the world on notice that it will tolerate no deal that gives the Communists Indochina."[40] That is just what Eisenhower wanted the communists—and the French and the Associated States and the Republican right wing—to believe.

There remained forces within the government, one of them the determined JCS chairman, still lobbying to put the president's public words into action, despite his private "no." Earlier, Radford had given up hope of saving Dien Bien Phu because of the time it would take to create a coalition for intervention, but the tenacity of the defenders, who had held out beyond all predictions, revived his optimism. Now he communicated indirectly to Dulles that, if "united action" could be organized in time, the fastest and most effective way of getting help to the French Union forces at Dien Bien Phu would be to drop three tactical atomic bombs on Indochina.[41] This offered the bonus of creating general acceptance of the use of nuclear weapons as part of the nation's arsenal, said Radford. Passing a note through subordinates, Radford enquired whether the secretary of state might not, while he was negotiating "united action" with the French, also get their approval for using atomic weapons in Indochina. Dulles did not acknowledge Radford's query and left on his diplomatic mission to France without raising it with the admiral.[42]

Throughout the political debate, committees of the Joint Chiefs of Staff continued developing operational plans for United States action and CINCPAC representatives deliberated with Navarre's staffs in Saigon and Hanoi over airstrike plans. The plan developed by the on-site team held close to the original Operation Vulture concept. The proposed action would be limited in time and space to a quick American airstrike operation to rescue the garrison at Dien Bien Phu. Three hundrerd US fighter-bombers from American bases in the Philippines, would stage a series of conventional bombing raids on the Vietminh base at Tuan Giao near the Chinese border and on Vietminh-Chinese supply and communication lines. In an amendment to the original airstrike plan, the area immediately surrounding Dien Bien Phu would not be targeted, since the CINCPAC team judged French short-range navigational radar to be inadequate to support close fire. Nevertheless, Navarre got the impression that the American Air Force generals with whom he consulted were sanguine about the operation's chance of success in rescuing the outpost.[43]

The French themselves tossed between optimism and anxiety. The defenders at Dien Bien Phu had survived yet another assault wave; the latest Vietminh offensive ended April 7. However, the general picture had not improved and would not, they knew, without substantial outside assistance. Confounded by all of the obstacles delaying Operation Vulture, Ély sent Radford an urgent plea to make good on his March promises. His message ended with the hope "that requested emergency intervention should not remain subordinated to political exchange of views which will not fail to take a lot of time."[44]

At nearly the same moment the French chief of staff wrote those words, Admiral Carney was cabling Pacific Fleet Commander Admiral Stump with orders to wrap up his reconnaissance program and recall the carrier force from the Gulf of Tonkin.[45] The US government had decided firmly that it would take no action to save the French at Dien Bien Phu.

VI

Disunity

All Dulles' efforts now went to creating the pre-Geneva coalition, although most White House officials knew from the start that he would fail. Even if he could overcome the antipathy of the British and French governments toward "united action" in general, which Dulles himself admitted was improbable, the proposed partners shared no consensus on specifically what the coalition should do. Dulles had helped create the latter problem by pitching his appeal to the individual interests and needs of each potential member. He recognized that it had become a problem—one more problem—when he arranged to fly to London and France to canvass for the multilateral association, and Eden put him in an embarrassing position by asking if the talks could be tripartitie (Dulles, Eden, and Bidault). Dulles had to wriggle out of a joint meeting by hinting to the British that he had some harsh facts about the French to reveal privately. To his own representatives he confessed, "Also, I believe possibility of getting French and British to move in right direction is greater if we see them separately."[1]

Eisenhower had first raised the idea of sending Dulles to the European capitals to stump for the Southeast Asian coalition in his April 14 message to Churchill. If his intention was to put the allies on the spot (and in the spotlight), the president chose an effective method.

Discreet messages passed through ambassadors had gotten nowhere. By April 7 the governments of only Thailand and the Philippines had responded with even preliminary interest. Australia and New Zealand, whom Dulles had counted on to join the coalition even if Britain did not, regretfully declined. The Australian government wanted to avoid controversy until after the national elections in six weeks; New Zealand would not break ranks with its mother country. Quiet diplomacy had achieved the single unwelcome effect of letting the key allies off the hook. Churchill perhaps realized this. Although he accepted Eisenhower's offer and said that Dulles was welcome to come to London the following Monday (April 12), Eisenhower noted that he did so with discernible coolness.[2] Dulles was to disguise the intention of his mission by saying publicly that he was preparing for the Geneva negotiations.

Before departing for London on the evening of April 10, Dulles hopefully prepared for a victorious return. He scheduled another meeting with key congressmen to brief them on the results of his probes as soon as he got back.[3] (If he could persuade the allies to join the coalition against the Vietminh, he wanted immediately to announce his fulfillment of the legislators' conditions and get their support for "united action.") He asked Radford in the meantime to discuss the military aspects of "united action" with the visiting chief of the British Armed Services Mission in Indochina, General Jock Whitely. According to Radford, Dulles hoped to preclude any attempt by the British government to claim it must consult with the military before it could decide whether to join the coalition.[4] Working intimately with a master prevaricator, Dulles had become expert at anticipating and preventing delaying tactics by others.

The secretary of state and British foreign secretary held their first meeting informally, over Sunday dinner, April 11, at Ambassador Aldrich's house.[5] Dulles led off with the usual arguments. Eden's response, though, broke new ground. Prepared for a timorous unwillingness to take action to help stop the spread of communism in Southeast Asia, Dulles was delighted to hear Eden talk seriously about forming a regional coalition based on the NATO model. Eden opposed implementing any coalition before the Geneva Conference decided the fate of French Indochina, of course, but Dulles believed he could persuade him to compromise on that. In any case, the foreign secretary's position did not differ widely from Eisenhower's as expressed in the last NSC meeting. "Eden indicated a real willingness to consider defense arrangements in SE Asia on the basis of united action," Dulles said enthusiastically in a cable to Washington. "I believe he would strongly and actively support such action if Geneva fails."[6]

Eden's response fit neatly into Dulles' game plan for his talks in London and Paris. Dulles did not waste his energies trying to *implement* the Southeast Asian defense pact. The British government would never go along; and even if Eden had been less hostile to joining a pre-Geneva coalition, Dulles did not believe he had enough time in the two weeks remaining before the start of the Geneva Conference to make the proper political arrangements. Most important, Dulles believed the *threat* of action would be sufficient to quash Vietminh ambitions at the negotiating table. Therefore, over the next two days of talks with Eden, Dulles concentrated on chipping away the foreign secretary's resistance to joining an ad hoc Southeast Asian coalition planning group.

By his own accounting, he had more than moderate success (though it was to prove short-lived). While Eden held firm against committing UK forces to the Indochina War in the event the Geneva negotiations failed and would not join Dulles in issuing a warning against communist adventurism in Indochina before the conference (to do either, he said, would prejudice the peace talks), he did agree significantly to sign a statement to the effect that communist aggression in Indochina threatened all of Southeast Asia. At the close of their talks, on April 13, Eden and Dulles issued a communiqué announcing.

we are ready to take part, with the other countries principally concerned, in an examination of the possibility of establishing a collective defense, within the Charter of the United Nations, to assure the peace, security, and freedom of Southeast Asia and the Western Pacific.[7]

Dulles basked briefly in the glow of his first triumph of the Indochina debate. Dubbing the talks "very satisfactory," he wrote to his chief,

Believe accomplished considerable in moving the British away from their original position that nothing should be said or done before Geneva. The communiqué issued today indicates a large measure of acceptance of our view of the danger and necessity of united action. . . . Despite remaining differences in emphasis and timing, feel satisfied that a very big step forward has been taken in bringing British thinking in harmony with our own.[8]

In truth, Dulles had greatly overestimated that measure of acceptance. Eden later insisted that he had agreed to sign the joint communiqué only on condition that he be allowed to add a verbal explanation to the House of Commons that no decision had yet been made on which nations, *including the United Kingdom,* would make up the collective defense organization. (Dulles' reports of the meetings of April 12 and 13 contain no mention of Eden requesting this significant privilege.)[9] Moreover, Eden was to claim that he had made it clear to Dulles that, before the British government would decide whether to join any coalition, it would have to consult with the governments of India, Pakistan, and other Commonwealth states. (State Department counselor MacArthur's memorandum of the opening conversation substantially contradicts this.)[10]

Whether agreed to beforehand or not, Eden made the disclaimer on the very afternoon of signing the communiqué. The Churchill government, he told Parliament, had made no commitment to the Americans to join a Southeast Asian coalition or even to help establish one. It had merely said that it was willing to look into "certain possibilities." Nothing would be done before the Geneva peace effort was given a complete chance, he insisted.

I hope that those critics who thought that we were going to issue some sort of fulminating declaration before the Geneva Conference took place will realize that we are as anxious as they are—and perhaps more so—to see the Geneva Conference succeed.[11]

The foreign secretary's "explanation" sapped away the force which Dulles had hoped to bring to bear on the Geneva Conference.

Dulles was aware of none of this as he confidently flew to Paris, fine-tuning his triumphant opening speech. Standing on the tarmac a few feet from the plane that had just borne him from London, he told the French that the agreements reached in London promised a speedy end to the Indochina War under the terms of "liberty and justice" for all people in the region. Pitching his words to the Geneva Conference he warned,

The Communist forces which fight the French Union in Indochina in fact endanger the peace and security of the entire of Southeast Asia and the Western Pacific. Mr. Eden said that in London an hour ago. That is why I am here in Paris. For it is right that all of those who are concerned should unite in common purpose. That purpose should be to end the war.[12]

What Mr. Eden actually had said an hour earlier made a mockery of Dulles' statement—just as Dulles' speech made Eden appear to be a liar to his own people. While Eden fumed over Dulles' embarrassing "twisting" of his words, Dulles cried out that the Briton had "double-crossed" him. Dulles seems the more sincere of the two. Ambassador Dillon recounted Dulles' elation upon arriving in Paris. The secretary of state told the ambassador that he finally had persuaded Eden "to move ahead in really helping the French"; Britain was ready at last to do something to help stop the communist takeover of Indochina. When the next day the American delegation saw a transcript of Eden's Commons speech, Dillon records that Dulles appeared shaken. It was the ambassador's opinion that this falling-out sparked the feud between the two foreign secretaries that would continue as long as they lived.[13]

Few believed Eden's insistence of innocence in the mix-up. Dillon, who, though not a party to the London conversations, was intimately acquainted with Dulles' negotiating skills, supposed that the secretary of state had persuaded Eden to go further than he had intended; but once Dulles had left the foreign secretary alone to face the fury the joint communiqué elicited from the Labour left, Eden had scrambled back into line.[14] (Aneurin Bevan, leader of the party's radical wing, resigned from the shadow cabinet in protest over Eden's "surrender to American pressure . . . for the purpose of imposing European colonial rule.")[15] State Department Policy Planning Director Robert Bowie, who *did* attend the bilateral talks, laid the blame on what he judged to be Eden's extreme indecisiveness in general and his weakness before the Labour back bench in this particular instance.[16]

The London *Economist* magazine cast the most flattering light on Eden's role in the misunderstanding, congratulating the foreign secretary on a "very adroit piece of evasive action," having averted the joint warning Dulles was pushing at him without sending the Americans off into angry unilateralism.[17] While it is true that the joint communiqué was so vague as to be open to an array of interpretations, the *Economist* struck far from the mark in asserting that Eden had found a comfortable middle ground. The foreign secretary's ostensible equivocation enraged Dulles and, to a lesser extent, Eisenhower, and created a strain in the Atlantic Alliance that would burst over the Suez crisis two years later.[18] The editors of the *Economist* also erred in thinking that Eden had prevented the Americans from taking unilateral action. Eisenhower had already vetoed that.

Irritation aside, until he could speak to Eden to find out what had transpired, Dulles chose to go on as if nothing had changed. He turned his attention to selling "united action" to the French.

Dulles' opening speech in Paris got a mixed reaction. His promise of a quick, honorable solution to the Indochina War was exactly what the nation of France was hoping for. But his accompanying call for a coalition of states to achieve that solution had little appeal to a people intent on keeping the war, however costly and hopeless it might be, *their* war. They wanted no truck with gung-ho allies who would drag out the already interminable fighting. Their single-minded desire continued to be to extricate themselves from the war under the best possible negotiated terms. And with each passing day their definition of acceptable terms grew more generous.

Four days before Dulles' arrival in France, Laniel had alarmed the State Department by showing just how slack the French resolve to prevent communist control of Indochina had become. In a well-publicized policy statement on the war, the premier told the National Assembly that, although the government intended to continue its military effort in Indochina, especially to hold Dien Bien Phu, it had instructed France's peace negotiating team "to approach the negotiations at Geneva in complete liberty, with the willingness to neglect no opportunity" that might bring peace.[19] The State Department read this as a declaration that, while Laniel continued to seek a short-term solution to the Dien Bien Phu crisis, he had closed the door on a larger-scale, longer-term operation—nor did he intend to let Dulles' hints that such an operation might be under consideration undercut the Geneva peace process. Yet, for all its resolve to hold its ground against widening the war, the Laniel government teetered on the edge of survival, its fate lashed to that of Dien Bien Phu. America's perceived power to rescue the fortress, and with it Laniel's ministry, gave Dulles an edge.

Laniel's strategy was to offer ratification of the European Defense

Community to lure the Americans into Dien Bien Phu. The premier summoned State Department Counselor Douglas MacArthur II to his home late on the night the Americans arrived in Paris.[20] There Laniel "unofficially" suggested that on April 15 (significantly, just *after* Dulles was to depart France) his cabinet might fix a date for the long-awaited Assembly debate on the EDC, but, he added, it would be a very risky move. Having caught MacArthur's interest, the premier drew in the line. The mere scheduling of the debate could create a political crisis that would bring down his government, he said. So far his administration had benefited from the courageous defense of Dien Bien Phu; even his most anticolonialist opponents did not want to do anything that would undermine the morale of the besieged forces. However, Laniel emphasized, that would no longer be true if Dien Bien Phu were to fall. Then "the situation with respect to both the EDC and Indochina would be virtually hopeless." Taken aback, MacArthur reminded Laniel of his earlier promises—the basis of American military aid to the French war—that he would never be a party, even indirectly, to a turnover of Indochina to the communists. Laniel replied that he would keep that promise as long as he remained premier, but that his government would surely fall if Dien Bien Phu were captured. He did not have to repeat the obvious corollary that a subsequent government would not be bound by his promises.

Laniel had shaken MacArthur, but the next day he and Bidault faced a tougher opponent in Dulles. In a grueling full day of meetings (two hours in the morning with Bidault and his staff, a private conversation with Bidault after lunch, and an evening meal in Laniel's office), Dulles relentlessly pursued his objectives—with some success.[21] In exchange for a shadowy undertaking to go to Congress for a vote on "united action,"[22] he wrested Bidault's signature to a joint communiqué similar to the one Eden had signed ("In close association with other interested nations, we will examine the possibility of establishing . . . a collective defense"), with the important addition of a vow to maintain Franco-American solidarity at Geneva.[23] Moreover, Dulles got at least a sop to American demands for decolonization. Bidault pronounced that "the independence of the three Associated States within the French Union, which new agreements are soon to complete, is at stake in these battles."[24]

The French and British communiqués, disregarding Eden's recantation, gave Dulles enough to go on to begin building his ad hoc coalition. He returned to his home in New York on Thursday, April 15, and immediately set to work inviting the representatives of the proposed coalition members to an organizational meeting five days hence. Their job, he told them, would be to set up a committee to draft the treaty of the Southeast Asian defense organization. Thus, if all went as planned, there would be some visible movement toward "united action" in time for the opening of the Indochina portion of the Geneva Conference.

To Dulles it seemed that things finally were going his way. While he had negotiated Britain's and France's support for the coalition, his assistant secretary for the Far East had secured even stronger endorsements from the ambassadors of the Associated States. Even the weather cooperated. A few days earlier the fog and rain had cleared and Navarre had succeeded in dropping a fresh battalion and several loads of ammunition and supplies into Dien Bien Phu, enabling the garrison to recapture one of its strongpoints. This, more than anything Dulles said, girded the Laniel government before the Geneva Conference and brought it tentatively to consider a coalition.

However, a storm was brewing. Its first bolt would come not from London or from Dien Bien Phu, where some 13,000 fresh Vietminh troops were heading in preparation for the final assault, but from within the White House. From an "off the record" remark by Vice President Richard Nixon the thunder would grow deafening. The wind of dissention it would raise would blow Secretary of State Dulles' fragile coalition to bits.

Responding to a newsman's query following his speech to the American Society of Newspaper Editors on April 16, the vice president said that if France were to withdraw from Indochina the United States government would "dispatch forces."[25] Though Nixon later insisted that all he did was give his "personal opinion" to a "hypothetical question," his statement captured headlines all over the world. Since it came from the number-two man in the Eisenhower administration, the opinion sounded like government policy. Reaction was immediate, intense, and widespread.

In rare unison, both parties in both houses of Congress, the American and world press, the Western allies, the communist bloc, and the nonaligned governments cried out in protest. (Only the Associated States were pleased.) Eisenhower had unilaterally rewritten his Indochina policy, they charged, and reneged on his earlier assurances. Each group had its separate cause for alarm. Congress believed that once again it was being left out of US foreign policymaking, an especially sore spot for the Republicans, who had come to power condemning Roosevelt's "secret agreements."[26] The nation's press, conduit for the White House's mixed signals, grew angry at being used by the administration to launch what the media decided was a "trial balloon" to gauge public reaction to intervention.

Though delighted that Washington finally had assumed the threatening posture Paris had so long desired to give it the appearance of strength at Geneva, the Laniel government was embarrassed by the insulting tone of Nixon's speech. (Not known for his subtlety, Nixon had said that "with respect to the current crucial battle at Dien Bien Phu, there is not the will to win. If the battle is lost, it will be lost in Saigon and Paris.") More upsetting still was the vice president's reflection that, for the United States to stop communist subversion in the long run, it must align itself with "the legitimate aspirations of its friends and potential friends in the Far East"—giving new life to the old fear of the American giant elbowing France out of Indochina.[27]

The anger of the Americans and French combined paled in comparison with that of the British government, however. Eden already had subjected himself to considerable criticism from his countrymen and commonwealth for agreeing even to examine the possibility of joining a long-term Southeast Asian defense pact. Particularly outspoken in his criticism, Prime Minister Jawaharlal Nehru of India had threatened to create a small tempest at the Colombo Conference of nonaligned nations (the majority of whom were in the British Commonwealth) opening on April 28. After his talks with Dulles, Eden had contained incipient disaffection by insisting that the coalition they had discussed would not be aimed at Indochina. Now, he and the rest of the world heard the vice president of the United States announce publicly that if the French pulled out of Indochina (making no distinction between negotiated partition or military defeat) they would be replaced by a definitely military form of "united action." It did not ease tension when Nixon added that if the allies refused to join the effort America "will have to take on the problem alone."[28]

Eden cabled the UK ambassador to the United States that he had had enough:

> Americans may think the time past when they need to consider the feelings or difficulties of their allies. It is the conviction that this tendency becomes more pronounced every week that is creating mounting difficulties for anyone in this country who wants to maintain close Anglo-American relations.[29]

He told Makins to pass the word to Dulles that Britain would not be represented at the April 20 coalition organizing meeting.

Given the level of international distress, the response of the Eisenhower administration was paltry. Eisenhower and his top advisers were caught as short by Nixon's comments as was everybody else. Yet the president refused to refute them. He ordered the State Department to put out an explanatory statement, but "without cutting ground from under Nixon."[30] He himself said nothing. He may have reasoned that, since he did not intend to intervene in the French-Indochina War in any case, Nixon's words had done no real damage, so there was no need to get into a fight with the vice president and his troublesome associates on the right of the party. (Nixon at that time was proving himself very useful in the administration's secret battle with McCarthy.) Eisenhower may have determined, as Dulles certainly did, that Nixon's indiscretion could prove useful for frightening the communists as they headed to Geneva and that to disavow the threat under pressure would damage the West's image of strength.[31] He may simply have been sticking to his policy of revealing no rifts within the administration. Perhaps all of these. It remains an open question because Eisenhower kept silent throughout the entire brouhaha. As in the Checkers incident, Eisenhower simply disassociated himself; he never even raised the subject with Nixon. Unlike the campaign financing scandal, however, Nixon's rash comments on Indochina had serious international implications. This is one example (McCarthyism is another) of when Eisenhower's "hidden hand" crippled his powers as president.

The remaining question is: why did Nixon do it? His own explanation is unpersuasive. He claims that he merely gave an honest, impromptu answer to a hypothetical question and that he had no idea that his words would reach the newspapers.[32] A display of such gross naiveté by a politician famed for his adroitness at manipulating the media challenges credulity. What ultimately disproves Nixon's story, though, is that reporters present at the question-and-answer session testified that the vice president answered the question at length, *from a prepared statement.*[33] Nixon's day-after explanation to Dulles, that he was endorsing the Eisenhower-Dulles policy of firmness in Asia, also does not ring true.[34] Nixon had known from the April 6 National Security Council meeting that Eisenhower would order intervention only as part of a coalition with Britain and France. As has been shown, Nixon abhorred that decision, accusing the president in his diary of seeming "resigned to do nothing at all." He felt that Eisenhower had abandoned his policy of firmness.

Nixon's "off-the-record" statement reads like a public protest of that abandonment, a bugle call to dissenters, of whom the vice president was certain there were many. He was convinced at the time and remained convinced that most administration officials, including Dulles, supported United States intervention to replace the French in Indochina. Further, he believed that all Congress and the public needed to bring out their support was a little persuasion. He had emphasized that at the April 6 NSC meeting: Eisenhower must not underestimate his own and his chief advisers' abilities to get the backing they needed to intervene in Indochina. But Eisenhower had not acted on his advice. After suffering silently for ten days what he interpreted to be the president's growing political impotence, Nixon may have decided to give Ike a demonstration of what a little vigor could accomplish. Radford, who was on close terms with the vice president, said that Nixon was conducting his own test of public opinion.[35] More precisely, he may have been testing his influence *over* public opinion. If so, he scored pretty dismally.

White House Chief of Staff Sherman Adams records that Nixon was "mortified" by the overwhelmingly negative reaction to his speech in the world press and, especially, in Congress.[36] Even his usual ally, Senator Knowland, joined the opposition. The majority leader led a Senate demand that Eisenhower come to Capitol Hill to make a full revelation of his secret plans for invading Indochina.[37] House Majority Leader Charles Halleck told the president at the next legislative leaders' meeting that Nixon's remarks "had really hurt" the administration's relations with Congress and diminished the likelihood of forging a bipartisan foreign policy. He urged that there be no more talk of unilaterally sending American troops to Vietnam.[38] Eisenhower's refusal to take up Hagerty's suggestion that he tell the congressional leaders "to get off their cans" led Admiral Radford to believe that the adverse response to Nixon's statement ended all remaining possibility of United States intervention in the Indochina War.[39]

Dulles raged as he saw his coalition collapse around him, led by the defection of Knowland. At least the Republican leadership could wait for the administration's explanation before lodging public protests, he fumed to Senator H. Alexander Smith, one of the few dependably friendly congressmen.[40] The next day, two days after Nixon's speech, Ambassador Makins informed Dulles that neither he nor any UK representative would attend the Southeast Asian coalition organizing meeting. Though he had feared since shortly after signing their communiqué that Eden was backing off from the coalition, only now did Dulles have confirmation. "Eden has reversed himself and gone back on our agreement," he confided in his pain to his sister Eleanor.[41]

Dulles scrambled to save what little remained of the Indochina alliance. The coalition organizing meeting was to be held in two days' time, too soon to cancel it without drawing unwanted press attention. Yet, without the presence of a UK representative, the meeting, designed primarily to impress the communists with a show of free world unity before the Geneva Conference, would succeed instead in advertising its disunity—and emboldening the opposition. To preserve the appearance of allied cohesion, Dulles offered to turn the April 30 multilateral conference into a general pre-Geneva briefing session. Under those terms, Eden allowed Makins to attend.[42] Perhaps, the secretary of state told Senator Smith, he might still be able to straighten Eden out and get the coalition back on course when he met the British foreign secretary in Paris in a couple of days (they both would be there attending the NATO ministers' meeting on Friday, April 23).[43] However, he realistically accepted that there would be no breakthroughs before the Geneva Conference on April 26. Asked by the press whether he thought it was important to have a collective defense system organized before the Indochina phase of the Geneva Conference began, Dulles said, "The essential thing is that the discussion of Indochina should be had against a background of unity of purpose."[44]

Before flying to Paris, the secretary of state met with the president, still on vacation in Augusta. Their conversation, the first since Dulles' return from Europe on his expedition to drum up support for the coalition, lasted only a little over an hour and ranged over a number of foreign policy issues.[45] Dulles no longer had much of interest to report on "united action." The Indochina portion of their discussion centered on whether the United States should refuse to participate in the Geneva Conference if the other conferees allowed China to attend officially.

Although the April 23 meeting of foreign ministers in Paris was dedicated to NATO affairs, the ministers arrived early and stayed late to discuss the real concern on all minds, the French-Indochina War. As had been the case throughout this complex and highly charged conflict, each concerned party tried to impose his own agenda on the unofficial two days' talks. Bidault saw them as a last chance to save Dien Bien Phu. Dulles planned to make his final appeal for the Southeast Asian defense coalition. Eden hoped, by ending all talk of "united action," to ensure that the Geneva Conference would open in a mood of sincerity and realism. The conversations that resulted from this mishmash of expectations would only increase Western divisiveness on the eve of the Indochina negotiations.

The French made the first move, on the morning of April 22, the day after Dulles' arrival.[46] Appearing as suppliants before the immutable secretary of state, Laniel and Bidault beseeched Dulles for American airstrikes to save Dien Bien Phu. The position of the courageous garrison was "virtually hopeless," Bidault said. He said that he spoke not simply of the loss of the battle or the position, but the death or capture of every French Union soldier in Dien Bien Phu. The number of wounded prevented a breakout; the able-bodied would not abandon them. A "massive" United States aerial action (Ély later specified 200–300 carrier aircraft) offered the sole ray of hope for saving their lives.[47] Bidault urged Dulles to forget about British participation, which, he said, "would not amount to much anyway." The only way to save the situation, he insisted, was for the United States to intervene at once.

Dulles did not reply directly, but turned the conversation to organizing his long-term defense coalition. Their roles reversed; Dulles became the appellant and Bidault the naysayer. The French foreign minister said that, if Dien Bien Phu fell, his nation would have no interest in a coalition. Dulles insisted that the coalition was essential to give France strength at Geneva so that it could win an "acceptable peace." That is not how France saw it, Bidault replied. If Dien Bien Phu fell, the only purpose of the coalition would be to keep the French fighting in Southeast Asia. (And, as Defense Minister Pleven had said the previous day to Donald Heath, the United States minister to the Associated States, "France was not interested in fighting beside the South Koreans.")[48] Bidault's spurned pleas gave way to intimidation. Dulles records that the foreign secretary told him, "if Dien Bien Phu fell, the French would want to pull out entirely from southeast Asia, and assume no continuing commitments and the rest of us would have to get along without France in this area."[49]

The following day Laniel issued a similar warning to MacArthur, and Ély repeated it to Radford when the admiral arrived in Paris on the 24th. The impression shared by the French leaders that they would lose everything when Dien Bien Phu went down had the corollary that they had nothing to lose by extorting the Americans in an effort to prevent the collapse. Laniel coolly agreed with MacArthur's objection that there was no logical reason why the defeat of a small outpost in an isolated corner of Indochina should lead to France's withdrawal from Southeast Asia. Unfortunately, the premier continued, it would do just that—and it would probably abort the European Defense Community as well. He could not be logical or reasonable in his warnings, said Laniel, because Dien Bien Phu "had become a tremendously emotional thing and Frenchmen were no longer capable of reasoning about it." When MacArthur riposted that the French were leaving Washington no choice but to rethink its entire relationship with France, Laniel parried. That would be a terrible tragedy, he assured the counselor, but unfortunately one he could not prevent, since his government would not survive the fall of Dien Bien Phu.[50] Ély replied more aggressively to a similar ultimatum by Radford that it would be the French who would need to rethink their relationship with the United States.[51]

Even before Dulles could pen an evaluation of his disturbing April

22 conversation with Laniel and Bidault, the foreign secretary leveled a second blow. Bidault was presiding over the North Atlantic Council session, on the afternoon of April 23, when he received a copy of a message from Navarre. Already appearing exhausted and confused, Bidault was driven "close to the breaking point" by what he read.[52] Interrupting the proceedings, he handed the note to Dulles. Navarre reported that the final battle for Dien Bien Phu had begun. His combat-worthy force was down by two-thirds to only 3,000 men; no more reserves remained. The only alternatives left to the French Union command were Operation Vulture or a request for a cease-fire. Dulles had no authority to grant Navarre's first alternative even had he wanted to, which he did not. He told Bidault that to his mind aerial intervention under present conditions was out of the question, but he would report immediately to the president at the conclusion of the session. They agreed to talk further over dinner.

When Dulles cabled Eisenhower that evening, he still hoped that the cease-fire Navarre referred to would be limited to Dien Bien Phu. A short while later, over a cheerless dinner for the foreign delegations at the Quai D'Orsay, Pleven disabused him even of that. The one offer by the French that even remotely resembled a compromise was Bidault's "belief" that, if the United States tried but failed to rescue Dien Bien Phu, France would stay in the war "as a matter of honor." Eden banished that to the edge of possibility by expressing his grave doubts that Britain would join in any fight to save Indochina, and admonishing Dulles that the United States should take no action without prior consultation.[53]

Finally unnerved, the secretary of state had a sudden change of heart. Until then he had stood pat against intervention at Dien Bien Phu every time it had been considered. The wellspring of his determination had been his conviction that the outpost's defeat could be contained to its true dimensions, and that there would be opportunity after that to strike a better deal with France. However, his unsettling conversations with the French leadership in the course of the NATO ministers' meeting dried up that confidence. Leaving the banquet hall, Dulles belatedly jumped onto the bandwagon for Operation Vulture. He still did not think that intervention could save Dien Bien Phu, but he reluctantly accepted that it alone could prevent the French from ordering a general cease-fire once it fell. Eisenhower's insistence on British participation in any military action thus became for Dulles a matter of greatest urgency.

For one furious afternoon, April 24, the secretary of state stood side-by-side with Radford trying to press Eden into joining an expeditious bombing mission over Indochina.[54] Only that would keep the French fighting, he told Eden. Radford added that it might also prevent a massacre of French civilians by disaffected VNA troops. If the Churchill government would agree to participate in an aerial action (Radford suggested the contribution of RAF squadrons from Malaya or Hong Kong), Eisenhower was prepared to seek congressional approval for intervention by US forces, Dulles said. But, he reemphasized, the United State would enter the conflict only if it were a joint action.

Eden replied synpathetically, wanting to preserve as much of the Atlantic Alliance as he could, but skeptically. He said he did not see how airstrikes would improve the military picture in Indochina, and he worried that the Chinese, and perhaps even their Russian ally, would retaliate and that the Vietnamese might rise up against the coalition members for siding with the French. To each of these concerns, Radford had a ready comeback: intervention would stabilize the military situation and prevent the Vietnamese National Army from collapsing and turning on the French; he did not believe that the Chinese could or would retaliate, but if they did it would be a limited intervention and "could be dealt with"; the Vietnamese were angry with the French because of their "terrible leadership," but would be glad to be helped by the Americans and British. However, neither Radford nor Dulles could argue away Eden's political demurrer. Intervention, he said, would be "hell at home"; he could not think of a more inflammatory issue with the British public.

Eden's personal lack of enthusiasm and his pessimism that his government would approve military action must have dampened Dulles' spirit. By Eisenhower's rules, the game must end if the British would not play. Nevertheless, it was not the foreign secretary's objections to "united action" that ended Dulles' short campaign for Operation Vulture, but a revelation by Eden's deputy, exploding Dulles' new-found conviction that only immediate intervention could prevent a French cease-fire.

Near the end of the April 24 Anglo-American debate on "united action," Sir Harold Caccia, the British deputy under secretary for foreign affairs, mentioned "the difficulty created by the difference in [French] presentation of the problem" to the British versus the Americans. He said that Bidault had told the British ambassador specifically that France would go on fighting *even if Dien Bien Phu fell.* Nonplussed, Dulles had the story checked out—and found it to be true. "[T]he line taken by the French certainly was different" depending on to whom they were speaking, Dulles told Eden, recounting the quite different scenario he had been given.

He [Dulles] said that Bidault had told him that if Dien-Bien-Phu fell and the United States was not in, all was over; that if the United States was in prior to the fall of Dien-Bien-Phu, then the French would go on fighting even if Dien-Bien-Phu fell; and finally when he asked Bidault if the French would fight on after the fall of Dien-Bien-Phu before our actual intervention, but after the receipt by the French of assurances from us that we would come in within a matter of a few weeks, Bidault had replied "No."[55]

Red-faced, Dulles summarily confronted Bidault. In Eden's presence he asked him what the position of the French government would be if Dien Bien Phu fell.[56] Bidault at first equivocated. He and Laniel wanted to continue the fight, but they would have to contend with an extremely adverse military and psychological reaction; "in all honesty and frankness he could not guarantee what position the government would take if Dien Bien Phu falls." That is not what Pleven had said, Dulles retorted. "Pleven had told me last night that the cease fire which Navarre envisaged in his letter covered all of Indochina and not just Dien Bien Phu." That was correct, Bidault replied incongruously, veering off into a reflection of how the whole battle had been a mistake. Dulles broke in. He asked the foreign minister "point blank" whether the Laniel government would declare a cease-fire before the Indochina phase of the Geneva Conference. Bidault revealed that it would not, that he would enter the negotiations with his hands relatively free.

Eden interjected that his government did not feel itself committed by the Dulles-Eden communiqué of the week before to intervene in the French-Indochina War. However, if the French government were to request such action (which, he added, he believed would be a mistake) he would refer the request back to London forthwith. Bidault's mood had changed markedly in twenty-four hours. The morning's cabinet meeting had not turned into the pillorying of himself and Laniel that he had expected. He now sounded more tired than desperate. He did not make a direct request of Eden. Nor did he repeat that the situation was hopeless. According to Dulles, "He simply said that he was not proud and that anything that could be done to assist the Expeditionary Forces in Indochina or strengthen them would be appreciated."

With the pressure of an immediate cease-fire off, Dulles could return to his preferred position of withholding military action until he could work out a political deal. He handed Bidault a draft of a letter he had prepared in reply to Navarre's request for intervention and had sent back to Washington for approval before his brief flirtation with Operation Vulture. In essence, the letter said "No" to airstrikes.

I must inform you that the situation as regards the United States belligerency in the area remains as I explained to you last week when we conferred on April 14. War action under such circumstances as now prevail should be preceded by a Congressional authorization. Such Congressional authorization is in no event obtainable within a matter of hours, nor in my opinion is it obtainable at all except within the framework of a political understanding which would embrace the other nations directly and vitally interested in Southeast Asia (and which would include a clear intention to grant independence to the Associated States of Vietnam, Laos, and Cambodia). . . .

I should add that in the opinion of our military advisers, there is no reason why the fall of Dien Bien Phu, should it fall, should be regarded as materially and vitally altering the military position in Indochina. . . . It is not apparent to us from any military reason why the fall of Dien Bien Phu should require a plea for a cease-fire. . . .

We believe that it is the nature of our nations to react vigorously to temporary setbacks and to surmount them. That can be done in relation to the present situation if our nations and people have the resolution and the will. We believe that you can count upon us, and we hope that we can count upon you.[57]

On first reading the letter, Bidault said he would hope for some modifications. Then he fell silent for some time, changed his mind, and said that, if Washington approved the message, Dulles could go ahead and deliver it. The meeting ended with Bidault agreeing to abide by his April 14 joint communiqué with Dulles on "united action" and also recognizing that Britain was not bound to intervene in the French-Indochina War by its communiqué.

Dulles emerged from the meeting in better spirits than he had been in since his arrival in Paris. After confronting Bidault, he cabled Eisenhower, "it would seem that we will at least enter the Geneva conference without the French government definitely committed to some disastrous course of action."[58] That was the most he could hope for, under the circumstances, and it certainly beat committing the United States militarily to a war to achieve much the same result.

His confidence revived, Dulles resumed his firm stance as he spoke with Laniel shortly before he left Paris that evening.[59] When Laniel repeated the by now tired threat that Dien Bien Phu could last only a few days more and that its collapse would lead to military disaster and political withdrawal from the war, Dulles replied that he could do nothing to help. Under the United States Constitution the president could not authorize acts of war without the approval of Congress, unless the country were under attack, he said. That approval rested on two conditions: British participation and Indochinese independence. The latter substantially had been met, he said. (Dulles that morning had spoken to Bao Dai who had told him that Vietnam and France had nearly reached agreement on the political portion of their independence negotiations, the Vietnamese having withdrawn their earlier objection to entering the French Union. Only the financial convention stood in the way of signing.)[60] As to the former, while he could not foretell how the British would respond if Paris formally asked them for assistance, Dulles said, his government would do everything within its power to make them see the importance of replying positively. That was not altogether true. Dulles had a very good idea how the British would respond and he had more than once expressed it in his messages to Washington. However, by giving the impression that the question remained open, the secretary of state accomplished two of his expressed goals. He induced Laniel to ask London officially for military intervention, forcing Churchill to turn down the request outright, and thereby "establishing the record clearly" so that the French could not pin the blame for nonaction on the Americans.[61] And he gave Laniel a reason to hold on until the end of the fighting season and the Geneva negotiations on Indochina. Dulles said that he hoped that the alliance of US and UK forces would come to France's aid "within the next few weeks." However, he reminded the premier, it could do so only if France held firm over that time.

Dulles deceived Laniel about something more than his knowledge of Churchill's position. While technically true that Eisenhower could not commit an act of war without congressional authorization, he could get around that via executive action. In the White House meetings on Indochina intervention, the president established that he would not act without Congress, because he respected the separation of powers, not because he *could not* do so. And, for a brief moment back in March, when he had considered ordering a bombing mission, his single qualification had been that it must be certain to be decisive, *not* that Congress approve it. None of that, of course, proves that Dulles was being disingenuous when he said that Eisenhower could not order airstrikes on his own authority. He proved that in a cable he sent to Washington from Geneva on April 25. His first sentence read, "it is my opinion that armed intervention [in the French-Indochina War] by executive action is not warranted."[62]

Laniel asked Eden that night for airstrikes around Dien Bien Phu. Eden immediately flew to London to confer with Churchill. The next day he and the prime minister laid the request before the full cabinet, called to an emergency Sunday session. Not one voice spoke out in favor of the expedition. The British chiefs of staff agreed that the action would be ineffective. After hearing their further estimation that the fall of Indochina would have no decisive effect on the British position in Malaya, Churchill announced that his government would take part in no military action, whether designed to rescue the Dien Bien Phu garrison or to give France a last-minute confidence boost. Such an operation would be unproductive militarily, counterproductive morally, and most likely would escalate into a major war, he said. The best hope for lasting peace in Indochina and the world as a whole, the British prime minister repeated, was partition of Vietnam.[63]

A few hours later, on his way to Geneva for the start of the Conference on Far East Problems on Monday, Eden stopped briefly at Orly Airport, where Bidault was waiting for him. The British foreign secretary told Bidault that his government had voted to abstain from all military action in Indochina at least until the conclusion of the Geneva Conference. Hearing his judgment, says Eden, the Frenchman "seemed resigned."[64]

Once in Geneva, Eden called on Dulles at his room at the Hotel Beau Rivage to deliver the news that, he admitted, he knew was not exactly what Washington wanted to hear—and to offer a compromise. Britain would give France all the diplomatic support it needed to help reach a satisfactory solution at the conference table, Eden said. After the settlement had been signed, the United Kingdom would join other interested nations in guaranteeing it. In the meantime, the Churchill government would engage with the Americans in a *secret* study of military measures to protect the freedom of Southeast Asian states, *exclusive of communist Indochina,* should France relinquish all or part of Indochina at Geneva. But it would take no measures now, even of a planning nature, to force a different settlement in Indochina. Dulles responded that Eden's proposal might help the noncommunist states in Southeast Asia, but it gave the French no hope, no reason not to capitulate to the communists. That was as far as his government would go, Eden answered. Dulles joined Bidault in resignation. The conversation turned to the best possible line for partitioning Vietnam.[65]

Eden believed, and most contemporaries agreed with him, that his steadfast refusal to join in a coalition prevented the Americans from intervening at Dien Bien Phu. To an extent, that is correct. By turning down Laniel's request for airstrikes, the Churchill government made it impossible for Dulles to satisfy Congress' and the president's preconditions for military intervention. Unarguably, that was the immediate cause of death for "united action."

What is subject to argument is whether Eisenhower would have intervened to save Dien Bien Phu had the British been more forthcoming. He certainly talked like he would have—once he knew they would not. When Smith told him on April 24 that Eden "had grave doubts that Britain would cooperate in any activity" in Indochina, for example, Ike retorted that the acting secretary of state should tell Radford "to consult with the British staff and to ask them baldly why they would prefer to fight after they have lost 200,000 French" soldiers in Indochina.[66] Yet, General Eisenhower of all people must have known that having the JCS chairman speak to the British military was an empty gesture that stood no chance of changing government policy. He indirectly admitted as much when, a few sentences later, he asked Smith to draft a message for him to deliver when Dien Bien Phu fell. Furthermore, the conversation memorandum testifies that Eisenhower remained skeptical of the benefits to the United States of immediate intervention into the French-Indochina War:

> The President said that the French want us to come in as junior partners and provide materials, etc., while they themselves retain the authority in that region. He cannot go along with them on that or any such notion.

These were the concerns, which had little or nothing to do with British participation or congressional disapproval, that had ill-disposed President Eisenhower to military intervention in the war from the start.

Colonialism erected another unscalable wall. Dulles may have believed it when he told Laniel that the independence issue no longer presented a problem, but the president did not share his secretary of state's easy dismissal, as he emphasized in a personal letter to his long-time confidante, "Swede" Hazlett, on April 27. Expressing himself freely, Ike accused the French of using "weasel words in promising independence and for this one reason as much as anything else, have suffered reverses that have been really inexcusable." The French, he told Hazlett, had doomed their chance of winning the war by alienating noncommunist Vietnamese in the same way the British had lost the War of American Independence by treating the majority of Loyalist Americans as "colonials and inferiors."[67]

The qualms of the US military had hardened Eisenhower's doubts that the French-Indochina War was the right cause on which to stake his presidency's and his country's prestige. Even the Air Force, which stood to gain the most from intervention, had come out against airstrikes on Vietnam. On April 13 a US Far East Air Force staff paper on the feasibility of military action to defeat the Vietminh had concluded that the Indochinese had been so alienated by France's "arrogant" colonial policy that it would be virtually impossible for the French to win a military victory. Six days later, an Air Force staff study reached the same conclusion: American airstrikes would be of very limited value to the French Union land forces in Indochina, because of the rugged terrain, poor weather, and few and poorly located targets, and, most vitally, because the people of Vietnam had no will to continue fighting the war.[68]

Finally, while it can never be ascertained what Eisenhower would have done if Dulles had been able to pull the coalition together, he most definitely had done nothing to help the secretary of state. He made no stirring speeches. He communicated directly to Churchill and Laniel only once each during the military crisis (the latter in a message sent through Dulles on April 24 urging the premier to make a public statement that "regardless of the possibility of the physical over-running of this gallant outpost, France will continue the war for the independence of Indochina"; it contained no mention of coalitions or intervention, yet Eisenhower said it "accurately described" his "present feelings in the Dien Bien Phu affair").[69] He neither threatened nor chastised his allies. When Churchill asked to visit Washington in late May, Eisenhower ignored Dulles' suggestion the he withhold reply until he had wrung some concessions on Indochina's defense, and told Smith to answer that he would be happy to extend an invitation (though later he said he had written his instructions too hurriedly and had intended to be a bit more "standoffish").[70] To Dulles' numerous cables from Paris telling of his difficulties in building a defense coalition, Eisenhower offered his sympathy for the "feeling of frustration that must consume you," but he gave him no substantive assistance. On April 23 he wrote,

There is little I can say now to help you rally the spirits and determination of our allies, but I am so confident of the unity of convictions you and I hold on these and related matters that I do not even feel the need of assuring you again of my complete support.[71]

Had he been feeling cynical, Dulles might have replied that Eisenhower had said very little to the allies at any point to rally those spirits. The secretary of state did make a sort of protest by refusing the one "help" the president offered: he chose not to deliver Ike's April 24 message to Laniel, saying it would be more appropriate as a eulogy over the defeated at Dien Bien Phu (a rare act of insubordination that Eisenhower told Smith disappointed him).[72]

The British answer to Laniel's request for airstrikes ended the serious debate over intervention to save Dien Bien Phu. Two days later Churchill made his decision public. Speaking before the House of Commons on April 27, the prime minister assured the British nation that

Her Majesty's Government are not prepared to give any undertaking about United Kingdom military action in Indochina in advance of the results of Geneva. We have not entered into any new political or military commitments. . . . [I]f settlements are reached there [at Geneva] Her Majesty's Government will be ready to play their full part in supporting them in order to promote a stable peace in the Far East.[73]

Dulles may have been resigned, but he was not happy. He charged that, far from helping to encourage France to hold on to Indochina, Churchill was inducing it to surrender. He alone remained to fight the battle to keep France in the war, and his only ammunition was to say that the United States would refuse to take part in any settlement that surrendered any part of Indochina.[74] His position seemed more hopeless now than that of the French union forces at Dien Bien Phu. On April 24 they received an unexpected airdrop of ammunition and supplies, giving them yet one more extension on life.

VII

The Fall of Dien Bien Phu

On Monday, April 26, as the Conference on Far East Problems opened in Geneva, the president met again with the legislative leaders to discuss foreign policy.[1] Already Indochina had lost its place at the head of the agenda. Instead, Eisenhower opened with an account of the increasingly worrisome political situation in Latin America, compared to which the French troubles in the jungles of Southeast Asia seemed old news and very far away. Guatemala, said Eisenhower, had been taken over by the "Reds" and was threatening to pull down El Salvadore "as a first step in the [communist] breaking out of Guatemala to other South American countries." As his actions in May and June would reveal, the president was preparing to stamp out this fire in the country's backyard. Coincidentally, the felicitous timing of his revelation diverted the nation's attention while Ike quietly backed his administration's prestige out of Indochina.

"The French are weary as hell," Ike told the congressmen when the conversation turned to the Indochina War. Dien Bien Phu probably would fall within a week. However, America's allies prevented the United States from intervening to help them, he said. The French behaved erratically; the British focused so narrowly on Hong Kong that they were blinded to the importance of holding Indochina. Yet, said Eisenhower, the congressional leadership had recognized three weeks earlier that the United States could not act without them.[2] The president recounted Dulles' efforts to prevent defeat through a "united action" untainted by colonialism. Unfortunately, the allies would not accept those conditions, so the situation had become very serious, said Eisenhower. His administration's efforts now centered on getting the governments of the proposed coalition nations to agree to a plan of action that could be presented for discussion to the legislatures of those countries. (Apparently this was a reference to what would become SEATO, since legislative discussion by all participants ruled out anything for immediate implementation.) The president said he did not envisage the use of American ground forces as part of that plan.

Eisenhower negotiated a pencil-thin line in this meeting. He had to show why he did not believe Indochina was a worthy fight for American forces now, yet why it might be down the road under different circumstances; he had at all costs to avoid repeating Truman's China mistake of implying that he had written off the loss. He succeeded by laying the blame on America's allies, principally Britain, for his own decision not to militarily intervene in Indochina prior to the Geneva Conference (being careful not to come down so hard on the UK that the congressmen began to rethink the Atlantic Alliance—a real danger given the makeup of the Republican leadership).

More than once he had to scramble to avoid slipping into isolationism. Nixon, still stinging over his "trial balloon" debacle, called for a reappraisal of America's entire alliance system in light of its apparent breakdown over Indochina. Senator Eugene Milliken suggested more radically that, if the United States had been deserted by its allies, perhaps it should return to "fortress America." According to Press Secretary Hagerty's diary notation of the meeting, that caused the president to end the discussion with a stern lecture:

Dien Bien Phu is a perfect example of a fortress. The Reds are surrounding it and crowding back the French into a position where they have to surrender or die. If we ever come back to the fortress idea for America, we would have, as I said before, one simple, dreadful alternative—we would have to explore an attack with everything we have. What a terrible decision that would be to make.[3]

Amidst the vicissitudes of the past month, Eisenhower's stance toward Indochina had changed remarkably little. The single noticeable adjustment was his lowered opinion of the Churchill government. He still believed that the French exaggerated the military importance of Dien Bien Phu, that the Vietminh would continue to win until France granted complete independence to the Associated States, that the Western democracies must recognize Southeast Asia's strategic importance to their security, but that only the armies of the people directly threatened, assisted but not replaced by the combined strength of the regional powers, could secure the region. As the Dien Bien Phu crisis progressed, his thinking coalesced into plans for a defense organization based on the NATO concept that would guarantee the security of the entire Southeast Asian region and avoid other inopportune requests to put out "brushfire" wars. Indeed, he thought such an organization, publicly announced, would prevent the communists from touching off more brushfires.[4]

On the other hand, the interminable last gasp of the awe-inspiring forces at Dien Bien Phu both pained him as a soldier and embarrassed him as the president who had to say he could not help them. The heroics of the defenders kept his own lack of action sharply in the public eye. Eisenhower grew furious with the British for refusing to participate openly in discussions on the development of a future, long-term Southeast Asian defense coalition. At least they could help him show that the West was doing *something,* that it had not given up on Southeast Asia and admitted its helplessness to stop the spread of communism, he said. In a memorandum for his files Eisenhower debated whether he would go forward with the Southeast Asian defense coalition if the British continued to stand aloof—and decided, reluctantly, he would.[5]

Ike would not budge on his decision against intervention under current conditions, however, even if it meant a communist victory in Indochina. At his April 29 press conference the president indirectly endorsed the Geneva peace process by calling for a solution to the conflict that fell in the broad region between the "unattainable" ("a completely satisfactory answer with the Communists") and the "unacceptable" (the loss of all anticommunist defenses in Southeast Asia). While he refused to give his opinion of partition as a settlement, he indicated that he was thinking along those lines when he likened the problem in Indochina to that of Berlin and Germany. "The most you can work out is a practical way of getting along," he said. He reemphasized that he would never involve the United States in the hostilities, except via the constitutional process of asking first for a congressional declaration of war.[6]

The president fought a virtual one-man battle against his security advisers to enforce his decision against war—and to give the Geneva peace process a chance—at the April 29 NSC meeting.[7] Even the usually obedient Dulles indirectly challenged the president's reasoning. (Dulles was in Geneva at the time, but sent a message through Smith that he believed that America's allies would follow a "strong and sound U.S. leadership" in Indochina.[8] According to the official minutes of the meeting, Eisenhower retorted that "in spite of the views of the Secretary of State," to intervene unilaterally seemed "quite beyond his [Eisenhower's] comprehension.") Radford pushed for intervention, as did Smith, Nixon, Stassen, and (via messages to Radford and Smith) Ambassador to France Dillon. For nearly two hours, the president rebuffed their arguments one by one, supported only by one comment each from Kyes and Cutler.

The most heated exchange took place between Eisenhower and Stassen. It revealed not only the strength of the president's opposition to intervention, but also the wide variety of concerns—far beyond whether or not the British participated—that underlie that opposition. Stassen's position, pared down to its essentials, was that the United States should intervene in Indochina, without the British if necessary, if the French withdrew; and that Congress and the American public would support such intervention "if the Commander-in-Chief made it clear to them that . . . [it] was necessary to save Southeast Asia from Communism." The Eisenhower administration, Stassen said, should not let "the appalling weakness of both the British and the French . . . render the United States inactive and impotent."

The president accused his foreign operations director "of making assumptions which leaped over situations of the gravest difficulty." He challenged Stassen's estimation of the congressional and public response to intervention, and added another that Stassen had not mentioned: the Indochinese response. "It was all well and good to state that if the French collapsed the United States must move in to save Southeast Asia," Ike said, as paraphrased by Cutler, "but if the French indeed collapsed and the United States moved in, we would in the eyes of many Asiatic peoples merely replace French colonialism with American colonialism." That raised a related, serious problem, he said: the Vietnamese people were so skeptical of French promises of independence they had no will to fight for themselves nor any comprehension of what the United States would be fighting for. Finally, on the most practical level, Eisenhower asked, where was he to find the military forces to rush to Indochina?

Stassen persisted. Just because the Vietnamese did not trust the French did not mean that they would not trust the Americans, he argued. He was confident that the governments of the Associated States would gladly invite United States intervention. Furthermore, Stassen believed that the French would be forced by circumstances to phase their withdrawal in such a way that US forces could be introduced in an orderly fashion. Eisenhower replied by expressing his "conviction" that unilateral military intervention into Indochina by the United States "would mean a general war with China and perhaps with the USSR"—and the United States would have to fight that war without any allies. Not if US forces confined their operations to Indochina, Stassen insisted, and did not try to roll back the Vietminh beyond the China border.

Unconvinced by Stassen's military analysis and repelled by his willingness to cast off America's allies whenever they got in the way, Eisenhower spoke with great passion:

To go in unilaterally in Indochina or other areas of the world which were endangered, amounted to an attempt to police the entire world. If we attempted such a course of action, using our armed forces and going into areas whether we were wanted or not, we would lose all our significant support in the free world. We should be everywhere accused of imperialistic ambitions.

The people of Korea and the Philippines did not accuse the Americans of being imperialists, Stassen countered. Indeed, he said, the only countries that made that accusation were in those areas of the world where the US supported British and French positions. "We plainly had thrust upon us the leadership responsibility for the free world, and . . . we should determine to meet this responsibility," the director for foreign operations demanded. Eisenhower replied sharply that "the concept of leadership implied associates." Without them, he said, "the leader is just an adventurer like Genghis Khan."

Stassen held his ground as tenaciously as a bulldog. The United States would have plenty of regional allies behind it if it went into

Indochina, he insisted (ignoring Australia's and New Zealand's rejection of "united action," and Burma's, India's, and Indonesia's outright hostility). If the administration did not shrink from exercising its leadership, he said, "there will be plenty of others who will gradually return to our fold." But America would lose its followers in the free world if "we lacked the courage to make the assault." Worse, said Stassen, in one of those leaps of logic that propelled the Cold War, "it would be impossible to let the Communists take over Indochina and then try to save the rest of the free world from a similar fate. This was the time and the place to take our stand and make our decision."

Eisenhower ended the exchange by asking his advisers whether they wanted to bear the burden of starting World War III—and whether they believed the legislature would want to bear it. For, he said, before he would ask Congress for a declaration of war in Indochina, he would tell them where it could lead. According to the NSC minutes,

> The president answered that before he could bring himself to make such a decision [for war in Indochina], he would want to ask himself and all his wisest advisers whether the right decision was not rather to launch a world war. If our allies were going to fall away in any case, it might be better for the United States to leap over the smaller obstacles and hit the biggest one with all the power we had. Otherwise we seemed to be merely playing the enemy's game—getting ourselves involved in brushfire wars in Burma, Afghanistan, and God knows where. . . .
>
> The president said that . . . before he would be prepared to commit U.S. divisions to Indochina—six, eight, ten, however many were required—he would earnestly put before the leaders of the Congress and the Administration the great question whether it would not be better to decide on general war and prepare for D-Day. The cause of the free world could never win, the United States could never survive, if we frittered away our resources in local engagements.

Smith asked if airstrikes in league with other Asian states were still not a possibility. Not now that Australia had indicated its unwillingness to participate, Eisenhower answered. Nixon followed with another speech in favor of aerial intervention, without Australia if need be. "To do no more than we have done would be tantamount to giving Britain a veto on US action in Southeast Asia," the vice president said. Eisenhower replied that he would put the proposal before Congress, "if he could be sure that the Vice President was correct in assuming that the French would stay and fight in Indochina." Of course, nearly all communications with the French indicated that they would not. (Even if the signals had been more favorable, how could Eisenhower be *sure?*)

The debate raged on, Eisenhower's counsellors pressing in on him as hard as they could, the president offering reason after reason why he should not order intervention—either by airstrikes to save the French position in Indochina or by land forces to prevent a "giveaway" at Geneva—until finally Smith offered a compromise that Ike would accept. The acting secretary of state would speak with the Australian and New Zealand ambassadors before he left to take over the American side of the negotiations at Geneva. He would tell them Britain had backed out of the coalition, but that the United States was still considering going ahead with other interested countries, and "let them think this point over." Secondly, when he got to Geneva, he or Dulles would "hint" to the French that the Eisenhower administration had not made its ultimate decision on intervening in Indochina. "This would help to keep the French going," Smith said, until Secretary of State Dulles returned to Washington the next week and the NSC would hold its final debate on whether to enter the war.

To Smith and the other pro-interventionists the compromise offered the chance that warlike responses from Ambassadors Spender and Munro and the returning Dulles might persuade the president to change his position at the next convening of the National Security Council. Eisenhower agreed to it, knowing that it bound him to do nothing but wait a while longer.[9]

Despite Dulles' strong words to the president about exercising leadership, however, the secretary of state had effectually resigned himself to accepting the will of the Geneva negotiators once the conference began. Dulles' remarks to the press upon arriving at Geneva came close to being a public declaration of that acceptance. Asked if the United States government might be preparing to intervene in the war to save Dien Bien Phu, Dulles replied that the Eisenhower administration's response would be confined to offering the defenders its "very great sympathy."

The Fall of Dien Bien Phu

We have taken, you might say, all steps short of actual belligerency to assist [the French]. We have drawn a line of belligerency which we have not crossed and I see no present reason to anticipate that we will cross that line.

Questioned whether he was now saying that the United States could afford the loss of Indochina to communism, Dulles answered weakly, "we certainly wouldn't like to see it fall, but some things have happened that we don't like and can't prevent."[10]

The secretary of state's abandonment of "united action" became even more evident after he returned to Washington on May 4. Stassen had left a note on Dulles' desk, repeating the points he had made at the April 29 NSC meeting along with his confidence that Dulles shared "many, if not all" of those views.[11] However, Dulles gave no sign that he shared Stassen's enthusiasm for intervention when he met with the president the next morning. The secretary of state was fed up with the British, fed up with the French, and fed up with the whole French-Indochina War. He told Eisenhower that "conditions did not justify the U.S. entry into Indochina as a belligerent at this time." Eisenhower "firmly agreed." They decided to go ahead with the regional grouping, but circumspectly. First they would find out quietly where the British and Americans were in accord, and proceed with talks with a wider group from there.[12]

Later in the day, Dulles told two dozen leading congressmen that the administration had decided against intervention. Not only had the legislative leaders' stipulations not been met, he said, but the conditions did not exist for the successful conclusion of the war. Dulles said that the administration must now turn its attention to creating a greater Southeast Asian defense community, which would probably not include Indochina, "to insulate the rest of Southeast Asia against the possible loss of Vietnam."[13]

On May 7, after a harrowing two months of fighting, Vietminh troops overran the French Union position at Dien Bien Phu, shrunk nearly to the size of a baseball field. They took 6,500 to 10,000 French Union prisoners, about 40 percent of them wounded.[14] Total French casualties in the battle neared 10,000.[15] Vietminh losses have been estimated at approximately 23,000.

The Indochina phase of the Geneva Conference opened the very next day. The cards held by the Vietminh were as good as Giap could have dealt. All of Bidault's exertions to create a position of strength for the French had collapsed along with the fortress. The White House's latest statements on intervention insured that France would get no help from its erstwhile partner. The foreign minister of France was left, in his words, with nothing more than a "two of clubs and a three of diamonds" with which to open the bidding at Geneva.[16]

Also buried in the rubble of Dien Bien Phu were Dulles' hopes of keeping France from negotiating away any part of Indochina, calling for a cease-fire, or pulling out of the war. In his opening statement of the Indochina debate, Bidault called for a general cessation of hostilities in Indochina, during which "the regular forces of the two parties would be brought together in clearly demarcated regrouping zones"—the first step toward formal partition.[17] American and French representatives continued to negotiate the terms of United States intervention into the war until the collapse of the Laniel government on June 12. France continued to wage war on the Vietminh until the final declaration of Geneva ended the war and divided Vietnam at the seventeenth parallel on July 21. Neither effort was pursued with much sincerity.

The rainy season limited most military activity, but was not able to halt the rapid deterioration of the French position in Indochina following the destruction of the Dien Bien Phu outpost. In early June the French Union command staff reported that the Tonkin Delta, where the French had attempted to consolidate their forces, was also on the point of falling to the Vietminh. Laniel, who held on to his premiership in its last month by a frail two-vote majority, still refused to order military conscription. The editors of Le Monde assessed the situation perceptively (and a good deal more generously than did the Eisenhower administration) when they opined after Laniel's tepid vote of confidence, "A two-vote majority may be sufficient to make peace. It is certainly not sufficient . . . to continue the war."[18]

France and the United States continued desultorily to pursue intervention negotiations, with no give on either side. Laniel asked Eisenhower to declare at once whether the United States would intervene militarily in Indochina if the Geneva Conference failed to reach a settlement.[19] In reply the president outlined a list of "indispensible" conditions for intervention, so demanding as to preclude French acceptance: among them, France must guarantee the Associated States "complete independence, including [the] unqualified option to with-draw from [the] French Union at any time; French forces must re-main in the war at full strength for the duration of the "united ac-tion" operation; and the government in power must formally accept, *and the National Assembly endorse,* all of the stipulated conditions for intervention.[20] The final condition was the *coup de grace,* given Laniel's weak hold on the government, the general opinion already expressed in the Assembly that Bidault was taking too hard a line at Geneva, and Washington's belief that even most of Laniel's cabinet had not known about and would not have supported his original request for airstrikes by the Americans. On the other side of the Atlantic, too, Laniel and Bidault had lost interest in the reality of American intervention after the fall of Dien Bien Phu, maintaining a pretense of desiring it, Dulles feared, to deflect some of the blame for the defeat from themselves.[21] Among Laniel's new conditions for accepting American military aid was that the United States must com-mit ground forces. Two weeks after the French defeat at Dien Bien Phu, Dulles admitted to MacArthur that the negotiations with the French on military intervention had become "an academic exercise":

it is not going to come to a positive result other than it affects those who are in Geneva. We don't want to wreck the talks there—just say it's dis-cussable. . . . We are trying to create in the minds of the French and those in Geneva that serious talks are going on. Let's not dispel that.[22]

In fact, the myth was being dispelled daily, and Dulles was doing as much as anyone to shatter it. On May 11, three days after the opening of the Indochina phase of the peace conference, Dulles told reporters, in a decisive break from past statements, that Southeast Asia could be held even if Indochina were lost to the West. "What we are trying to do is create a situation in Southeast Asia where the domino situation will not apply," he said. "That is the purpose of this collective security arrangement . . . to save all of Southeast Asia if it can be saved; if not, to save essential parts of it."[23] The next day, he amplified his position in testimony before the Senate Foreign Relations Committee. In language oddly reminiscent of his "united action" speech, the secretary of state said,

The great mistake the French made was to make Dien Bien Phu a symbol for Indochina. When it was lost most of the French people said, "We might as well quit." I am not willing to make Indochina the symbol for all of

The Fall of Dien Bien Phu

Southeast Asia. Southeast Asia has a population of 200 million, of which roughly 25 million are in Indochina. It has vast resources in the way of rubber, oil, tin, none of which are in Indochina. It has important strategic positions, and so forth, of which only one, Saigon, is in Indochina.

Therefore, I think it is a great mistake to take the position, particularly because of its effect on the neighboring areas, that Indochina is the symbol of all Southeast Asia, and if Indochina goes we concede the whole area to the Communists, which we do not intend to do.[24]

Before the end of May, at the president's request, the Joint Chiefs of Staff had prepared an analysis of how Southeast Asia could be defended after Indochina joined the communist camp. On June 23, during a recess of the stalled Geneva Conference, Dulles outlined the new military plan in a joint meeting of the president, secretary of state, and top congressmen. "Something constructive can be built in Southeast Asia," he said.

First, we would have to draw a military line across which the Communists could not pass, and if they did, we would have to hold this area and fight any subversion within with all the strength we have. If that area is kept free, the Pacific will be a friendly ocean.

As was the case of Korea, partition "was not without redeeming features from the American standpoint." Dulles concluded, "Today there is a possibility of solving something which will be free of the taint of French colonialism."[25]

When Knowland cried out that partition amounted to nothing more in reality than a "Far East Munich," Eisenhower deftly silenced him. Munich had been a giveaway to avoid a war, the president told the senator. Partitioning Vietnam merely would be accepting a military fact. The French, he said, from the comfortable shelter of truth, had been defeated.[26]

On June 18 a new French government rose from the ashes of defeat at Dien Bien Phu. The premier, Radical Socialist Pierre Mendès-France, won the election by a landslide, 419 votes to 47, after promising to end the French-Indochina War one month after taking office, or resign. He came within a hair's breadth of making it, close enough to satisfy the French people. And he surprised the Americans by not "selling out."

On July 21, 1954, the Geneva conferees concluded cease-fire agreements for the separate, independent states of Vietnam, Cambodia, and Laos. The accords "temporarily" partitioned Vietnam at the 17th parallel for a cooling-off period, to end after nationwide elections in the summer of 1956. Heavily pressured by China and Russia, the Vietminh came away with less than virtually everyone had predicted at the start of the conference. The United States gained access to the remaining more than three-quarters of Indochina, now "free from the taint of colonialism" and separated by a northern Vietnamese buffer from China. Though domestic political protests against the partition (led by Knowland) induced the Eisenhower administration to abstain from being a direct party to the accords—it merely "took note" of the agreements and promised not to disturb them by force— the White House actually felt it got the best of a bad deal.

Washington set to work at once to create the defense pact that would prevent another communist victory in the region. London and Washington had got back into approximate step once it became clear that the United States was not going to sabotage the Geneva Conference and Britain was not going to turn it into a giveaway. They came closer as they saw that Mendès-France intended to let the EDC die without a fight (the National Assembly rejected the pact 319–264 on August 30). Near the end of June the British dropped their insistence that they would take part only in secret talks on creating a Southeast Asian coalition. Dulles and Eden signed an agreement to establish a joint study group on the area. Two and a half weeks after the conclusion of the Geneva Conference, on May 8, Britain and France joined the United States, the Philippines, Thailand, Australia, New Zealand, and Pakistan in forming the Southeast Asian Treaty Organization (SEATO) creating a defensive shield around Asia. In a separate protocol, they extended the protected area to include Laos, Cambodia, and South Vietnam, prohibited by the Geneva settlement from actually joining the military alliance.

As the French had feared, once the United States had its foot in the door it rapidly crowded France out of Indochina. In January 1956 the United States MAAG took over from the French the role of training and organizing the Vietnamese military forces. Though the MAAG presence in Vietnam during Eisenhower's tenure remained small— always below 700 men[27]—American dollars gave the United States predominant influence over South Vietnam's military and inextricably linked it to the government of Ngo Dinh Diem. Between 1955 and 1961 the Eisenhower administration channeled more than a billion dollars in aid (78 percent of it military) to the Diem regime. Sanctioning Diem's refusal to hold the Geneva-mandated Vietnam-wide elections in the summer of 1956, the United States became the sole prop of an unstable South Vietnam. Eisenhower at last had the unencumbered testing ground he had sought to prove his New Look. "We have a clean base [in Vietnam] now," Dulles told an interviewer in 1956. "Dien Bien Phu was a blessing in disguise."[28]

Like all presidents, Eisenhower had both successes and failures. His attempt to create a stable democracy in Vietnam by blindly supporting the Diem regime is an example of the latter (one, however, that is grist for another mill). This book concerns what must, on balance, be judged a success—one won against considerable odds.

Caught between the rocks and whirlpools of France and Britain, communism and colonialism, Radford and Ridgway, "No More Chinas" and "No More Koreas," Eisenhower skillfully negotiated a path that kept American forces out of the French-Indochina War while maintaining America's commitment to the security of Southeast Asia. He had to make compromises he did not like—he keenly felt the "loss" of North Vietnam to communism—but he avoided a war of possibly tremendous dimensions. Preserving the peace, historians have concurred, was Ike's greatest achievement as president. That is a conclusion Eisenhower shared. "The United States never lost a soldier or a foot of ground in my administration," he recollected proudly. "We kept the peace. People asked how it happened—by God, it didn't just happen, I'll tell you that."[29]

It certainly "didn't just happen" in Indochina. Ike grappled with choices to which there were only wrong answers, made hard decisions, stood fast against the contrary advice of the majority of the NSC (including his most trusted advisers), shook the Atlantic Alliance—and somehow made it look as if he had done nothing, like he was the prisoner of events, or Congress, or the allies, or his own indecision. He actually *improved* executive-legislative relations by appearing to defer so fully to congressional authority. That he managed to do all of this by subterfuge is the negative side of the equation.

Eisenhower's practice of sending "mixed signals" backfired on more than one occasion, most seriously in the Radford-Ély talks, contributing to an impression in Paris especially that Washington could not be trusted to keep its word. That mistrust would build throughout the Eisenhower presidency, reaching its peak with DeGaulle's eviction of NATO and creation of an independent nuclear force. The irony is that, in large part, Ike treaded so lightly around Dien Bien Phu because of his concerns over upsetting the EDC and the Western alliance with France.

Yet, one may honestly question whether the president could have handled the situation more dextrously, given the paradox that bound him. He put a high priority on inducing the French to win the war in Indochina or at least to negotiate from strength at Geneva. To refuse military intervention outright would have threatened that goal. It also would have damaged his administration's credibility at home and abroad as a force against communist expansion. The method Eisenhower chose publicly demonstrated his respect for Congress and for multilateralism, a lauditory if not wholly sincere gesture. In the short run, Eisenhower's handling of the Dien Bien Phu crisis preserved the popularity that would allow him to continue to govern effectively through a difficult time in American history. That may not be bold leadership, but it is wisdom.

Notes

I. Setting the Stage

1. NSC 124/2, June 25, 1952, Office of the Special Assistant for National Security Affairs, NSC Series, Eisenhower Papers.
2. Truman, *Memoirs*, vol. 2, p. 519.
3. US Department of Defense, *Pentagon Papers*, vol. 1 [hereafter referred to as *Pentagon Papers*], pp. 4–5.
4. *Ibid.*, pp. 37–38.
5. *Ibid.*, pp. 36–37.
6. *Ibid.*, pp. 38–40.
7. Karnow, *Vietnam*, p. 177.
8. The French colonial administration in Indochina in early 1950 dubbed Robert Blum, the chief of the American aid program, "the most dangerous man in Indochina." (Hammer, *Struggle*, p. 315.)
9. The single American killed was OSS Lt. Col. Peter Dewey, mistaken for a French officer during a Vietminh ambush in 1945. (Karnow, *Vietnam*, p. 140.)
10. Acheson, *Present at the Creation*, p. 673.
11. By late 1953 the Vietminh had seven mobile divisions and one complete artillery division "that could take on anything the French could oppose them with." (Fall, *Hell*, p. ix.)
12. Gurtov, *First Vietnam Crisis*, p. 47.
13. Fall, *Hell*, pp. viii–ix.
14. Karnow, *Vietnam*, p. 192.
15. Fall, *Hell*, p. ix.

I. Setting the Stage

16. Hyman and Sheatsley argue from polling evidence that Eisenhower could have won on either ticket. ("The Political Appeal of President Eisenhower.")
17. 1952 Republican Party Platform, p. 6, Speeches and Press Conferences File, Dulles Papers.
18. According to a January 1953 *New York Times* survey, of the Senate's 48 Republicans, 19 stood solidly in the Eisenhower camp, 19 in the Taft wing, and 10 were uncommitted; the House broke down at 116 with Eisenhower, 93 with Taft, and 12 uncommitted. The Taft bloc had the added strength of seniority (its adherents held the key chairmanships) and greater solidarity. (Henry, *Presidential Transitions,* pp. 539–540.)
19. Donovan, *Eisenhower,* p. 151.
20. Lubell, *Revolt,* p. 36 Eventually, on February 26, 1954, the amendment failed by a single vote to receive the necessary two-thirds majority. Despite Eisenhower's public "unalterable opposition" to the bill, 32 Republicans, including Senate Majority Leader William F. Knowland, voted for it.
21. Eisenhower, *Mandate,* p. 192.
22. Ambrose, *Eisenhower,* pp. 97–107; White House Staff, Report on Press Coverage on the President, compiled October 1953, White House Correspondence 1953, White House Memoranda Series, Dulles File, Eisenhower Papers.
23. Testimony before the Department of the Air Force Appropriations Subcommittee of the House Appropriations Committee for FY 1954, in Kolodziej, *Uncommon Defense,* pp. 168–169.
24. Eisenhower, *Mandate,* p. 37.
25. Eisenhower stated this explicitly in a letter to Dulles prior to the nomination:

    Since it is just as tragic for us to lose [a friendly nation] to Communism by political action as to marching armies, our programs will not satisfy our minimum requirements unless they protect us and the area in which we are concerned from both kinds of aggression—that is, military and political. This means that we must be successful in developing collective security measures for the free world—measures that will encourage each of these countries to develop its own economic and political and spiritual strength. Exclusive reliance upon a mere power to retaliate is not a complete answer to a broad Soviet threat.

    (Eisenhower to Dulles, June 20, 1952, Correspondence with Eisenhower File, Dulles Papers.)
26. Dulles, Speech to Council on Foreign Relations, January 12, 1954, Speeches and Press Conferences File, Dulles Papers.
27. Kinnard, *Eisenhower and Strategy,* p. 24.
28. Nixon, *Six Crises,* p. 160.
29. Eisenhower interview, Dulles Oral History Collection [hereafter referred to as DOHC].

I. Setting the Stage

30. Divine, *Eisenhower and Cold War*, p. 21.
31. Larson, *Eisenhower*, p. 27; see also, for example, the Bowie, Clay, and Hagerty interviews, DOHC.
32. Bowie interview, DOHC.
33. Clay interview, DOHC.
34. Bowie interview, DOHC.
35. Kinnard, *Eisenhower and Strategy*, p. 21.
36. Radford interview, DOHC.
37. Larson, *Eisenhower*, pp. 84–106.
38. A May 1953 Gallup poll graphically reveals this dividing line in American thinking. Asked of those who knew about the French-Indochina War whether they supported the United States sending war materials to aid the French, 56 percent (two-thirds of those who had an opinion) expressed their approval and only 28 percent opposed. When questioned as to whether they believed US troops should take part in the fighting, however, only 12 percent said yes and an overwhelming 78 percent turned thumbs down. ("Gallup Public Opinion on Indochina," June 5, 1953, in Gallup, *Gallup Poll*, p. 1146.)
39. Dulles, Address to the American Legion, September 2, 1953, in US Department of State, *Bulletin*, September 14, 1953, pp. 339–342.
40. Quoted in Gelb and Betts, *Irony of Vietnam*, p. 51. Dulles, who strenuously opposed Indochina negotiations, gave the EDC as the principal reason for his reluctant agreement to broaden the Geneva Conference. To have refused, he told the NSC, "would have probably cost us French membership in the EDC as well as Indochina itself." (Quoted in Gibbons, *US Government and Vietnam*, p. 163.)
41. Eisenhower, *Mandate*, p. 343.
42. Dulles, Testimony before the Senate Foreign Relations Committee Executive Session, January 7, 1954, in US Senate, Committee on Foreign Relations, *Executive Sessions*, vol. 6, pp. 5, 23.
43. Jackson, Memorandum on January 16 Meeting in the President's Office, January 18, 1954, US Department of State, *Foreign Relations of the United States*, vol. XIII [hereafter referred to as *FRUS*], pp. 981–982; for a more extended treatment of Eisenhower's Euro-centered perspective on the world see McMahon, "Eisenhower and Third World Nationalism."
44. NSC 5404, January 16, 1954, *Pentagon Papers*, pp. 434–443.
45. Jackson, Memorandum on January 16 Meeting, January 18, 1954.
46. Eisenhower interview, DOHC.
47. NSC 177, December 30, 1953, NSC Series, White House Records, Eisenhower Papers.
48. Memorandum for the Record, January 30, 1954, Meeting of the President's Special Committee on Indochina, January 29, 1954, Office of the Assistant Secretary of Defense, in US House, *US-Vietnam Relations*, vol. 9, pp. 443–447.

I. Setting the Stage

49. *Ibid.*
50. Minnich, Memorandum on Legislative Conference, February 8, 1954, *FRUS*, pp. 1023–1025.
51. *Ibid.;* Eisenhower telephone conversation with Wilson, February 9, 1954, DDE Diary (Phone Calls), DDE Diary Series, Eisenhower Papers [hereafter referred to as DDE Phone Calls].
52. Presidential press conference, February 10, 1954, *Public Papers of the President: Eisenhower,* vol. 2, pp. 245–255.

II. The Ely Mission

1. Radford, *Memoirs,* p. 391.
2. Ély, *L'Indochine,* p. 25.
3. Kern to Dulles, March 14, 1954, International Memoranda and Documents File, Dulles Papers; Dillon to Dulles, March 11, 1954, Dulles-Herter Series, Eisenhower Papers.
4. Dillon to Dulles, March 11, 1965.
5. Ely, *L'Indochine,* p. 25; Radford to Wilson, March 5, 1954, *Pentagon Papers,* pp. 447–448.
6. Ély, *L'Indochine,* p. 24.
7. O'Ballance, *Indochina War,* pp. 215–216; Fall, *Hell,* p. ix.
8. Ély, *L'Indochine,* p. 21.
9. Bidault, *Resistance,* p. 195.
10. Eisenhower, *Mandate,* p. 344.
11. Sources for this dinner meeting are Radford, Memorandum for the President, March 24, 1954, "Discussions with General Ély Relative to the Situation in Indochina," Chairman File: Radford, Modern Military Records, US National Archives [hereafter referred to as Radford Papers]; Radford, *Memoirs,* p. 329; Ridgway, Memorandum of Conversation at Home of Adm. Radford, March 20, 1954, Ridgway Papers; US Joint Chiefs of Staff [hereafter referred to as USJCS], "History," p. 370; Ély, *L'Indochine,* p.26.
12. Ély, *L'Indochine,* p. 26.
13. Memorandum of Discussion at the 189th Meeting of the National Security Council, March 18, 1954, *FRUS,* pp. 1132–1133.
14. USJCS, "History," p. 370.
15. Eisenhower, *Mandate,* p. 344.
16. Ély, *L'Indochine,* pp. 28–30.
17. *Ibid.,* p. 28.
18. Radford, *Memoirs,* pp. 400–401.
19. Hagerty, Diary entry for March 22, 1954, Diary Entries, Hagerty Papers, Eisenhower Archives [hereafter referred to as Hagerty Diary].
20. Dulles, Statement to the Press, March 23, 1954, Department of State Press Release no. 154, Speeches and Press Conferences File, Dulles Papers.

II. The Ely Mission

21. Radford, *Memoirs,* p. 393.
22. Dulles, Memorandum for the President, March 23, 1954, Dulles-Herter Series, Eisenhower Papers.
23. Ély, *L'Indochine,* p. 28.
24. *Ibid.,* p. 30.
25. Dulles telephone conversation with Radford, 10 AM, March 24, 1954, Telephone Conversation Memoranda Series, Dulles File, Eisenhower Archives [hereafter referred to as JFD Phone Calls]. Quotations relating to this and other Dulles telephone conversations are from the synopsis made by Dulles' personal secretary, who took notes while listening on a connecting line.
26. *Pentagon Papers,* pp. 458–459.
27. Dulles, Memorandum of Conversation with the President, March 24, 1954, *FRUS,* pp. 1150.
28. Ambrose, *Eisenhower,* pp. 49–50.
29. Dulles, Memorandum of Conversation with the President, March 24, 1954.
30. Msgs. CNO 1923232 and 2020232, March 1954; Msgs. CINCPAFLT 2219442 and 2221414, March 1954; and USS *Essex* deck log 1954, all cited in Hooper, *Setting the Stage,* pp. 247–248.
31. Ély, *L'Indochine,* p. 30.
32. *Ibid.,* pp. 32–34.
33. The US government gave Ély everything he asked for except the C-47s, which were in critically short supply, and the helicopters, which would require another loan of American maintenance personnel to maintain.
34. Randle, *Geneva,* p. 57.
35. Ridgway, Memorandum of Conversation at Home of Admiral Radford, March 20, 1954, and Memorandum for the Record on Indochina, March 29, 1954, Ridgway Papers.
36. Ridgway, *Soldier,* p. 272.
37. Ridgway, Memorandum for the Record, March 29, 1954.
38. Radford, Memorandum for the President, March 24, 1954.
39. Ély, *L'Indochine,* p. 34; Dulles telephone conversation with Radford, March 25, 1954, JFD Phone Calls.
40. USJCS, "History," p. 371.
41. *Ibid.,* p. 372.
42. Ély, *L'Indochine,* p. 35.
43. Correctly, Operation Vulture was the contingency plan for Intervention put together unofficially by Navarre's staff and Trapnell's MAAG team in Saigon in late March and early April 1954, after the Ély mission. (Navarre, *Agonie,* p. 244; Fall, *Hell,* p. 301; *Pentagon Papers,* p. 97.) Radford did not refer to his airstrike plan by that name (although Ély did) and told the authors of the *Pentagon Papers* that no plan named "Operation Vulture" ever existed. (*Pentagon Papers,* p. 97.) However, since

II. The Ely Mission

the plan he devised with Ély so closely resembled what is known of the later plan, and since Ély and the French government referred to the air-strike plan consistently as Operation Vulture, the name is used here for convenience.

44. Ély, *L'Indochine*, p. 38.
45. Radford, *Memoirs*, p. 394; USJCS, "History," p. 373; Hooper, *Setting the Stage*, pp. 250–251.
46. Ély, *L'Indochine*, p. 35.
47. *Ibid.*, pp. 35–39; Minutes of the Meeting between Admiral Radford and General Ély held on Friday, 26 March, 1954, Radford Papers.
48. Radford, *Memoirs*, p. 394; Ély, Draft Minutes of the Meeting between Admiral Radford and General Ély held on Friday, 26 March, 1954, Radford Papers.
49. Ély, *L'Indochine*, p. 35.

III. United Action

1. The source for all material relating to this meeting is: Memorandum of Discussion at the 190th Meeting of the National Security Council, March 25, 1954, *FRUS*, pp. 1163–1168.
2. The description of this meeting comes from Ridgway, Memorandum for the Record, March 29, 1954.
3. Ridgway, *Soldier*, p. 276.
4. Ridgway, Memorandum for the Record, March 29, 1954.
5. Ridgway, *Soldier*, p. 276.
6. *Pentagon Papers*, p. 127.
7. Ridgway, *Soldier*, p. 276.
8. Most of the details of this meeting are taken from the notes made by presidential assistant Sherman Adams, Indochina File, Adams Papers; all quotations are direct quotations recorded in Hagerty Diary, March 26, 1954.
9. Hagerty Diary, March 27, 1954.
10. Dulles, Memorandum of Conversation with the President, March 24, 1954.
11. Dulles, "The Threat of a Red Asia," March 29, 1954, Speeches and Press Conferences File, Dulles Papers.
12. See, for example, George and Smoke, *Deterrence*, pp. 256–257; Larson, *Eisenhower*, p. 76; Anderson, O'Conner, and Adams interviews, DOHC.
13. Dulles telephone conversation with McCardle, March 27, 1954, JFD Phone Calls.
14. Dulles telephone conversation with Knowland, March 30, 1954, JFD Phone Calls.
15. James Reston, "Dulles Asks for Unity to Block Red Rule in Southeast Asia," *New York Times*, March 30, 1954, pp. 1, 5; Anne O'Hare

McCormick, "For a United Western Policy in Asia," *New York Times*, March 31, 1954, p. 26; William S. White, "Democratic Brand New Look Defense Unsafe for Nation," *New York Times*, March 31, 1954, pp. 1, 8.

16. US Congress, Senate, *Record*, March 30, 1954, p. 4209.
17. US Senate, Committee on Foreign Relations, "Mansfield Study Mission," p. 5.
18. US Congress, Senate, *Record*, April 6, 1954, p. 4677.
19. White, *New York Times*, March 31, 1954. According to Dulles' version of his conversation with Mehta, he told the ambassador that he did not consider a peaceful settlement of the Indochina War to be acceptable "if it meant a giveaway of Indochina to the Communists. We cannot be content with mere promises and we would not make any down payments until time and Communist action had provided evidence of good intentions." (Dulles to the Embassy in India, April 2, 1954, *FRUS*, pp. 1217–1218.)
20. Dulles telephone conversation with Makins, March 29, 1954, JFD Phone Calls.
21. Eden, *Full Circle*, p. 102.
22. Laniel, *Le Drame*, pp. 79–86; Ély, *L'Indochine*, p. 39; Devillers and Lacouture, *End of a War*, pp. 75–77; Fall, *Hell*, p. 299.
23. Sources for this meeting are Laniel, *Le Drame*, pp. 82–86; Ély, *L'Indochine*, p. 39; Devillers and Lacouture, *End of a War*, pp. 75–76; and Gurtov, *First Vietnam Crisis*, p. 84.
24. Radford, Memorandum for the Secretary of Defense, "Subject: Indochina," March 31, 1954, Ridgway Papers.
25. Twining, Memorandum for Admiral Radford et al., April 2, 1954, Ridgway Papers.
26. Carney, Memorandum for Admiral Radford et al., April 2, 1954, Ridgway Papers.
27. Shepherd, Memorandum for Admiral Radford et al., April 2, 1954, Ridgway Papers.
28. Ridgway, Memorandum for Admiral Radford et al., April 2, 1954, Ridgway Papers.
29. Radford, Memorandum for the Secretary of Defense, March 31, 1954.

IV. Three Conditions

1. Diary entry for March 17, 1951, Eisenhower, *Diaries*, p. 190.
2. Dulles telephone conversation with McCardle, March 27, 1954, JFD Phone Calls.
3. Presidential Press Conference, March 27, 1954, *Public Papers of the President*, vol. 2, pp. 364–370.
4. Diary entry for January 18, 1954, Eisenhower, *Diaries*, p. 268.

IV. Three Conditions

5. "The Decision to Win in Indochina," *New Republic,* April 12, 1954, vol. 63, p. 3.
6. Heath to Dulles, March 31, 1954, Midnight, *FRUS,* pp. 1190–1191; Heath to Dulles, April 1, 1954, 1 PM, *FRUS,* pp. 1199–1200.
7. Memorandum of Discussion at the 191st Meeting of the National Security Council, April 1, 1954, *FRUS,* pp. 1200–1202.
8. Dulles to Heath, April 1, 1954, 8:10 PM, *FRUS,* pp. 1205–1206.
9. *FRUS,* p. 1202, fn. 3.
10. See especially Roberts, "The Day We Didn't Go To War."
11. Dulles telephone conversation with Radford, April 1, 1954, JFD Phone Calls.
12. Dulles telephone conversation with Stassen, April 1, 1954, JFD Phone Calls.
13. Source for this meeting is Dulles, Memorandum of Conversation with the President, April 2, 1954, White House Memoranda Series, Dulles File, Eisenhower Papers.
14. Draft Joint Resolution, April 2, 1954, Indochina Papers, Geneva Conference Subfile, Radford Papers.
15. Robert Bowie, one of Dulles' top advisers, offers a third interpretation: that Dulles could have devised the resolution as a bluff to make the US diplomatic position appear stronger. Bowie explained to a Congression Research Service interviewer in 1983,

    The Resolution was an excellent device, like the united action speech, for ambiguity, because it suggested the United States was united, that it would have a point at which it will resist, without committing us to when, or under what circumstances, or anything else. So it was a wonderful device for vaguely threatening the Chinese and the Soviets and the Vietnamese without being a bluff that anybody could call.

    (Quoted in Gibbons, *US Government and Vietnam,* p. 194, fn. 45.) While this is possible, it is contradicted by numerous statements Dulles made, both officially and unofficially, advocating United States military involvement in Indochina once certain conditions were satisfied.
16. Dulles telephone conversation with Brownell, April 1, 1954, JFD Phone Calls.
17. Dulles, Memorandum of Conversation with the President, April 2, 1954.
18. *Ibid.*
19. Further evidence of Eisenhower's attempts to cover up his decision on Dien Bien Phu and Indochina is found in the April 1, 1954, Hagerty Diary entry. Hagerty records that at an Oval Office luncheon with Roy Howard and Walker Stone, the director and the editor of the Scripps-Howard newspaper chain, Eisenhower said that he might have to send US aircraft into bomb the area around Dien Bien Phu, adding "of course, if we did, we'd have to deny it forever." Ike's disingenuousness in re-

vealing a supposedly top-secret plan to executives of right-wing tabloids is patent.

20. Sources for this meeting are Drumright, Memorandum of Conversation, April 2, 1954, *FRUS*, pp. 1214–1217; Dulles to Aldrich and Dillon, April 3, 1954, *Pentagon Papers*, pp. 293–294; Dulles to Dillon and Aldrich, April 4, 1954, *Pentagon Papers*, pp. 295–296; Eden, *Full Circle*, pp. 102–103.

21. See Dulles telephone converations with Strauss, March 27, 1954, and Dewey, March 31, 1954, JFD Phone Calls.

22. Drumright, Memorandum of Conversation, April 2, 1954.

23. Dulles to Dillon and Aldrich, April 4, 1954.

24. Hooper, *Setting the Stage*, pp. 252–253.

25. Sources for this meeting are O'Conner, Memorandum for the Secretary's File, "Subject: Conference with Congressional Leaders concerning the crisis in Southeast Asia, April 3, 1954." April 5, 1954, White House Memoranda Series, Dulles File, Eisenhower Papers; Roberts, "The Day We Didn't Go To War"; Russell, Notes from April 3, 1954, Meeting at the State Department, Russell Papers; *Pentagon Papers*, pp. 367–69; Gibbons, *US Government and Vietnam*, pp. 191–195.

26. O'Conner, Memorandum for the Secretary's File, April 5, 1954.

27. *Ibid.*

28. Russell, Notes from April 3, 1954, Meeting. (Russell's notation on Dulles' lack of enthusiasm about British support is not substantiated by the secretary of state's file memorandum, however.)

29. Russell, Notes from April 3, 1954, Meeting; O'Conner, Memorandum for the Secretary's File, April 5, 1954. Columnist Chalmers Roberts' account ("The Day We Didn't Go To War") alleges that Radford asked for airstrikes specifically to save Dien Bien Phu. Since Roberts wrote his article several months after the event, however, it may contain imprecisions, particularly since Radford was again to change position on whether the outpost could be saved.

30. Quoted in Roberts, "The Day We Didn't Go To War," p. 31.

31. Roberts, "The Day We Didn't Go To War"; see also Gurtov, *First Vietnam Crisis*, pp. 95–96; *Pentagon Papers*, pp. 100–101; Lyon, *Eisenhower*, pp. 603–604.

32. Randle, *Geneva*, pp. 64–65; Hoopes, *Devil and Dulles*, p. 212.

33. Dillon to Dulles, April 2, 1954, 8 PM (telegrams 3692 and 3693), and telegram 3470 to Paris, April 3, 1954, *FRUS*, pp. 1218–1219.

34. For an in-depth look at the congressional response to the Dien Bien Phu crisis, see Gibbons, *US Government and Vietnam*.

35. Roberts, "The Day We Didn't Go To War," p. 35.

36. Sources for this meeting are Bonbright, Memorandum of Conversation, April 3, 1954, *FRUS*, pp. 1225–1229; and Dulles to Dillon and Aldrich, April 4, 1954.

IV. Three Conditions

37. Eisenhower telephone conversation with Dulles, April 3, 1954, *FRUS*, p. 1230.
38. Sources for this meeting are Bonbright, Memorandum of Conversation, April 4, 1954, *FRUS*, pp. 1231–1235; Interview with Sir Leslie Knox Munro, DOHC; Dulles to Peaslee and Scotten, April 6, 1954, *Pentagon Papers*, pp. 367–369.
39. This meeting was held "off the record"; no contemporary account of it exists. The principal available source for what transpired is the published memoirs of presidential assistant Sherman Adams (*Firsthand Report*. p. 122). Though Adams is not listed among the meeting's attendants, the gist of his account is corroborated by Eisenhower's statement of his response to the congressional leaders' conditions, as recounted in his own memoirs (*Mandate*, p. 347). See also *Pentagon Papers*, p. 101.
40. Eisenhower, *Mandate*, p. 347.
41. *Ibid.*
42. Gibbons concludes that Congress generally supported going to war in French Indochina in 1954, if the US acted as a part of a coalition that would remove the taint of its being a colonial (vs. anticommunist) war. Indeed, he found that the legislators "may have been even more inclined than the President to consider United States ground forces in Southeast Asia if that became necessary to stop the Communists, although they, too, wanted to avoid 'another Korea.' " (*US Government and Vietnam*, pp. 203–204.)
43. Quoted in *Ibid.*, p. 195.
44. Hoopes, *Devil and Dulles*, p. 212.

V. "Resigned To Do Nothing"

1. Navarre, *Agonie*, p. 229; "Living Dangerously," *Time*, March 1, 1954, p. 25.
2. Ély, *L'Indochine*, p. 39.
3. *Ibid.*, Fall, *Hell*, p. 299.
4. Fall, *Hell*, p. 299; Lancaster, *Emancipation of Indochina*, pp. 302–304; Eisenhower, *Mandate*, pp. 344–345; Devillers and Lacouture, *End of a War*, p. 76; Navarre, *Agonie*, pp. 242–244.
5. Laniel, *Le Drame*, pp. 84–85; Ély, *L'Indochine*, p. 40; Devillers and Lacouture, *End of a War*, pp. 76–77; Fall, *Hell*, p. 302.
6. Sources for this meeting are Laniel, *Le Drame*, pp. 84–85; Dillon to Dulles, April 5, 1954, *FRUS*, pp. 1236–1238.
7. Laniel, *Le Drame*, pp. 84–85.
8. Dillon to Dulles, April 5, 1954, *FRUS*, p. 1237.
9. Ély, *L'Indochine*, p. 40.
10. Eisenhower telephone conversation with Dulles, April 5, 1954, DDE Phone Calls.

V. "Resigned To Do Nothing"

11. More than a decade later, Eisenhower's anger had barely subsided. According to his oral history account, the president's reaction to the French request for airstrike was:

    Are you crazy? If we're going to participate in this thing at all, we're certainly going to be in a decisive position, as far as the use of our troops is concerned. . . . We're not just going to give you something to use as you please, and then we have no power over that decision.
    . . . I just won't do it. I'm not going to make my county just another Hesse to hire out mercenaries for you people. I'm not going to do it.

    (Eisenhower Interview, EOHP, pp. 64–65.)

12. In a conversation with the author, historian Richard Immerman, an authority on Eisenhower, suggested that Ike's rage may have been a projection of self-anger for his own culpability in deliberately misleading Radford and thus, to some extent, encouraging the admiral's behavior. Eisenhower never liked to accept blame, says Immerman, so in this case might have externalized it.

13. Radford, *Memoirs*, p. 403.

14. Dulles to Dillon, April 5, 1954, *FRUS*, p. 1242.

15. *Ibid.*

16. Dulles suggested to Eisenhower during their April 3 telephone conversation that the president should write the prime minister. (*FRUS*, p. 1230). Eisenhower agreed and asked Dulles to work up a cable. The message as sent was drafted by State Department Counselor Douglas MacArthur II in collaboration with Secretary Dulles, and modified and approved by the president. (See statement by MacArthur, *FRUS*, p. 1238, fn. 1.)

17. See statements by Eisenhower recorded in Memorandum of Discussion at the 192nd Meeting of the National Security Council, April 6, 1954, *FRUS*, pp. 1253–1254, 1257.

18. Dillon to Dulles, April 6, 1954, *FRUS*, p. 1248.

19. Hagerty Diary, April 6, 1954.

20. US National Security Council, NSC Action No. 1074-A, in *Pentagon Papers*, pp. 298–331.

21. Source for this meeting is Memorandum of Discussion at the 192nd Meeting of the National Security Council, *FRUS*, pp. 1250–1265.

22. Eisenhower's sharp rebuke of Humphrey for making a point that the president had made many times previously and would make again—that the United States could not become a world policeman—seems to be yet another instance of his projecting self-directed anger onto another. Eisenhower's decision to let North Vietnam go communist was an extremely uncomfortable one for the president, both politically and ideologically; therefore, he was embarrassed by Humphrey's *realpolitik* arguments in his support.

23. At the 194th NSC meeting, Eisenhower disparaged unilateral intervention as "an attempt to police the entire world." (*FRUS*, p. 1440.)

24. Kyes met with members of Congress the next day to seek their opinion of extending the assignment of the Air Force mechanics already in Indochina. He called Dulles after the meeting to report the result. According to Dulles' record of the conversation, "Kyes said the results were 50-50. . . . There was an undertone in one statement that if No. 1 [Eisenhower] did something, it would be backed up." (Dulles telephone conversation with Kyes, April 7, 1954, JFD Phone Calls.)

25. Nixon, *RN*, p. 151.

26. Dillon to Dulles, April 7, 1954, *FRUS*, pp. 1272–1273.

27. Ély, *L'Indochine*, p. 40.

28. Dulles statement to House Foreign Affairs Committee, April 5, 1954, International Memoranda and Documents File, Dulles Papers.

29. The next day Dulles heard from his brother, CIA Director Allen Dulles, that US intelligence sources in Saigon could not confirm French reports of Chinese intervention. (Dulles telephone conversation with Allen Dulles, April 6, 1954, JFD Phone Calls.) A. Dulles reconfirmed his doubt that the Chinese had directly intervened at the NSC meeting that evening; Radford's intelligence sources agreed. (*FRUS*, p. 1252.)

30. Ély, *L'Indochine*, p. 40; Navarre, *Agonie*, p. 243; Laniel, *Le Drame*, p. 84.

31. Dulles telephone conversation with Radford, April 5, 1954, JFD Phone Calls.

32. Dulles to Dillon, April 7, 1954, 1:28 PM, *FRUS*, pp. 1274–1275.

33. Eden, *Full Circle*, pp. 103–104.

34. Aldrich to Dulles, April 6, 1954, *Pentagon Papers*, p. 366.

35. "Letter to Washington," April 8, 1954, in Rovere, *Affairs of State*, p. 193.

36. US Congress, Senate, *Record*, April 6, 1954, p. 4674.

37. *Ibid.*, pp. 4675–4676.

38. See, for example, statement by Senator Stennis in *ibid.*, p. 4681. Even Kennedy, the most outspoken opponent of intervention, demanded as a precondition on liberation only that France make "minimal decrees for real independence." (Quoted in Gibbons, *US Government and Vietnam*, p. 205.)

39. Presidential Press Conference, April 7, 1954, *Public Papers of the President*, vol. 2. p. 383.

40. "Why U.S. Risks War for Indochina," *US News and World Report*, April 16, 1954, p. 21.

41. MacArthur, Memorandum to the Secretary of State, April 7, 1954, *FRUS*, pp. 1270–1272.

42. MacArthur's April 7 memorandum (*ibid.*) is accompanied by the following note by Roderic O'Conner, special assistant to the secretary of state: "Sec did not want to raise this now with Adm R—& the latter I gather did not raise it with the Sec." On April 9 MacArthur appended another memorandum for the file:

VI. Disunity

I called Captain George Anderson. . . . I said I was leaving with Secretary Dulles for Europe tomorrow and wanted him to know I had passed on to the Secretary the information Captain Anderson had given me. . . . I said that the Secretary had said an opportunity to talk to Admiral Radford about this would undoubtedly occur some time and I thought we could leave it to the two of them to get together when appropriate.

(*FRUS*, p. 1272, fn. 3.)

43. MacArthur, Memorandum to the Secretary of State, April 7, 1954; *FRUS*, p. 1271, fn. 1; Radford, *Memoirs*, p. 405; Navarre, *Agonie*, p. 244; Fall, *Hell*, pp. 305–306.
44. Ely to Valluy for Radford, c. April 7, 1954, in USJSC, "History," p. 385; Radford, *Memoirs*, p. 402.
45. Carney to CINCPACFLT, April 8, 1954, in Hooper, *Setting the Stage*, p. 255.

VI. Disunity

1. Dulles to Dillon, April 7, 1954, 8:25 PM, *FRUS*, pp. 1286–1288; see also fn. 2, p. 1287.
2. No copy of Churchill's reply exists in the available archives, but there are two secondary accounts of it. Unfortunately, they conflict. Eisenhower describes it in his memoirs as a "brief message [that] showed that the British had little enthusiasm for joining us in taking a firm position" (*Mandate*, p. 347). However, Dulles, in his April 7 cable to Dillon (*FRUS*, p. 1287), said that Churchill had replied that "he would be glad for me to come to London next Monday to talk about the Southeast Asian coalition." Either Dulles' enthusiasm for pulling off a major diplomatic coup by creating a pre-Geneva coalition clouded his perception, or, just as likely, Eisenhower's hindsight was altered by his desire to lay the blame for the failure of "united action" on another's administration.
3. Dulles telephone conversation with Knowland, April 10, 1954, JFD Phone Calls.
4. Radford, *Memoirs*, pp. 403–405.
5. Accounts of this meeting are in MacArthur, Memorandum of Conversation, "Subject: Indochina," April 11, 1954, *FRUS*, pp. 1307–1309; Dulles to Smith, April 12, 1954, *FRUS*, p. 1308, fn. 2; "Chronology of Actions on the Subject of Indochina . . . ,"January 27, 1956, International Meetings and Conferences File, Dulles Papers; Eden, *Full Circle*, pp. 106–108.
6. Dulles to Smith, April 12, 1954.
7. Joint Statement by Eden and Dulles, April 13, 1954, Eisenhower File, Dulles Papers.
8. Dulles to Eisenhower, April 13, 1954, *FRUS*, pp. 1322–1323.
9. Eden, *Full Circle*, p. 109; Dulles to Department of State, April 13, 1954, 1 AM, *FRUS*, pp. 1319–1320; Dulles to Eisenhower, April 13, 1954. The

synopsis of the final Dulles/Eden meeting contained in the State Department's January 27, 1956, "Chronology of Actions on the Subject of Indochina" contains a passage that leaves the impression that Eden had agreed to take part in planning the Southeast Asian defense organization at once:

> In his final meeting with Eden the Secretary suggested getting in touch with the British after his present trip, to see how best we might proceed in organizing a united will to resist aggression in SEA. Mr. Eden agreed and said Makins would be available for this purpose.

10. Eden, *Full Circle*, p. 109. In MacArthur's memorandum of the April 11 conversation at Aldrich's residence (*FRUS*, pp. 1307–1309), Eden had begun by arguing that Burma, India, and Pakistan should be invited to participate in any collective defense arrangements, to which Dulles replied that he had already met with the ambassadors of the South Asian commonwealth countries to inform them of American plans for "united action." However, he said, to invite them to join the coalition at the beginning would raise the question of inviting the Koreans, Taiwanese, and Japanese, and thus overextending the nascent organization. Eden seemed to accept this logic. According to MacArthur's record, the foreign secretary said, "If he could say that India was being kept fully informed, he thought his own problem would be met and that the Labor Party, which would certainly raise this question, could be given an answer which would be defensible."

11. UK House of Commons, *Parliamentary Debates*, April 13, 1954, pp. 969–975; see especially p. 972.

12. Dulles, Statement on arriving in France, April 13, 1954, Dien Bien Phu File, Dulles Papers.

13. Dillon interview, DOHC.

14. *Ibid.*

15. UK House of Commons, *Parliamentary Debates*, p. 971.

16. Bowie interview, DOHC.

17. Quoted in "Cold War," *Time*, April 26, 1954, p. 32.

18. This is asserted in both the Dillon and Bowie interviews, DOHC.

19. Cited in Gurtov, *First Vietnam Crisis*, p. 104.

20. Source for this meeting is MacArthur, Memorandum of Conversation with Laniel, April 14, 1954, White House Memoranda Series, Eisenhower Papers.

21. Godley, Minutes of Conversations held in Paris (April 14, 1954), April 21, 1954, *FRUS*, pp. 1328–1334; Dulles, Memorandum of Conversation with Bidault, April 14, 1954, *FRUS*, pp. 1335–1336; MacArthur, Memorandum of Conversation in Laniel's Office, April 14, 1954, Dulles-Herter Series, Eisenhower Papers.

22. What Dulles actually told Bidault was that "*under certain circumstances*

the US Administration was prepared to ask the Congress for powers which would enable us to participate in a united effort to save Southeast Asia" [emphasis added]. However, he said, Congress would approve US participation in "united action" only if it were a regional undertaking, including British participation, and if it were clearly for the independence of the Associated States. (Dulles, Memorandum of Conversation with Bidault, April 14, 1954.)

23. Dulles and Bidault, Communiqué Issued Following Talks in Paris, April 14, 1954, in Council on Foreign Relations, *Documents,* pp. 258–259.
24. *Ibid.;* Dulles also won the EDC point. Warning Laniel that his uncooperativeness on the European Defense Community could force the Eisenhower Administration to find other allies on which to base America's European defense or even to turn away from Europe entirely, Dulles demanded that Laniel call the debate. The premier agreed to announce a date for the EDC debate at the next day's cabinet meeting.
25. No official text of the statement is extant. Excerpts and/or summaries can be found in Luther Huston, "High Aide Says Troops May Be Sent If the French Withdraw," *New York Times,* April 17, 1954, pp. 1, 3; "Digest of Nixon's Talk on Indochina," *New York Times,* April 18, 1954, p. 3; Nixon, *RN,* p. 152.
26. See, for example, Senate statements on April 19, 1954, in US Congress, Senate, *Record,* pp. 5289–5294.
27. Quoted in "Digest of Nixon's Talk," *New York Times,* April 18, 1954.
28. *Ibid.*
29. Eden, *Full Circle,* pp. 110–111.
30. Hagerty Diary, April 17 and April 19, 1954.
31. Dulles telephone conversation with Nixon, April 19, 1954, JFD Phone Calls.
32. Nixon, *RN,* p. 152.
33. "Digest of Nixon's Talk," *New York Times,* April 18, 1954.
34. Dulles telephone conversation with Nixon, April 19, 1954.
35. Radford, *Memoirs,* p. 406.
36. Adams, *First-Hand Report,* p. 122.
37. Cited in Randle, *Geneva,* p. 92.
38. Nixon, *RN,* p. 153.
39. Hagerty Diary, April 20, 1954; Radford, *Memoirs,* p. 406.
40. Dulles telephone conversation with Senator Smith, April 19, 1954, JFD Phone Calls.
41. Hoopes, *Devil and Dulles,* p. 216.
42. Merchant, Memorandum of Conversations, April 18, 1954, *FRUS,* pp. 1349–1350.
43. Dulles telephone conversation with Senator Smith, April 19, 1954.
44. "Mr. Dulles Answers Some Questions," *US News and World Report,* April 30, 1954, p. 63.

VI. Disunity

45. Dulles, Memorandum of Conference with Eisenhower, April 19, 1954, White House Memoranda Series, Dulles File, Eisenhower Papers.
46. Source for this conversation is Dulles to Smith, April 22, 1954, 2 PM, Dulles-Herter Series, Eisenhower Papers.
47. MacArthur, Memorandum of Conversation with Laniel et al., April 23, 1954, *FRUS*, p. 1371.
48. Memorandum of Information for Secretary of the Navy, April 23, 1954, File A16-3 to A16-9, 1954, International Affairs, Office of the Chief of Naval Operations, Records of the Immediate Offices of the CNO/CIC, US Fleet, 1942–1956, Operational Archives, Naval History Division.
49. MacArthur, Memorandum of Conversation with Laniel, April 23, 1954.
50. *Ibid.*
51. Radford, *Memoirs*, p. 407.
52. This assessment and the account of this incident is from Dulles to Smith, April 23, 1954, 8 PM, Dulles-Herter Series, Eisenhower Papers.
53. Dulles to Smith, April 23, 1954, Midnight, Dulles-Herter Series, Eisenhower Papers.
54. Sources for this meeting are Merchant, Memorandum of Conversation, April 26, 1954, *FRUS*, pp. 1386–1391; Dulles, Dulte 18 from Paris, April 24, 1954, *FRUS*, p. 1386, fn. 1; "Chronology of Actions on the Subject of Indochina . . . ," January 27, 1956; Eden, *Full Circle*, pp. 114–115; Radford, *Memoirs*, p. 407.
55. Merchant, Memorandum of Conversation, April 26, 1954.
56. Source for this meeting is Dulles to Smith, April 24, 1954, 10 PM, *FRUS*, pp. 1391–1393.
57. Dulles to Smith, April 24, 1954, Midnight, *FRUS*, pp. 1398–1399. The final version of the message, as later officially delivered to Bidault, dropped the parenthetical phrase "and which would include a clear intention to grant independence to the Associated States of Vietnam, Laos, and Cambodia," on recommendation of the State Department (*FRUS*, p. 1398, fn. 2.)
58. Dulles to Smith, April 24, 1954, 10 PM.
59. Source for this meeting is Dulles to Smith, April 24, 1954, 11 PM, *FRUS*, pp. 1394–1396.
60. Heath, Memorandum of Conversation, April 24, 1954, *FRUS*, pp. 1384–1385.
61. Dulles expressed this desire for "establishing the record clearly since the French might attempt to pin on us the responsibility for their withdrawal from Indochina," in connection with his previous day's discussion of preparing an official letter to Bidault. (Merchant, Memorandum of Conversation, April 26, 1954.)
62. Dulles to Smith, April 25, 1954, 8 PM, *FRUS*, pp. 1404–1405. The reasons Dulles gave in this cable for opposing intervention by executive action mostly echo his earlier, oft-repeated objections to involving the United

States militarily in Indochina before proper political arrangements were made. In addition, he said that it could strain relations with the UK.

63. Eden, *Full Circle*, pp. 116–117; Radford to Dulles, April 26, 1954, Dulles-Herter Series, Eisenhower Papers.
64. Dulles, Memorandum of Conversation with Eden et al., April 25, 1954, Dulles-Herter Series, Eisenhower Papers; Eden, *Full Circle*, pp. 116–119; *FRUS*, p. 1398, fn. 1.
65. Dulles, Memorandum of Conversation with Eden, April 25, 1954; Dulles to Smith, April 25, 1954, Midnight, *Pentagon Papers*, pp. 288–289; Dulles to Smith, April 26, 1954, Dulles-Herter Series, Eisenhower Papers.
66. Eisenhower telephone conversation with Smith, April 24, 1954, *FRUS*, pp. 1381–1383.
67. Eisenhower to Hazlett, April 27, 1954, *FRUS*, pp. 1427–1428.
68. Hooper, *Setting the Stage*, p. 256; Far Eastern Air Force, "To Recommend a Feasible Military Course of Action to Achieve United States Objectives in Indochina," April 13, 1954, and Director of Plans, United States Air Force, "History," January–June, 1954, pp. 90–92, both cited in Futrell, *US Air Force in Southeast Asia*, pp. 23–24.
69. Smith to Dulles, April 24, 1954, 10:14 PM, *FRUS*, p. 1383.
70. "Chronology of Actions on the Subject of Indochina . . . ," January 27, 1956; USJCS, "History," p. 387.
71. Eisenhower to Dulles, April 23, 1954, DDE Diary Series, Eisenhower Papers.
72. Dulles to Smith, April 24, 1954, 11 PM, *FRUS*, pp. 1394–1396; for Smith's reply telling of Eisenhower's displeasure see *FRUS*, p. 1396, fn. 2.
73. UK House of Commons, *Parliamentary Debates*, April 27, 1954, p. 1456.
74. Dulles to Smith, April 26, 1954, 9 PM, *Pantagon Papers*, pp. 390–391.

VII. The Fall of Dien Bien Phu

1. Hagerty Diary, April 26, 1954; Cutler, Summary of Principal Points Made by the President in His Talk with the Republican Leaders, April 26, 1954, Indochina 1954 File, WHO, Project Clean-up, Records of the Special Assistant for National Security Affairs, Eisenhower Archives; "Memorandum by the Assistant Staff Secretary to the President," undated, *FRUS*, pp. 1412–1414; Nixon, *RN*, p. 153.
2. Ike overestimated the congressional leaders' firmness on their conditions. Later that same day Undersecretary Smith discussed the Indochina War with members of the Senate and House Far Eastern subcommittees. He reported to Dulles afterward that

I was actually surprised by the restrained gravity of all who participated. With no carping questions or criticisms, there appeared to be full realization of the seriousness of the situation, and among the Congressional group there was open discussion of the passage of a resolution authorizing use of air and naval strength following a declaration of common interest, with, or possibly even without British participation.

(Quoted in Gibbons, *US Government and Vietnam*, p. 216.) Gibbons concludes that the key members of the congressional foreign policy committees were coming around to supporting intervention, or at least a threat of intervention, regardless of Britain's position.

3. Hagerty Diary, April 26, 1954.
4. See Eisenhower's letter to Greunther, April 26, 1954, *FRUS*, pp. 1419–1421; and to Hazlett, April 27, 1954, *FRUS*, pp. 1427–1428.
5. Eisenhower, Memorandum for the Files, April 27, 1954, *FRUS*, pp. 1422–1423.
6. Presidential Press Conference, April 29, 1954, *Public Papers of the President,* vol. 2, p. 92.
7. Memorandum of Discussion at the 194th Meeting of the National Security Council, April 29, 1954, *FRUS*, pp. 1431–1445.
8. Raymond Aron, editor of *Figaro,* had made this point a few days earlier during an audience with Dillon to plead for airstrikes. When the US ambassador said that the United States would act only in league with other countries interested in the region, Aron replied (according to Dillon's summary of their conversation):

   that if that means, as he had seen in the press, that we [Americans] required British agreement before acting, then it would be quite clear that the US was not yet ready to assume the obligations and risks of world leadership. He said it was obvious that the British would have to follow any strong lead taken by the US.

   Dillon reported this to Dulles in Geneva and to Smith at the Department of State on April 26 (*FRUS*, pp. 1415–1416).
9. That afternoon, while knocking some golf balls around the White House lawn with Hagerty, Eisenhower told his press secretary that the morning's NSC meeting "had been quite controversial, but the decision had been reached to hold up for the time being any military action on Indo-China until we see how Geneva coming along." (Hagerty Diary, April 29, 1954.)
10. Presidential Press Conference, April 29, 1954.
11. Stassen to Dulles, May 3, 1954, *FRUS*, pp. 1463–1466.
12. Memorandum of a Conference at the White House, May 5, 1954, *FRUS*, pp. 1466–1470.
13. Record of the Secretary of State's Briefing for Members of Congress, May 5, 1954, *FRUS*, pp. 1471–1477.
14. Figures range so widely because, in the chaos of battle, no records reached Saigon of who exactly was captured on May 7–8, as opposed to those who deserted or were captured earlier in the battle.
15. The descrepancy between the casualty tolls and the earlier figure of 13,000

VII. The Fall of Dien Bien Phu

French Union forces at Dien Bien Phu is accounted for by airborne reinforcements.

16. Cited in Herring, *America's Longest War*, p. 36.
17. Excerpts from the 1st Plenary Session of the Geneva Conference, Indochina Phase, May 8, 1954, *Pentagon Papers*, p. 504.
18. Quoted in "France," *Time*, May 24, 1954, p. 32.
19. Dulles to Dillon, May 12, 1954, Dulles-Herter Series, Eisenhower Papers.
20. Dulles to Dillon, May 11, 1954, *Pentagon Papers*, pp. 451–455.
21. Fearing that the French were using the intervention negotiations for another purpose, Dulles warned Dillon that,

   while we are anxious to bolster up the French position, we must also be on our guard lest Laniel is creating an alibi and he, or his successor, will in the end tell the French people that they had to capitulate because U.S. terms were so rigorous that they were obviously unacceptable, and therefore U.S. is to blame.

   (Dulles to Dillon, May 17, 1954, Dulles-Herter Series, Eisenhower Papers.)
22. Dulles telephone conversation with MacArthur, May 20, 1954, JFD Phone Calls.
23. Dulles, Press and Radio News Conference, May 11, 1954, Speeches and Press Conferences File, Dulles Papers.
24. "Report by the Secretary of State," May 12, 1954, in US Senate, Committee on Foreign Relations, *Executive Sessions*, vol. 6, p. 275.
25. Hagerty Diary, June 23, 1954; "Outline of General Smith's Remarks to the President and Bipartisan Congressional Groups," June 23, 1954, Indochina 1954 File, WHO, Project Clean-up, Records of the Special Assistant for National Security Affairs, Eisenhower Archives.
26. Bryce Harlow, Memorandum for the Record, June 23, 1954, Legislative Meetings Series, Eisenhower Papers.
27. By the terms of the Geneva Accords the United States could post no more that 342 MAAG officers in Vietnam. Ike added an additional 350 in 1956 under the guise of a "Temporary Equipment Recovery Mission." The number remained at 692 until the Kennedy presidency.
28. Hughes, *Ordeal of Power*, p. 208.
29. Quoted in Ambrose, *Eisenhower*, pp. 625–626.

Bibliography

Primary Sources

Archival and Manuscript Collections

Dwight D. Eisenhower Library, National Archives and Records Administration, Abilene, Kansas:

Eisenhower Papers, Ann Whitman File:
    Ann Whitman Diary Series
    Cabinet Series
    DDE Diary Series
    Dulles-Herter Series
    International Series
    Legislative Meetings Series
    NSC Series

Eisenhower Records, White House Central Files:
    Confidential File
    General File
    Official File

John Foster Dulles File:
    Drafts of Presidential Correspondence and Speeches Series, 1953–1955
    Telephone Conversation Memoranda Series, January 16, 1953–April 29, 1955
    White House Memoranda Series

Bibliography

James C. Hagerty Papers

C. D. Jackson Papers

Republican National Committee, News Clippings and Publications

White House Office, Office of the Special Assistant for National Security Affairs, Records:
Administrative Series
NSC Series
White House Office, Project Clean-up, Records of Gordon Gray, Robert Cutler, Henry McPhee, and Andrew J. Goodpaster

Operational Archives, Naval History Division, Washington, DC:

Records of the Immediate Offices of the CNO/CIC, US Fleet, 1942–1956
Records of the Strategic Plans Division, Office of the CNO

Seeley G. Mudd Manuscript Library, Princeton University:

Allen W. Dulles Papers

John Foster Dulles Papers

Livingston T. Merchant Papers

H. Alexander Smith Papers

Sherman Adams Papers, Dartmouth College.

Chairman File, Admiral Radford, 1953–1957, Record Group 218 (US JCS), Modern Military Records, National Archives.

Matthew B. Ridgway Papers, US Army Military History Collection, Carlisle Barracks, Pennsylvania.

Richard B. Russell Papers, University of Georgia, Athens, Georgia.

Oral Histories

John Foster Dulles Oral History Project, Princeton University:

Achilles, Theodore
Aiken, George D.
Alsop, Stewart
Armstrong, W. Park, Jr.
Brownell, Herbert

Adams, Sherman
Alsop, Joseph
Anderson, Dillon
Bowie, Robert
Bruce, David K.

Bibliography

Brundage, Percival
Cabell, Charles P.
Casey, Richard G., Lord (Berwick)
Clay, Lucius D.
Couve de Murville, Maurice
Dirksen, Everett M.
Eisenhower, Milton
Fulton, James G.
Gates, Thomas S.
Hagerty, James C.
Hanes, John W.
Harr, Karl, Jr.
Hauge, Gabriel
Holmes, Julius
Hughes, Emmet John
Javits, Jacob K.
Judd, Walter H.
Larson, Arthur
LiSagor, Peter
Luce, Henry
Mansfield, Michael J.
McCardle, Carl W.
Morton, Thruston B.
Murphy, Robert D.
Nixon, Richard M.
O'Connor, Roderic L.
Poto, Sarasin
Prochnow, Herbert
Ridgway, Matthew B.
Romulo, Carlos P.
Saltzman, Charles E.
Service, John Steward
Sherfield, Lord
Spaak, Paul Henri
Streibert, Theodore C.
Twining, Nathan F.
Weintal, Edward
Yost, Charles W.

Burke, Arleigh
Carpenter, Isaac W., Jr.
Childs, Marquis W.
Collins, J. Lawton
Dillon, C. Douglas
Eisenhower, Dwight D.
Frank, Sir Oliver Shewell
Garcia, Carlos P.
Goodpaster, Andrew J.
Halleck, Charles A.
Harlow, Bryce
Harsch, Joseph C.
Hickenlooper, Bourke B.
Houghton, Amory
Humphrey, George M.
Johnson, U. Alexis
Khoman, Thanot
LeMay, Curtis
Lodge, Henry Cabot
MacDonald, Sir Thomas
Martin, Joseph W., Jr.
Mendes-France, Pierre
Munro, Sir Leslie Knox
Nash, Sir Walter
Nolting, Frederick E., Jr.
Phleger, Herman
Potter, Philip
Radford, Arthur W.
Roberts, Chalmers
Rovere, Richard H.
Sebald, William J.
Shanley, Bernard M.
Smith, Bromley
Spender, Sir Percy
Stump, Felix B.
Tyler, William R.
Won Waithayakon, Prince

Dwight D. Eisenhower Oral History Project, Columbia Oral History Project, Columbia University:

Anderson, Dillon
Dillon, C. Douglas

Bowie, Robert
Eisenhower, Dwight D.

Bibliography

Harlow, Bryce
McCardle, Carl
Persons, Wilton B.
Twining, Nathan

Knowland, William F.
Merchant, Livingston
Robertson, Walter

William H. Darden Oral History, Richard B. Russel Oral History Project, University of Georgia.

Captain Stephen Jurika, Jr. Oral History, US Naval Institute Oral History Program, Operational Archives, Naval History Division.

General Matthew B. Ridgway Interview, Senior Officers Debriefing Program, US Army Military History Research Collection.

Admiral Felix Stump Oral History, Columbia Oral History Project.

Newspapers and Periodicals (January–September 1954)

The Economist
Le Monde
The New York Times
The Times (London)
The Washington Post

L'Express
The New Republic
Time
US News and World Report

Published Sources

Acheson, Dean. *Present at the Creation*. New York: Norton, 1969.
Adams, Sherman. *First-Hand Report: The Story of the Eisenhower Administration*. New York: Harper, 1961.
Albertson, Dean, ed. *Eisenhower as President*. New York: Hill & Wang, 1963.
Alexander, Charles C. *Holding the Line: The Eisenhower Era, 1952–61*. Bloomington: Indiana University Press, 1975.
Allison, Graham. *Essence of Decision: Explaining the Cuban Missile Crisis*. Boston: Little, Brown, 1971.
Ambrose, Stephen E. *Eisenhower the President*. New York: Simon and Schuster, 1984.
Anderson, Dillon. "The President and National Security." *The Atlantic*, January 1956, 197:42–46.
Bachrack, Stanley D. *The Committee of One Million: China Lobby Politics, 1953–71*. New York: Columbia University Press, 1976.
Bartlett, C. J. *A History of Postwar Britain, 1945–74*. London: Longman Group, 1977.

Bibliography

Bator, Victor. *Vietnam, A Diplomatic Tragedy: The Origins of United States Involvement*. Dobbs Ferry, N.Y.: Oceana Publications, 1965.

Berding, Andrew H. *Dulles on Diplomacy*. Princeton: D. Van Nostrand, 1965.

Bernstein, Barton J. "Foreign Policy in the Eisenhower Administration." *Foreign Service Journal*, May 1973, 50:17ff.

Betts, Richard. "Soldiers, Statesmen and the Decision-Making Process." PhD dissertation, Harvard University, 1976.

Bidault, Georges. *Resistance*. Marianne Sinclair, trans. London: Weidenfeld & Nicolson, 1965.

Bodard, Lucien. *The Quicksand War: Prelude to Vietnam*. Boston: Little, Brown, 1967.

Buttinger, Joseph. *Vietnam: A Dragon Embattled*. New York: Frederick A. Praeger, 1967.

Capitanchick, David B. *The Eisenhower Presidency and American Foreign Policy*. London: Routledge and Kegan Paul, 1969.

Childe, Marquis. *The Ragged Edge: The Diary of a Crisis*. Garden City, N.Y.: Doubleday, 1955.

Childs, Marquis. *Eisenhower: Captive Hero*. New York: Harcourt, Brace, 1958.

Churchill, Randolph A. *The Rise and Fall of Sir Anthony Eden*. London: MacGibbon & Kee, 1959.

Clark, Keith C., and Lawrence J. Legere, eds. *The President and the Management of National Security*. New York: Frederick A. Praeger, 1969.

Clotfelter, James. *The Military in American Politics*. New York: Harper & Row, 1973.

Cole, Allen B., ed. *Conflict in Indochina and International Repercussions: A Documentary History, 1945–55*. Ithaca, N.Y.: Cornell University Press, 1956.

Cooper, Chester L. *The Lost Crusade: America in Vietnam*. New York: Dodd, Mead, 1970.

Council on Foreign Relations. *Documents on American Foreign Relations, 1954*. New York: Harper, 1955.

Cutler, Robert. *No Time for Rest*. Boston: Little, Brown, 1965.

Dale, Edwin L. *Conservatives in Power*. Garden City, N.Y.: Doubleday, 1960.

Dejean, Maurice. "The Meaning of Dien Bien Phu." *US Naval Institute Proceedings*, July 1954, 80:717–725.

Dulles, Allen. *The Craft of Intelligence*. New York: Harper & Row, 1963.

Dulles, John Foster. "A Policy for Security and Peace." *Foreign Affairs*, April 1954, 37:353–364.

—— "A Policy of Boldness." *Life*, May 19, 1952, 32:146–161.

—— *War or Peace*. New York: MacMillan, 1950.

Devillers, Philippe, and Jean Lacouture. *End of a War: Indochina 1954*. Alexander Lieven and Adam Roberts, trans. New York: Frederick A. Praeger, 1969.

Bibliography

Divine, Robert A. *Eisenhower and the Cold War.* Oxford: Oxford University Press, 1981.
—— *Foreign Policy and U.S. Presidential Elections, 1952–60.* New York: New Viewpoints, 1974.
—— *Since 1945: Politics and Diplomacy in Recent American History.* New York: John Wiley, 1975.
Donovan, Robert J. *Eisenhower: The Inside Story.* New York: Harper, 1956.
Drummond, Roscoe, and Gaston Coblentz. *Duel at the Brink: John Foster Dulles's Command of American Power.* Garden City, N.Y.: Doubleday, 1960.
Eden, Anthony. *Full Circle.* Boston: Houghton Mifflin, 1960.
Eisenhower, Dwight D. "The Central Role of the President in the Conduct of Security Affairs." In Col. Amos A. Jordon, Jr., ed., *Issues of National Security in the 1970s.* New York: Frederick A. Praeger, 1967.
—— *The Eisenhower Diaries.* Robert H. Ferrell, ed. New York: Norton, 1981.
—— *Mandate for Change, 1953–61.* Garden City, N.Y.: Doubleday, 1963.
Ély, Paul. *L'Indochine dans la Tourmente.* Paris: Librairie Plon, 1964.
Ewald, William Bragg, Jr. *Eisenhower the President.* Englewood Cliffs, N.J.: Prentice-Hall, 1981.
Fall, Bernard B. *Hell in a Very Small Place: The Seige of Dien Bien Phu.* Philadelphia: Lippincott, 1967.
—— *Street Without Joy.* Harrisburg, Pa.: Stackpole, 1967.
—— *The Two Vietnams.* New York: Frederick A. Praeger, 1963.
Fenno, Richard F., Jr. *The President's Cabinet.* Cambridge, Mass.: Harvard University Press, 1959.
France, Journal Officiel. *Debats Parlementaires Assemblee Nationale,* Paris, September 1953–September 1954.
Furniss, Edgar S., Jr. "Weaknesses in French Foreign Policy-Making." Princeton Center for International Studies, Memorandum no. 5, February 5, 1954.
Futrell, Robert F. *The United States Air Force in Southeast Asia: The Advisory Years to 1965.* Washington: Office of Air Force History, US Air Force, 1981.
Gaitskill, Hugh. "The Search for an Anglo-American Policy." *Foreign Affairs,* July 1954, 32:563–576.
Gallup, George H. *The Gallup Poll,* vol. 2: *1949–58.* New York: Random House, 1972.
Gelb, Leslie H., with Richard K. Betts. *The Irony of Vietnam: The System Worked.* Washington: The Brookings Institution, 1977.
George, Alexander L., and Richard Smoke. *Deterrence in American Foreign Policy: Theory and Practice.* New York: Columbia University Press, 1974.
Gerson, Louis L. *John Foster Dulles.* Robert H. Ferrell, ed. *The American Secretaries of State and Their Diplomacy,* vol. 17. New York: Cooper Square, 1967.

Bibliography

Gibbons, William Conrad. *The U.S. Government and the Vietnam War: Executive and Legislative Roles and Relations*, part 1: *1945–60*. Princeton, N.J.: Princeton University Press, 1986.

Goldman, Eric F. *The Crucial Decade*. New York: Alfred A. Knopf, 1959.

Goold-Adams, Richard. *John Foster Dulles: A Reappraisal*. New York: Appleton-Century-Crofts, 1962.

Grabner, Norman. "Eisenhower's Popular Leadership." *Current History*, October 1960, 39:230–36ff.

—— *The New Isolationism: A Study in Politics and Foreign Policy since 1950*. New York: Ronald Press, 1956.

Greenstein, Fred I. *The Hidden Hand Presidency: Eisenhower as Leader*. New York: Basic Books, 1982.

Grosser, Alfred. *The Western Alliance: European-American Relations since 1945*. Michael Shaw, trans. New York: Continuum Press, 1980.

Guhin, Michael A. *John Foster Dulles: A Statesman and His Times*. New York: Columbia University Press, 1972.

Guillain, Robert. *La Fin des Illusions*. Paris: Center d'Etudes de Politique Etrangere, 1954.

Gurtov, Melvin. *The First Vietnam Crisis*. New York: Columbia University Press, 1967.

Halperin, Morton H. *Bureaucratic Politics and Foreign Policy*. Washington: Brookings Institution, 1974.

Hammer, Ellen J. *The Struggle for Indochina*. Stanford, Calif.: Stanford University Press, 1954.

—— "The Struggle for Indochina Continues." *The Pacific Spectator*, Summer 1955, 9: supplement.

Henry, Laurin L. *Presidential Transitions*. Washington: Brookings Institution, 1960.

Herring, George C. *America's Longest War: The United States and Vietnam, 1950–75*. New York: John Wiley, 1979.

Herring, George C., and Richard Immerman. "Eisenhower, Dulles and Dien Bien Phu: 'The Day We Didn't Go To War' Revisited." *Journal of American History*, September 1984, 71:343–63.

Hess, Stephen. *Organizing the Presidency*. Washington: Brookings Institution, 1976.

Hilsman, Roger. "Congressional-Executive Relations and the Foreign Policy Consensus." *American Political Science Review*, September 1958, 52:725–44.

Hitch, Charles J. *Decision-Making for Defense*. Berkeley: University of California Press, 1970.

Honey, P. J. *Genesis of a Tragedy: Historical Background to the Vietnam War*. London: Ernest Benn, 1968.

Hooper, Edwin, et al. *The United States Navy and the Vietnam Conflict*, vol. 1: *The Setting of the Stage to 1959*. Washington: US Navy History Division, 1976.

Bibliography

Hoopes, Townsend. *The Devil and John Foster Dulles*. Boston: Little, Brown, 1973.

Howe, Quincy, and Arthur M. Schlesinger, eds. *Guide to Politics, 1954*. New York: Dial Press, 1954.

Hsiao, Gene T., ed. *The Role of External Powers in the Indochina Crisis*. New York: Andronicus, 1973.

Hughes, Barry. *The Domestic Context of American Foreign Policy*. San Francisco: Freeman, 1978.

Hughes, Emmet John. *The Ordeal of Power: A Political Memoir of the Eisenhower Years*. New York: Atheneum, 1963.

Huntington, Samuel. *The Common Defense*. New York: Columbia University Press, 1961.

—— *The Soldier and the State*. Cambridge, Mass.: Harvard University Press, 1961.

—— "Strategic Planning and the Political Process." *Foreign Affairs,* January 1960, 38:285–99.

Hyman, Herbert H., and Paul B. Sheatsley. "The Political Appeal of President Eisenhower." *Public Opinion Quarterly,* Winter 1953–54, 17:443–60.

Irving, R.E.M. *The First Indochina War: French-American Policy, 1945–54*. London: Croon Helm, 1975.

Kahin, George M., and John W. Lewis. *The United States in Vietnam*. New York: Dial Press, 1967.

Karnow, Stanley. *Vietnam: A History*. New York: Viking, 1983.

Kempton, Murray. "The Underestimation of Dwight David Eisenhower." *Esquire,* September 1967, 68:108–109ff.

Kinnard, Douglas. *President Eisenhower and Strategy Management*. Lexington: University Press of Kentucky, 1977.

Kolodziej, Edward A. *The Uncommon Defense and Congress, 1945–63*. Columbus: Ohio State University Press, 1966.

Korb, Lawrence J. *The Joint Chiefs of Staff: The First Twenty-Five Years*. Bloomington: Indiana University Press, 1976.

Lancaster, Donald. *The Emancipation of French Indochina*. New York: Octagon, 1974.

Laniel, Joseph. *Le Drame Indochinois*. Paris: Librairie Plon, 1957.

Larson, Arthur. *Eisenhower: The President Nobody Knew*. New York: Charles Scribner's Sons, 1968.

Levering, Ralph B. *The Public and American Foreign Policy, 1918–78*. New York: William Morrow, 1978.

Lodge, Henry Cabot. *As It Was: An Inside View of Politics and Power in the Fifties and Sixties*. New York: Norton, 1976.

Lubell, Samuel. *The Revolt of the Moderates*. New York: Harper, 1974.

Lyon, Peter. *Eisenhower: Portrait of a Hero*. Boston: Little, Brown, 1974.

MacKintosh, John P. *British Prime Ministers in the Twentieth Century*, vol.

Bibliography

7: *Churchill to Callaghan*. New York: St. Martin's, 1978.

MacMillan, Harold. *Tides of Fortune, 1945–55*. New York: Harper & Row, 1969.

May, Ernest R., ed. *The Ultimate Decision: The President as Commander in Chief*. New York: George Braziller, 1960.

McMahon, Robert J. "Eisenhower and Third World Nationalism: A Critique of the Revisionists." *Political Science Quarterly*, Fall 1986, 101:453–73.

Morgan, Roger. *West European Politics since 1945: The Shaping of the European Community*. London: Betsford, 1972.

Murphy, Charles J. V. "The Eisenhower Shift." *Fortune*, January-April 1956, 53:82–87ff.

Nagai, Yonosuke, and Akira Iriye, eds. *The Origins of the Cold War in Asia*. New York: Columbia University Press, 1977.

Navarre, Henri. *Agonie de l'Indochine, 1953–54*. Paris: Librairie Plon, 1956.

Neustadt, Richard E. *Presidential Power: The Politics of Leadership*. New York: John Wiley, 1976.

Neustadt, Richard E., and Ernest R. May. *Thinking in Time*. New York: Free Press, 1986.

Nixon, Richard M. *RN: The Memoirs of Richard Nixon*. New York: Grosset & Dunlap, 1978.

—— *Six Crises*. Garden City, N.Y.: Doubleday, 1962.

O'Ballance, Edgar. *The Indochina War, 1945–54*. London: Faber & Faber, 1964.

Osgood, Robert E. *Alliances and American Foreign Policy*. Baltimore: Johns Hopkins University Press, 1968.

Parmet, Herbert S. *Eisenhower and the American Crusade*. London: Collier-Macmillan, 1972.

Peeters, Paul. *Massive Retaliation: The Policy and its Critics*. Chicago: Henry Regnesy, 1959.

Pentagon's Secrets and Half-Secrets. Hanoi: Vietnam Courier, 1971.

Prados, John. *The Sky Would Fall: Operation Vulture, the U.S. Bombing Mission in Indochina, 1954*. New York: Dial Press, 1983.

Public Papers of the President: Dwight David Eisenhower, 1953–54, 2 vols. Washington: USGPO, 1960.

Pusey, Merlo J. *Eisenhower the President*. New York: Macmillan, 1956.

Quester, George H. "Was Eisenhower a Genius?" *International Security*, Fall 1979, 4:159–79.

Radford, Arthur W. *From Pearl Harbor to Vietnam: The Memoirs of Admiral Arthur W. Radford*. Stephen Jurika, Jr., ed. Stanford, Calif.: Hoover Institute Press, 1980.

Randle, Robert F. *Geneva, 1954*. Princeton, N.J.: Princeton University Press, 1969.

Bibliography

Reichard, Gary W. *The Reaffirmation of Republicanism: Eisenhower and the Eighty-third Congress.* Knoxville: University of Tennessee Press, 1975.

Richardson, Elmo. *The Presidency of Dwight D. Eisenhower.* Lawrence: Regents Press of Kansas, 1979.

Ridgway, Matthew B. *Soldier.* New York: Harper, 1956.

Roberts, Chalmers. "The Day We Didn't Go To War." *Reporter,* September 14, 1954, 2:31–35.

Rosenau, James N., ed. *Domestic Sources of Foreign Policy.* New York: Free Press, 1967.

Rostow, W. W. *The United States in the World Arena.* New York: Harper, 1960.

Rovere, Richard. *Affairs of State: The Eisenhower Years.* New York: Farrar, Strauss & Cudahy, 1956.

Roy, Jules. *The Battle of Dien Bien Phu.* New York: Harper & Row, 1963.

Shepley, James. "How Dulles Averted War." *Life,* January 16, 1954, 40:70–80.

Slessor, John. "Air Power and World Strategy." *Foreign Affairs,* October 1954, 33:43–53.

Snyder, Glen H. "The 'New Look' of 1953." Warner R. Schilling et al., eds. *Strategy, Politics, and Defense Budgets.* New York: Columbia University Press, 1962.

Soapes, Thomas F. "A Cold Warrior Seeks Peace: Eisenhower's Strategy for Nuclear Disarmament." *Diplomatic History,* Winter 1980, 4:57–71.

Sorenson, Theodore. *Decision-Making in the White House.* New York: Columbia University Press, 1963.

Steele, John L. "The New-Model Cabinet." *Life,* October 8, 1956, 41:89–103.

Taft, Robert A. *A Foreign Policy for Americans.* Garden City, N.Y.: Doubleday, 1956.

Truman, Harry S. *Memoirs,* vol. 2: *Years of Trial and Hope.* Garden City, N.Y.: Doubleday, 1956.

Turner, Gordon B., and Richard D. Challener, eds. *National Security in a Nuclear Age.* New York: Frederick A. Praeger, 1960.

Twining, Nathan F. *Neither Liberty Nor Safety.* New York: Holt, Rinehart & Winston, 1966.

—— "US Air Offense Stronger than Russia's." *US News and World Report,* December 25, 1953, 35:40–45.

Ulam, Adam. *Expansion and Coexistence.* New York: Frederick A. Praeger, 1968.

—— *The Rivals: America and Russia since World War II.* New York: Viking, 1971.

United Kingdom, House of Commons. *Parliamentary Debates.* 5th Series: 1954. London: HMSO, 1954.

Bibliography

United Nations, Department of Economic Affairs, Research and Planning Division, Economic Commission for Asia and the Far East. *Economic Survey of Asia and the Far East, 1952–55*. Bangkok: United Nations, 1953–56.

United States Congress. *Congressional Record*, vol. 100: 83rd Congress, 2nd Session, 1954.

United States Congress, House, Committee on Foreign Affairs. *Report of the Special Study Mission to Pakistan, India, Thailand, and Indochina, May 6, 1953*. 83rd Congress, 1st Session, 1953.

—— *Report of the Special Study Mission to Southeast Asia and the Pacific by Hon. Walter H. Judd et al*. 83rd Congress, 2nd Session, 1954.

—— *Selected Executive Session Hearings of the Committee, 1951–56*, vol. 18: *United States Policy in the Far East*, part 2: *Developments in Southeast Asia* (Historical series), 1980.

—— *United States-Vietnam Relations, 1945–67*, vol. 9: *The Eisenhower Administration*. US Department of Defense Series. 92nd Congress, 1971.

United States Congress, Senate, Committee on Foreign Relations. *Congressional Hearings*, vol. 2: *Hearings to Amend the Mutual Security Act of 1951 and for Other Purposes, May 5–29, 1953*. 83rd Congress, 1st Session, 1954.

—— *Congressional Hearings*, vol. 6: *Hearings on Foreign Policy and its Relation to Military Programs: Statements of Secretary of State John Foster Dulles and Admiral Arthur W. Radford, CJCS, March 19–April 14, 1954*. 83rd Congress, 2nd Session, 1954.

—— *Executive Sessions of the Senate Foreign Relations Committee*, vol. 6: 83rd Congress, 2nd Session, 1954 (Historical series), 1977.

—— *Report of Senator Mike Mansfield on a Study Mission to the Associated States of Indochina*. 83rd Congress, 1st Session, 1953.

United States Department of Defense. *The Pentagon Papers*. Senator Gravel edition, vol. 1. Boston: Beacon Press, 1971.

United States Department of State. *American Foreign Policy, 1950–55, Basic Documents*, vol. 2. Washington: USGPO, 1957.

—— *Foreign Relations of the United States, 1952–54*, vol. 13: *Indochina*. Washington: USGPO, 1982.

United States Joint Chiefs of Staff, Historical Division. "The History of the Indochina Incident, 1940–54," in series "The Joint Chiefs of Staff and the War in Vietnam," in series "The History of the Joint Chiefs of Staff." Washington: Naval History Division, 1955.

United States Republican Policy Committee Staff. *Republican Platform Pledges and Highlights of Performance: The Record from January 1953–July 1955*. Washington, September 1955.

Werth, Alexander. *France, 1940–55*. New York: Henry Holt, 1956.

Williams, Geoffrey. *The Permanent Alliance: The Euro-American Partnership, 1945–74*. Leyden, Netherlands: Sijthoff, 1977.

Bibliography

Williams, Philip. *Crisis and Compromise: Politics in the Fourth Republic.* Hamden, Conn.: Archon, 1964.

Williams, Ralph E., Jr. "The Great Debate: 1954." *United States Naval Institute Proceedings,* March 1954, 80:247–55.

Wolfers, Arnold, ed. *Alliance Politics in the Cold War.* Baltimore: Johns Hopkins Press, 1959.

Index

Acheson, Dean, 2, 8, 79
Adams, Sherman, 133
Afghanistan, 152
Air Force (US): and New Look, 20, 69-70; mechanics controversy, 25-27, 94; and Operation Vulture, 49-50, 70-73, 120-21, 144
Aldrich, Winthrop, 124
American Bar Association, 94
American Society of Newspaper Editors, 130
Anderson, George, 172-73n42
Anderson, Robert, 90
ANZUS, see individual entries for Australia; and New Zealand
Aron, Raymond, 178n8
Army (US): and New Look, 20, 47, 56; McCarthy and, 55, 60; Ridgway report, 56-57
Asia-Firsters, 12-14, 19, 34-35, 53, 118
Associated States, see Indochina
Atlantic Charter, 3
Australia: and domino principle, 61, 87-88, 117; and "united action," 66, 91, 96, 98-100, 108, 124, 152-53; joins SEATO, 158

Bao Dai, Emperor, 2, 5, 10-11, 141
Bevan, Aneurin, 127
Berlin: Conference, 87; partition of, 149
Bidault, George: rivalry with Laniel, 30-31; and Dien Bien Phu, 32, 135, 139, 142; requests US airstrikes 104-6, 135-37, 156; requests B-29s, 109, 113, 115-16; morale of, 116, 137, 139-40, 142; and "united action," 114-16, 129, 140, 174-75n22; and Geneva Conference, 155-56
Blum, Robert, 161n8
Bonnet, Henri, 96-98, 101, 108
Bowie, Robert, 63-64, 168n15
Bricker Amendment, 15, 26, 94-95, 162n20
British Armed Services Mission in Indochina, 124
Brohon, Raymond, 69, 103-4
Brownell, Herbert, 84
Budget (US): Eisenhower's desire to cut, 12, 16-17; and New Look, 17-18, 20, 56; effect of Indochina intervention on, 75; for 1955, 94
Burma, 117, 152, 174n10

Cabinet (US), 58-60
Caccia, Harold, 138-39

Index

Cambodia, 1, 37, 57, 77, 157-58; *see also* Indochina

Canada, 114

Carney, Robert: and New Look, 20; puts fleet on alert, 43-44, 121; and airstrikes, 69-73

Central Intelligence Agency (US), 24, 33

Chaing Kai-Shek, 21

Chamberlain, Neville, 64

China: threat of intervention in French-Indochina War, 1, 48-49, 54, 61-63, 68, 76, 99, 103-4, 110, 117, 138, 151, 172n29; Communist takeover of, 4, 6, 16, 96, 148; recognizes Democratic Republic of Vietnam, 4; intervention in Korean War, 6, 44, 67; aid to Vietminh, 8-9, 11, 41, 76, 105, 107, 114-15; and Geneva Conference, 11, 135, 158; US warnings to, 21-23, 44, 61-63, 66-67, 78-79, 114-15; Pleven demands recognition of, 30; French seek promise of US retaliation against, 30-31, 38-39, 42, 48-49; Dulles seeks action against, 41, 44-45; and "united action," 61-63, 88-90; and domino principle, 117

China Lobby, 16, 118

Churchill, Winston: Eisenhower's relationship with, 15; and French-Indochina War, 67, 108-9, 123-24, 141-42, 145-46, 173n2; weakness of, 116; and French request for airstrikes, 142-43

CINCPAC, 48, 120-21

Clay, Lucius, 20

Clements, Earl, 90

Collective security, 14

Colombo Conference, 131

Congress (US): votes aid to French-Indochina War, 4-7, 9, 22-27; independence of 83d Congress, 12-16, 27, 86, 94-95, 162n18; and McCarthy, 15, 60; and New Look, 18; and mechanics controversy, 26-27, 94, 113, 172n24; Radford-Ély meeting with leadership, 37; and Dien Bien Phu, 54, 57; and "united action," 65-66, 96-97, 117-19, 140-41, 150, 154, 156-57, 170n42, 174-75n22, 177-78n2; April 3 leaders' meeting, 82-86, 90-96, 98-101, 168n15, 169n36; reaction to Nixon's remarks, 130-31,

133-34, Eisenhower meeting with leadership, 147-48

Conservative Party (French), 30-31

Containment policy, 13-14, 17

Cutler, Robert, 83, 110, 150

Defense Committee (French), 30-31, 34, 39

Defense Department (US), 24, 35-36, 45

DeGaulle, Charles, 160

Dejean, Maurice, 80

Democratic and Socialist Union of the Resistance (French), 30-31

Democratic Party (US): Eisenhower and, 12, 14

Democratic Republic of Vietnam (DRV), 2-3, 4

Dewey, Peter, 161n9

Diem, Ngo Dinh, 158-59

Dien Bien Phu: Navarre selects as final battle sight, 12, 24-5, 35; Eisenhower opposes battle plan, 24-25, 35, 53-54; battle for, 29, 31-33, 53, 58, 80, 90-91, 104-5, 110, 121, 129, 137, 141, 146-47, 149; repercussions in France, 33-34, 53, 91, 114, 128, 136, 139, 156-57; and US intervention, 34-45, 48-51, 54-61, 65, 67-75, 77-83, 90-93, 96, 103-6, 109-11, 115, 119-21, 128-29, 135-46, 153; fall of, 36, 94, 143, 154-56, 159; Nixon's remarks on, 131; and British airstrikes, 142-43

Dillon, C. Douglas, 104-9, 114-16, 150, 178n8

Domino principle, 1-2, 5, 34-35, 54, 75-76, 111, 117, 156-57

Dulles, Allen: and mechanics controversy, 25; and Dien Bien Phu, 33-34, 73, 110; and Chinese intervention, 172n29

Dulles, Eleanor, 134

Dulles, John Foster: opposes Korean division, 16; and New Look, 18, 20-21; role in administration, 19-20, 42-43, 57; supports US aid to French-Indochina War, 23-24, 37-45, 47, 57-59, 81-93, 101, 114-15, 144, 146, 150, 153-54, 179n21; and Dien Bien Phu intervention, 25, 37-41, 44-45, 50, 54-55, 57-59, 73, 81-82, 85, 137-42, 176-77n62; and Geneva Conference, 37, 76-77, 141, 153, 155, 163n40, 167n19; frustration with France, 41, 115-16, 154,

Index

Dulles, John Foster (*Continued*)
176*n*61; seeks action against China, 41;
difficulties in pinning down Eisenhower, 44-45, 77, 84-86, 144-45; pressures France, 57-58, 175*n*24; Overseas Press Club speech, 60-68, 74, 78-79, 87, 97, 111, 156; and Congressional leaders' meeting, 83-86, 90-93, 95, 98-99, 101, 117-18, 168*n*15; and "united action," 86-90, 96-102, 106-9, 111, 114, 116-17, 119-20, 123-30, 134-36, 154, 156, 171*n*16, 174*n*10, 174-75*n*22; animosity toward Eden, 87-88, 127-28, 134, 154; and use of atomic weapons at Dien Bien Phu, 120, 172-73*n*42; response to Nixon's remarks, 132, 134; and post-Geneva regional security, 156-59

East Germany *see* Germany, Democratic Republic of
Economist, 127-28
Eden, Anthony: and "united action," 67, 87 116, 124-27, 135, 137-40, 143; and Geneva Conference, 87-88, 135; retracts joint communique, 126-28, 131, 134, 173-74*n*9, 174*n*10; responds to Nixon's remarks, 131-32; Laniel requests airstrikes of, 142-43; and SEATO, 158
Eisenhower, Dwight D.: and French-Indochina War, 1-2, 21-27, 35-37, 42-45, 59-60, 64-65, 75-86, 94-96, 99-102, 107-13, 115-16, 119-20, 123-25, 128, 144-45, 147-56, 159-60, 171*nmm*11, 22, 23, 178*n*9; and EDC, 7, 160; power as president, 12-21, 57, 59, 94, 142, 162*nmm*16, 18; evasive style of, 15-16, 18-20, 44-45, 66-67, 77-79, 82, 84-86, 94-95, 101-2, 107, 109, 132, 144-45, 159-60, 171*nmm*12, 22; and New Look, 17-18, 20-21, 162*n*25; and Geneva Conference, 23, 76-77, 135, 149, 158; creates Special Committee, 24; and mechanics controversy, 25-27, 172*n*24; and Dien Bien Phu 24-25, 35-37, 40, 43-44, 51, 53-54, 68, 75-83, 106-7 110, 119, 137-43, 141-43, 147-49, 160, 168*n*19; Ridgway report to, 56-57; criticisms of French, 59-60, 112, 144, 147, 171*n*11; "fear speech," 60; and "united action"

speech, 60, 62, 64-65, 116; and congressional conditions for intervention, 83-86, 92-95, 98-102, 106-7, 111-14, 119, 170*n*39, 177-78*n*2; and domino principle, 119; and Nixon's remarks, 132-34; disappointment with Britain, 143, 147-49; support of South Vietnam, 158-59, 179*n*27
Ély, Paul: Ély mission, 29-41, 45-51, 53-57, 65, 68-69, 73, 77, 96, 106-7, 165*n*33; and Operation Vulture, 48-50, 68, 103-7, 114, 121, 135-36, 165*n*43
Europe: and domino principle, 1-2; American military commitment to, 6-7; Republican party attitude toward, 13-14; Dulles warns, 42-43
European Defense Community (EDC): as lever in US-French negotiations, 7, 22, 30, 54, 128-29, 136, 175*n*24; Russian desire to prevent, 11; Pleven and, 31; Dulles and, 41-43, 54, 57, 163*n*40; failure of, 158
Expressen, 11

Formosa, *see* Taiwan
Fourth Republic (France), 9, 30
France: colonial rule in Indochina, 2-3, 5, 141, 144; US aid controversy in, 5-6, 31, 68-69, 103; US efforts to build morale of, 22-24, 76, 106, 108, 116, 120, 153; Dulles' opinion of, 41-43, 54, 57-59, 61, 63-65; Eisenhower's opinion of, 59-60, 75-76, 81; and "united action," 67-68, 91-92, 96-98, 100-1, 105, 114-16, 123, 126-30, 154; requests airstrikes, 103-8, 121, 135-37, 142-43, 155-56; responds to Nixon's remarks, 131; joins SEATO, 158; mistrust of US, 159-60
French Indochina, *see* Indochina
French-Indochina War: US military aid to, 1-8, 21-27, 31, 35-36, 39, 45-48, 69-73, 90-92, 96-100, 109-13, 115, 118-21, 153-54, 165*n*33; origins of, 2-3; tactics, 6, 8-10, 32; French exhaustion with, 6, 8-11, 22-23, 29-30, 128; war costs, 7-8; settlement of, 155, 157; *see also* Dien Bien Phu
French Union Forces: tactics against Vietminh, 6, 8; discrimination against

Index

French Union Forces (*Continued*)
Vietnamese troops, 10; and US MAAG, 22; and battle for Dien Bien Phu, 32-33, 53, 80, 104-5, 110, 121, 130, 135, 137, 146, 149, 154, 178*n*14, 178-79*n*15; JCS criticisms of, 45-48, 72, 110; problems of, 76; post-Dien Bien Phu defeats, 155; *see also* Dien Bien Phu; French-Indochina War

Geneva Conference on Far Eastern Problems: French-Indochina War added to agenda, 11, 23, 163*n*40; French positioning for, 30-33, 37-38, 49, 53, 67, 105-6, 128, 131, 139, 155; American positioning for, 38, 54-55, 58-59, 62-65, 67, 73-74, 77, 80, 86-90, 95-99, 106, 112, 116, 119-20, 123, 125, 129, 132, 134-35, 141, 156; British positioning for, 67, 87, 116, 124-26, 135-36, 143, 145-46, 153, 155; attendance of China at, 135; negotiations at, 147, 153-54, 156; accord, 155, 157-59, 179*n*27
Germany, Democratic Republic of, 7, 21, 157
Germany, Federal Republic of, 7, 41, 157
Giap, Vo Nguyen, 8, 12, 32, 154-55
Great Britain: aids French reconquest of Vietnam, 3; recognizes French Associated States, 5; and "united action," 57, 63-64, 66-67, 86-90, 91-92, 96-101, 108-9, 116, 123-28, 134, 137-43, 145-46, 148, 153; and Berlin Conference, 87-88; response to Nixon's remarks, 131-32, 134; public opinion on war, 138; joins SEATO, 158
Guatemala, 94, 147

Hagerty, James, 110, 134, 148, 178*n*9
Haiphong Incident, 3
Halleck, Charles, 133-34
Hazlett, "Swede," 144
Heath, Donald, 45, 80-82, 136
Ho Chi Minh, 2-4, 9, 11, 61, 63
Hong Kong: and domino principle, 87-88; and "united action," 138, 147
Hoopes, Townsend, 93, 101-2
Howard, Roy 168*n*19

Humphrey, George, 19, 112, 171*n*22

India: and domino principle, 1-2, 61, 76, 117; and "united action," 66-67, 126, 131, 151, 174*n*10
Indochina: US strategic interest in, 1-5, 41-42, 58-64, 117, 119-20, 156-57; becomes French Associated States, 5; fear of French abandonment of, 40, 58-59, 86-87, 96; US desires to deal directly with, 41-42, 44-45, 131; Ridgway report on, 56-57; US policy toward, 57, 76; independence of, 57-59, 70, 92, 95, 100, 119, 129, 140-41, 144, 155, 176*n*37; and "united action," 114, 130; reaction to Nixon remarks, 131; *see also* Vietnam
Indonesia, 1-2, 76, 117, 152
Iran, 21, 94

Jackson, C. D., 25
Japan: and domino principle, 1-2, 61, 112, 117; in World War II, 2-3, 62-63; American commitment to, 6-7; and "united action," 174*n*10
Jenner, William, 16
Johnson, Lyndon, 90
Joint Chiefs of Staff (US): and mechanics controversy, 25; and Ély Mission, 30, 41, 45-48, 50, 55; and airstrikes, 56, 69-73, 81, 89-90, 92, 120; and SEATO, 157

Kennedy, John F., 66, 117-18, 172*n*38
Knowland, William F.: succeeds Taft, 13; and "united action," 64, 118; and congressional leaders' meeting, 90-91; response to Nixon's remarks, 133-34; and partition of Vietnam, 157-58; and Bricker Amendment, 162*n*20
Korea, Republic of: US military aid to, 1, 6-7; army as model for VNA, 46; and "united action," 65, 136, 174*n*10; and domino principle, 117; opinion of US, 151; partition of, 157
Korean War, 5-9, 11, 16, 19, 21-23, 44, 47, 56, 67, 71-72, 76, 79, 91, 96, 117-18
Kyes, Roger: and mechanics controversy, 25, 113, 172*n*24; opposes airstrikes, 73,

Index

Index